Aging Our Way

Aging Our Way

Independent Elders, Interdependent Lives

Meika Loe

WITHDRAWN

OXFORD
UNIVERSITY PRESS

OXFORD
UNIVERSITY PRESS

Oxford University Press is a department of the University of Oxford.
It furthers the University's objective of excellence in research, scholarship,
and education by publishing worldwide.

Oxford   New York
Auckland   Cape Town   Dar es Salaam   Hong Kong   Karachi
Kuala Lumpur   Madrid   Melbourne   Mexico City   Nairobi
New Delhi   Shanghai   Taipei   Toronto

With offices in
Argentina   Austria   Brazil   Chile   Czech Republic   France   Greece
Guatemala   Hungary   Italy   Japan   Poland   Portugal   Singapore
South Korea   Switzerland   Thailand   Turkey   Ukraine   Vietnam

Oxford is a registered trade mark of Oxford University Press
in the UK and certain other countries.

Published in the United States of America by
Oxford University Press
198 Madison Avenue, New York, NY 10016

Library of Congress Cataloging-in-Publication Data
Loe, Meika, 1973-
Aging our way : lessons for living from 85 and beyond / Meika Loe.
    p.   cm.
Includes bibliographical references and index.
ISBN 978-0-19-979790-5 (cloth : alk. paper); 978-0-19-997572-3 (paperback)
1. Aging—Social aspects. 2. Older people—Psychology. 3. Older people—Health and hygiene.
4. Quality of life. 5. Well-being. I. Title.
HQ1061.L59   2011
646.70084'6—dc22   2011008731

Printed in the United States of America
on acid-free paper

To Levi, who comes from a long line of phenomenal women

CONTENTS

ACKNOWLEDGMENTS

I want to thank the thirty inspirational elders who make this book what it is. Some taught me about conquering loneliness, some tutored me in Yiddish, some served me shortcake, and others served as editors. All reminded me of the importance of living purposeful lives, and their lessons live on.

Their voices are made that much richer by those who assisted with this book's preparation. Students of all ages patiently listened to ideas and excerpts early on, and offered encouraging feedback and support, including Colgate University and Skidmore College students who have taken my Sociology of the Life Course class, as well as Colgate's Lifelong Learners, Skidmore's Mature Adults, and Hunter College Alumni in the Capital Region. Special thanks go to student research assistants Rachel Greenburg and Katherine Flynn.

Many colleagues and friends took time to provide thorough and thoughtful feedback. Special thanks go to Toni Calasanti, Deborah Carr, Kelly Joyce, and several anonymous reviewers for believing in this project and giving it strength. Eliza Kent spent many hours in cafes reading drafts and providing invaluable guidance. Carol Bergen's news clippings and questions over breakfast kept me grounded. Laura Carpenter's and Jennifer Reich's support and encouragement never wavered. Thank you to Janel Benson, Courtney Burke, Rebecca Costello, Carolyn Kissane, Karen Luciani, and Crystal Moore, for your constructive feedback. Thanks as well to the Oxford team and James Cook, who carefully read every word of the manuscript, cut a few, and deftly shepherded it through.

I am indebted to the organizations that directly supported this project, specifically the Upstate Institute at Colgate University and the Institute on Research on Women at University at Albany. The project was strengthened with encouragement from Bill Thomas and Jude

Rabig and Eldershire workshop participants; Erin Mitchell at AARP; Loretta Carney of Albany Fortnightly; Sue Kenneally and Rick Ianello of the Albany Guardian Society; Kim Hansen Woods at Albany Senior Housing; Bethany Meade, Laurie Milward, and Nikki Smith from Albany Senior Services; Laurie Mante, Maryclaire Hassett, Libby Kesner, Liza McKinley, and Kris Santaromita of Eddy Village Green; Amy Vastola of Jewish Family Services; Sue Baumann and Steven Spiller at Madison Lane Apartments; Courtney Burke of the Rockefeller Institute; Lois Wilson of Senior Issues Forum; Claire Sigal and Dick Allen at the Sidney Albert Albany Jewish Community Center; Julie Meyer at the U.S. Census Bureau; Tanya Zelman of the West Hill Neighborhood Health Advocate Program; and the lifelong learners and researchers at Fortnightly Club of Hamilton, Thursday Morning Club of Troy, and Fortnightly Club of Albany.

We are all a product of our time and place. That could not be more true in my case. Heartfelt thanks to my Lancaster Street family and my Hamilton community, two places I call home and the initial inspiration for this book. That said, my life is made most meaningful by my New York, Colorado, and California families. On a daily basis, they model the most important lessons for living, and keep me accountable.

PROLOGUE

30–60–90: ON AGE AND PERSPECTIVE

30. When I turned thirty, I felt old. I felt experienced, grounded, and honestly, more legitimate. I was an assistant professor with several years of teaching and a book under my belt. I was a decade older than my students. Fewer people asked me if I was a student or what I was majoring in. Then I rented a room in an elder's home near the university and discovered a thriving elder community. Over the next three years, as I taught courses on aging, started a family, and resided in two vibrant intergenerational communities, elders became my primary teachers, mentors, friends, and extended family. Experiencing pregnancy and childbirth within these communities, I began to embrace the complexities of age, wrapped up in questions about body, health, culture, social perception and roles, generations, life stages, location, and relationships. Meanwhile, I came to view aging and the human life course in new ways. I realized the importance of social networks, continuity across one's life, and self-reliance and control when it comes to well-being and living, aging, birthing, and dying comfortably. In sum, I have been busy rethinking age.

60. My parents and in-laws are in their sixties. Each actively loves and cares for their surviving parents, children, and grandchildren, most of whom live at a distance. At moments, tables turn, and those who cared for us look to us for care. I see them balancing their adult lives with new and emerging issues. Their lives and bodies, roles and responsibilities are in flux. Reminders of aging that had previously remained under the surface are emerging. All have dealt with loss and grieving and serious health issues, and all have taken advantage of

senior discounts. Yet, they prefer not to refer to themselves as seniors, and are not even remotely considering moving to Florida. Instead, what lies before them is time, new family configurations, and opportunities for reinvention. They are rethinking age.

90. We have longevity in the family, as they say. My father's mother lived to ninety, and her mother lived to ninety-two. My mother's father just turned ninety. My grandparents' and great-grandparents' long lives enabled me to learn from them and enjoy their company well into adulthood. My grandparents have been among my most trusted lifelong companions, friends, and mentors. We have watched and supported each other over the years. I have observed them confronting physical challenges associated with longevity. I have asked questions about living meaningful lives in old age, and they have raised issues related to independence, safety, companionship, care, and mortality. In many ways, their questions have become my questions, and have led me to the thirty "oldest old" who anchor this book.

When I met these study participants, most were living at home and hoping to stay there. They were making it work, and I wondered how they managed to do that. All were willing to let me into their lives from time to time. Some instantly incorporated me into their day-to-day activities, others kept in touch from a distance. Many have become dear friends. Together and apart, we have been rethinking age.

30–60–90. In the midst of this three-year journey, a new life started, and many others ended. The cycle of birth and death became very real, and the social aspects of each were revealing. Julia's life ended in the church pews, as the choir sang. Lillian passed away with her lover by her side. Meanwhile, my daughter's beginning was eagerly anticipated. As the baby and I grew, I saw those around me starting new life chapters and ending others. My father ended a career in business. My only existing grandparent was now living alone. My in-laws became active grandparents. Ann and Eddie committed to more exercise. And Christine and Fred moved into a new nursing facility. While confronting change, many things stayed the same. All of us, no matter what our age, were practicing things like memory, mobility, balance, sensory perception, patience, and confidence. We were searching for words, for meaning. We wanted to be heard, known, trusted, and cared for. And we experienced setbacks and obstacles, and then started anew. I learned that a life course perspective helped me to see similarities and differences across lives and across age. I found a new way of seeing—a wide-angle lens that allowed me to see 30–60–90.

REALIGNMENT NOTE: 90–60–30. This book comes out of my journey, as a young yet aging professor of sociology, through an awareness of age and agelessness. Many people—young, old, and in between—have been important guides. They provided the links, the clues, and the glue to put it all together. But mostly nonagenarian women and men led this journey; they are the center of this book and my heart. They have been my teachers and I, the student. Through their life lessons, I have learned how to be a better parent, professor, and person. These lessons were taught in words and in actions, as they went about their daily lives. Observing their joys and challenges has modeled for me the diverse ways individuals can create full and meaningful lives at any age.

I have approached this book in direct contradiction to how our society is structured. Elder voices and experiences center it, in a 90–60–30 sort of way. They are not marginalized, not an afterthought, not an end-point. Instead, they provide a variety of starting points for understanding age, aging, and the life course, at a time when aging is changing. We will check their experiences with gerontologists, sociologists, psychologists, and other authorities along the way. But the real experts, testing out new and familiar theories on age and aging, are eighty-five and beyond.

Aging Our Way

Introduction: Living at Home and Making it Work

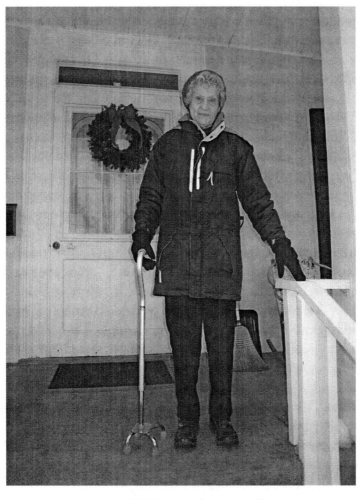

Ruth H. prepares for a winter walk

In 1998, Hallmark unveiled their new "One-Hundredth-Birthday" cards. By 2007, annual sales were at 85,000 cards.[1] America has the highest number of centenarians in the world (mostly due to our large population), estimated at 100,000,[2] and in general, our population is "graying." Today, American men can expect to live to age seventy-five and women to age eighty. The number of people in the United States over age sixty-five is expected to double between now and 2030, and the number over eighty is expected to almost triple.[3] By 2050, one in four or five Americans will be over sixty-five, and about 5 percent will be aged eighty-five and older, up from 2 percent now. If these trends continue, the United States at midcentury roughly will be where Japan, Italy, and Germany—the three "oldest" industrialized countries in the world—are today.[4] Everywhere in the world the number of solitary elders is climbing fast. Given the growing population of elders situated to age in place in future generations, we all have a vested interest in understanding how the experience of old age is changing.[5]

We are well on our way toward a fundamentally new, permanent, and older age structure in our society.[6] By 2020, for the first time in history, Americans over sixty-five will outnumber those under fifteen.[7] The baby boomer generation's vast numbers will accelerate this shift.[8] This new social structure will reflect demographic changes in class status and education, ethnicity and gender, in combination with age. Younger generations will be substantially more ethnically diverse (with many minority youths working low-wage jobs, particularly in health care), and older generations will remain disproportionately nonminority and female.

Given broad changes in mortality and morbidity rates, some scholars project overall increases in life expectancy for years to come. Advances in biomedical technology make scientists optimistic that increased longevity in America will both accelerate and continue beyond the middle of this century. For example, *The Lancet* medical journal projected in 2010 that most babies born since 2000 in wealthy countries such as France, Germany, Italy, the UK, the United States, Canada, and Japan will celebrate their hundredth birthdays.[9] On the other hand, it is possible that recent increases in obesity and diabetes will actually lead to declines in life expectancy in this century.

The fastest-growing age group in America is composed of those eighty-five years and over.[10] Today, Americans who live to age eighty-five live on average another 6.8 years for women and 5.7 years for men.[11] As longevity and good health increase, the meaning age is changing; being old does not necessarily entail being dependent. In fact, the chance that older adults will live independently increases as they age. Nearly 40 percent of Americans eighty-five or older live by themselves, compared to only 20 percent of those ages sixty-five to seventy-four.[12]

We are no longer a society with a functionally impaired older generation alongside a fit, active, younger population. In fact, the MacArthur Foundation Research Report on Aging found that the trend is toward a more active and healthier older population, and a less healthy younger and middle-aged population.[13] Perhaps surprisingly, *active* life span is increasing faster than total life span. More people are living longer and healthier, while avoiding or delaying severe disability. The health and functional status of the old have been improving steadily since the early 1980s, mainly thanks to improvements in medical care. At the same time, it is crucial to remember that not everyone is living longer and healthier. Disability rates have increased among those younger than sixty-five, due to substantial increases in rates of asthma, obesity, and diabetes.[14] A great deal of research suggests that social inequalities contribute to chronic illness and shorter life expectancy. Added to this, some of the most important determinants of diminished capacity—cognitive and functional decline—are more closely related to socioeconomic factors and education level than to age. In sum, good health is a privilege and a luxury in America, as is a long active life.

Our current culture of medicalization potentially overstates the physical declines of later life.[15] In fact, evidence suggests that important abilities, such as perspective, social values, emotional regulation, and experience, may all increase with age and can contribute to adaptability in old age. Assessing elders' functionality in relation to young adults, or focusing on quantity of health problems or scores on individual tests, obscures their overall capacity to function and adapt in ways that allow them to lead full, meaningful lives into old age.[16] These traditional assessment models also obscure the importance of social contexts in shaping quality of life and overall health.

Given these changes in our society, a close look at how old people creatively and strategically maintain self-efficacy, health, and well-being is timely and important. This book follows the everyday lives of thirty individuals, aged 85 to 102, the majority of whom live alone, at home, in rural, suburban, and urban upstate New York, over the course of three years. These elders are role models; they are typical of the aging populace as well as the "aging in place" movement. They represent the vast majority of Americans who, for reasons of familiarity, ease, networks, and economic necessity, hope to—and are—aging in their own homes and communities. Their daily lives answer the question many of us are asking or will ask someday: "How can I stay at home *and* continue to lead a meaningful life in old age?"

WHAT IS YOUR LONGEVITY SECRET?

Very old people are often asked, "What's your secret?" People want to know what they do to stay healthy, engaged, and—to be blunt—alive. The answers vary. A few point to genetics; their parents, uncles, or sisters lived long lives. Some say they never took risks. Most say, "I have no idea; I never expected this." They see their long lives as a fluke.

Contrary to common wisdom on what contributes to longevity— such as exercise, diet, and a good attitude—recent research suggests that these old individuals are still with us because they have lived conscientiously. This spirit of prudence and persistence, coupled with meaningful social connections, are the factors that seem to contribute to health and longevity, according to health researchers Howard Friedman and Leslie Martin, authors of *The Longevity Project: Surprising Discoveries for Health and Long Life from the Landmark Eight-Decade Study.*

Since I did not follow this group of mostly nonagenarians into old age, I cannot assess what factors contributed to their longevity.[17] However, as I observed their daily practices and asked them questions, I began to see patterns in how they create meaningful, comfortable lives—in their degree of connectedness, in the creative ways they care for themselves and others, and in the innovative ways they go about living, on their own terms. However, while there are similarities across age, there are just as many differences.

Arranged into thirteen "lessons for living," the book's organization was not what I set out to do, but over several years, I became convinced that knowledge about aging should come from the experts themselves. On the whole, these elders tell stories of creativity and resilience that are inspiring, but also, at times, painful.

This book is different from popular and scholarly works focused on longevity, health, and well-being. It does not focus on the holy triumvirate of diet, exercise, and medicine to "defy age," or a heroic "successful aging" recipe for youthful productivity. Instead, this book and its participants actively embrace age and aging, and mobilize a much wider range of resources to achieve self-care, well-being, and ultimately, comfort. Diet, exercise, and medicine certainly feature in some of the stories, but not necessarily in ways you would imagine. Instead, participants in this research fit with what it means to live lives of continuity, meaning, and connection. So, for example, Eddie's regular workout is just as much about connecting with others and having a daily routine as it is about exercise. Ruth L.'s creatively assembled doctor's network is less about medical services and more about holistic health, understanding, support, and honor for her as a Holocaust survivor. Alice's diet is an exercise in saving money, being healthy, and using technology, which together enable her to reinforce the control she has over her daily life.

This diverse group of elders had at least one other thing in common: they were deeply committed to aging in their communities and at home (in apartments, condos, houses, and group homes), and many expressed a wish to die there.[18] In fact, most saw death as preferable to placement in a nursing facility.[19] Many had spent the majority of their years "rooted" in their communities. In order to stay at home, they needed to be creative, independent, and active in maintaining their health. At the same time, the majority learned to balance self-directedness with asking for help. This lesson was sometimes learned the hard way, especially after instances of over-extending themselves, such as when Ann fell after walking an unusually long distance.

Our time together took place in kitchens and living rooms, at fitness centers, birthday parties, funeral homes, doctors' offices, gardens, churches, community centers, and diners. By 2010, as I was writing this book, three had moved into assisted living environments, three had moved in with family members, and twenty-one were still living at home, though often with increased assistance. Over the course of my three-year study, about half of the study participants were hospitalized for minor illnesses or surgeries, one sustained a stroke, three developed dementia, two fell and broke a bone, two became legally blind, six passed away, and two became centenarians.

(See Epilogue for updates.) I was able to discuss the final book outline, including the thirteen lessons, with twenty-five of the original thirty study participants, and receive their feedback and blessings. One nonagenarian, Ruth L., who originally asked not to be in the book but requested that I call or visit on a weekly basis, agreed to be part of the project only after three years of friendship. Ann, whose life goal was to have something she had written published, agreed to write the Postscript. Seymour wrote about the book in his monthly newsletter column and later played the role of copyeditor, as did Ruth H. And many hoped to live long enough to be able to hand this book to the next person who asks, "What's your secret?"

This book is a synthesis of what I have learned from all thirty study participants about quality of life, health, and well-being. Moreover, through discussions with college students enrolled in my sociology courses on aging and the life course, I have come to see that these lessons resonate more broadly. Working at continuity, comfort, connections, and a balance of autonomy and dependency can be crucial at all stages of human development.

These lessons for living push us to broaden our collective sense of the factors that contribute to health and well-being. The participants' stories remind us to actively work at creating lives worth living and to reflect on mortality more often. Their experiences and challenges highlight grassroots and policy opportunities for supporting the millions who are and will age at home. Most important, these elders remind us that old age can be empowering, meaningful, connected, and even joyful.

ON FINDING THE OLDEST OLD

Between 2006 and 2008, I was a fixture at several senior centers in upstate New York. In an age-segregated and stratified society, elder-oriented organizations are some of the only places to meet old people, particularly those living independently. There, I met elders in fitness classes, over meals, and in discussion groups. Ultimately, I described my research to the leaders of these community organizations, who agreed to contact their nonagenarian members (even those no longer actively involved in the organization) to ask if they would be willing to participate in my study.

I also met the oldest old in intergenerational neighborhoods, churches, and women's organizations. Two were highlighted in local newspaper articles. Others were introduced to me by people they knew. While all thirty study participants lived within one hundred miles of one another, they generally did not know each other.[21] At first, most study participants wondered why anyone would be interested in their lives, but in the end, all agreed to meet with me. I told them I wanted to know how they made aging at home "work." More specifically, I wanted to know how they maintained their autonomy and managed self-care.

Each participant first underwent a life history interview, answering questions about their past as well as their current daily lives. Initial interviews took place mostly in their homes. Most participants then took part in three or more follow-up interviews, scheduled annually, during which they discussed their daily lives. These were more open-ended discussions, covering topics they were interested in. It was not uncommon for elders to share pictures of family members at our meetings, to offer me food and drink, and to give me tours of their living spaces. As we got to know each other, I asked to accompany each study participant outside of their homes, to places that were important to their lives and regular routines, including cemeteries, grocery stores, cafes, and fitness centers. In this way, I was able to observe their self-care inside and outside of the home. I also offered to pick up groceries and provide rides if needed, and several took me up on these favors. For those who had no or few family members nearby, my regular presence in their lives may have been magnified. They got to know my daughter, and asked after my grandfather. I visited with them at least once a month. For others, I was simply an annual appointment.

During this three-year period, I also logged approximately 150 hours observing a combination of regional aging-related meetings and conferences, touring institutions dedicated to elder care, and conducting interviews with professionals in elder support and care. This time in the field provided a crucial backdrop to thirty individual lives. For example, interviews with the head administrators at the local Green House as well as sitting in on staff trainings and house meals helped me to understand how this innovative care community compared to traditional nursing homes, and added crucial context to Christine and Fred's experiences. While I do not focus closely on the people and the institutions surrounding these thirty elders in this book, interviews and observations have added depth and perspective to my thinking on aging in place, policy, and care. (See the section in the appendix on "Best Practices" for more on specific institutional contexts.)

I found spending time with elders to be, for the most part, a breath of fresh air. In our youth-obsessed culture, old people can be the least interested in defying or denying age. Many did not put up a front; they seemed to level with me. Usually this made for great interviews. One explained that her uncensored frankness was something she couldn't control; it came from the "decomposition of her frontal cortex." Sometimes this brutal honesty proved challenging. Some elders were downright cantankerous. One castigated me for my limited knowledge of Jewish ritual, asking, "What kind of Jew are you?" Several nonagenarians also expressed concern or confusion when I told them that my child was in daycare, that I worked far from home, and that my husband was a very involved dad. These elders have had a lifetime to embrace their own vulnerabilities, and to know themselves. Many welcomed an opportunity to reflect upon their lives, and seemed to enjoy our regular meetings. As they talked, I found myself thinking about my own grandparents, my marriage, and my life as a parent, and I shared stories when appropriate. Our exchanges were meaningful on many levels.

WHO ARE THE OLDEST OLD?

The "oldest old" is the term the U.S. Census Bureau uses to describe all individuals over eighty-five years of age, the fastest-growing age segment of the nation and the world today, with 5.7 million people in that age bracket in the United States in 2008. (In 1900, just over 100,000 were aged eighty-five and older.) This group is projected to expand to 19 million by 2050.[22]

This book uses the term oldest old whenever specifics regarding age group or demographics are needed. Otherwise, study participants are referred to as "elders." Sociologists of aging Toni Calasanti and Kathleen Slevin make a strong case for using the adjective "old" to reclaim its positive connotations, to naturalize and neutralize it.[23] On the other hand, when I surveyed several hundred people aged fifty-five to ninety-five, asking which words they prefer to use to describe their age group, most noted dislike for common terms that highlight age like "elderly," "old," or "senior citizen." When pressed, the majority were most comfortable with "mature adult" or "elder." Likewise, The 2009 Pew Research Report revealed that 75 percent of Americans associate the term "old" with those who are aged eighty-five and older, and those who are no longer independent. It was then no surprise when a handful of the participants in this study took issue with the use of this term. "Elder" was more warmly received, as it tends to connote respect and refer to a broad age spectrum. The fact that it is more commonly associated with men further compelled me to use it in a study that is dominated by women and that actively engages with sexism and ageism. The foregoing discussion only underscores how charged age-based language is in an age-stratified society.

The thirty research participants are largely representative of the national population in their age group, in terms of cultural heritage, housing, socioeconomic diversity, gender, and marital status. As social scientists have shown, being white and middle or upper class is a powerful predictor of late-life health and well-being. Almost 90 percent of the oldest old are currently white, followed by blacks and Latinos.[24] This is changing as the ethnic makeup of America shifts.[25] Likewise, this sample includes twenty-six individuals (87 percent) who identify as white, with Polish, Danish, British, Irish, Italian, Russian, Latvian, German, and Jewish ethnic backgrounds. Most identify themselves ethnically by their cultural heritage. With several exceptions, they are primarily a mix of first- and second-generation immigrants, many of whom were perceived as non-white (or alien, unwelcome groups, due to ethnic and religious backgrounds) for a portion of their lives in America.[26] Two, Joseph and Ruth L., are Holocaust survivors. The percentage of Jewish participants (23 percent) is higher than in the population of oldest old at large, reflecting their over-representation in New York State and in university areas, as well as their involvement in service organizations.[27] Three study participants (10 percent), Rose, Pauline, and Emma, identify as black. They all migrated from the southern United States to New York State in early adulthood. And one study participant (3 percent), Juana, identifies as Puerto Rican. She followed her children to New York when she was in her forties.[28]

Like many Americans, most participants consider themselves to be middle class, but their late-life realities (e.g. Social Security, health,

TABLE 1: Who are the oldest old (85+) in the U.S.?
Adapted from *Census Bureau* (2008), *Pew Research Report* (2009), and *Older Americans 2010*.

They are called the "Greatest Generation"
They came of age during the Great Depression and survived two World Wars

Women outnumber men 2:1

90% of this population is White, followed by Blacks, Hispanics, and Asians.

28% are married (54% men; 14% women)
64% are widowed (38% men; 76% women)
4% are divorced
4% never married

Over 1/3 live in the south; the rest are equally distributed around the U.S.

70% have a high school diploma or more
14.8 % have a bachelors degree or more

90% native born
10% foreign born (65% arrived before 1970)

78% live in their own home
5% live with a child or other family member
7% live in community housing with some services
15% live in a long term care facility

88% take at least one prescription drug
66% rate their health as good
60% report trouble hearing
28% report trouble seeing
40% say they are experiencing some memory loss
34% have no natural teeth (linked to poverty)
30% say they often feel sad or depressed

86% pray daily
48% pursue hobbies
36% volunteer
25% say they no longer drive
16% go online at least occasionally

and inheritance) place them in a wide range of socioeconomic contexts, from poor to affluent.[29] Their diverse housing situations provide a clue to economic status and are consistent with national averages for this age group. Upon meeting them, eighteen study participants (60 percent) occupied and owned family homes, five

(17 percent) lived in HUD Section 8 subsidized senior housing (studios or apartments), two (6 percent) in state and federally funded long-term care (Green House group homes), three (10 percent) in apartments or condos, and the remaining two (6 percent) rented apartments in retirement communities.

Interestingly, nationwide, women outnumber men in this age group by over 2 to 1. They represent 67 percent of the oldest old population.[30] Beyond this, old men are somewhat more difficult to locate than old women because they are less likely to participate in organizations and activities in senior centers, for example. Of the thirty participants, twenty-three are women; seven are men, a ratio just over 3 to 1, or closer to 76 percent women.[31] Marriage and widowhood rates are on par with national averages. Two individuals have never married. Four of the men (57 percent), and three of the women (10 percent), are married and living with spouses.[32] Three of the five couples are on their second marriages.

This sample differs from national averages in four significant ways. Because this study focuses on aging in place, the population of individuals living at home was deliberately oversampled. At the time we met, nineteen (60 percent) lived alone (the rest lived with spouses, family members, or in group home environments), higher than national estimates of 40 percent of the oldest old living alone in the United States. Second, as mentioned above, women and Jewish participants are more numerous than in the oldest old population at large. Third, the women are more educated than national averages; more than half have college degrees, and four have advanced degrees.[33] This is important, because research shows that education correlates with health and longevity. At the same time, a handful of participants did not make it to ninth grade, revealing that a diversity of factors contributes to longevity.

This research sample is representative when it comes to rates of chronic illness like arthritis, hypertension, and diabetes. On the other hand, because I was unable to interview those with severe cognitive impairments, this sample does not represent the extent of dementia among the oldest old, estimated to affect a third or more, with higher rates for women.[34] Women report higher levels of arthritis and hypertension, and men report higher levels of heart disease and cancer.[35] While some of these illnesses are controlled by medication, such as hypertension, others, like arthritis and severe dementia can be obstacles to independent living.

Well-being encompasses, but is not reducible to, physical health. The most common health-related challenges and illnesses in the seventy-five to eighty-five age group are hypertension and arthritis (about 60 percent), followed by diabetes (38 percent), and enlarged prostate for men (35 percent).[36] (The leading causes of death among people aged sixty-five and over are heart disease, cancer, stroke, chronic respiratory diseases, Alzheimer's, diabetes, influenza, and pneumonia.)

In terms of health and disability, today's oldest old are not the frail, ailing, homebound elders of another era. They represent a new model of aging, experiencing disease and illness and surviving to live relatively able-bodied, mentally sharp, and healthy lives.[37] For these participants, a self-care ethic is about accomplishing and maintaining a broader sense of health that involves comfort, confidence, continuity, autonomy, and connectedness in the context of old age. They actively coordinate self-care in dealing with the usual aging-related sensory, cognitive, and physical difficulties. At the same time, most experience aging-related strengths including domain-specific knowledge and daily task management skills.[38] When I first met these individuals, only one, Christine, was wheelchair-bound. The rest were ambulatory, which dramatically shaped their self-care regimens. Most were active participants in their communities, though their degree and modes of participation may have changed over time.

When we met, I learned that most had arranged a variety of care configurations to meet their needs. Eight rented apartments in senior communities or complexes and were able to access limited transportation, food, and activities in these contexts. Christine and Fred lived in a group home (premised on the elder-centered Green House model) with twenty-four-hour on-site care. Of the twenty-eight not living in a care facility, six (20 percent) employed a home health aide for a few hours each day. Eight (25 percent) lived with a spouse or family members who provided some care. And all study participants relied on nearby friends and/or family members to help with transportation and care intermittently, as well as for regular check-ins. At the same time, a surprising number offered care to others; some were actively helping to care for family members—grandchildren, spouses, or siblings; others cared for friends; and a few regularly volunteered with elders they did not know.

In general, these elders prefer to be totally independent. If this is not possible, then depending on their proximity and general closeness with family, some prefer to utilize informal networks, formal transportation services (including paid drivers and public transportation), or delivery services for day-to-day needs. Others fit with Cantor's hierarchical compensatory model,[39] first turning to a spouse or children, then other relatives, then friends. In general, these elders do not want to be a "burden" on others, particularly family, and they want to protect their autonomy, privacy, and pride. As a regular visitor, I sometimes became complicit in protecting their privacy when they confided stories that they asked me not to share with family members: worrying stories about falling, faltering, or weakness.

All of these elders believe strongly in autonomy and dignity, and retain control over their day-to-day lives. They decide when to start and end their days and design routines that work for them. Many continue to do some version of what they always did, until they experience challenges. Then they scale back; ask for assistance; interview, hire, and fire aides; or tour care facilities and weigh the options. I have observed these elders mobilize an array of resources for support and make important changes in their lives. Even those in the Green House care setting work with staff to design their own daily routines and contribute to the community in their own ways.

While this book focuses on elder autonomy and self-care, it must be noted that the oldest old are not necessarily always alone when it comes to problem solving and personal care. Family members, friends, house-cleaners, nursing aides, health care workers, and others also provided care. These supporters are primarily younger women and are in health and domestic work fields. Increasingly women of color, poor women, and women from developing countries, this group is crucial to the success of aging-in-place initiatives. Even the two married couples in this sample who proudly provide health monitoring and emotional support for their spouses depend on regular assistance from others, including a driver, neighbors, and family or a nursing aide and housekeeper.

THE GREATEST GENERATION

Generational membership is a crucial factor in shaping views and experiences.[40] All thirty study participants were born before 1925 and belong to the group sometimes referred to as the "Greatest Generation" or the "GI Generation." Those who grew up in the United States were raised during the Great Depression. World War II and the Holocaust intersected with and interrupted their romances, family lives, and careers; these historical events dramatically shifted lives. Some served in the military, some were imprisoned in concentration camps, some took on new jobs, and some lived alone or with families, waiting and hoping. Those who served the country were able to access education, purchase homes, and start their lives over with the GI Bill. In fact, two-thirds of men eighty-five and over are veterans.[41]

Some families and individuals moved to New York in the early to mid-twentieth century, seeking jobs, opportunities, and new, freer lives. African Americans migrated northward, Puerto Ricans moved to the mainland, and members of the Jewish European diaspora emigrated overseas. While this generation came of age in a context of gender and racial injustice and sexual silences, those living particularly in urban areas also grew up with Freudianism, flappers, Amelia Earhart, the contraceptive revolution, the growth of coeducational institutions that provided for new gendered and sexual freedoms, and the growing middle-class ideal of heterosexual "companionate marriage."[42]

Generational differences become particularly salient when looking at the daily lives and social and physical locations of the oldest old. Many, particularly those who are financially secure, have experienced a degree of "rootedness" in the second half of their lives; they are perhaps the last generation to live a lifetime, or at least several decades, in one location (or two locations, if they seasonally migrate to a "camp" in the Catskills or a flat in Florida). Proximity and rootedness can enable long-standing familial and nonfamilial support systems. On the other hand, while siblings and friends may be nearby, this generation's children and grandchildren are likely scattered across the United States, and this can contribute to stress and feelings of isolation. Finally, high marriage rates and low divorce rates in this generation mean that singlehood generally signals death of a spouse, which is not the case for their children's generation. This has particular ramifications for women, who tend not to remarry and continue to live independently for an average of fourteen years.[43]

Approaches to aging, health, and technology can also be cohort-specific.[44] Many participants growing up in the Depression era continue to live frugally. In some ways, this approach of living with less enables elders of this generation to be resourceful and to accomplish self-care with limited resources (see Lesson 4, "Live in Moderation," for more on this ethic of restraint). Yet this outlook can act as a barrier when it comes to asking for assistance. This generation also came to appreciate and use newly developed technologies, including radios, sewing machines, and slow cookers. Today, few own or regularly use microwaves, dishwashers, or computers. Some are ambivalent about new biotechnologies like prescription drugs and medical devices (especially those not utilized by their parents), but may also defer to their doctors when it comes to unfamiliar health issues. On the plus side, frugality may translate into economic safety nets and even some health benefits.[45] While there may be notable exceptions, this cohort effect is a crucial part of understanding common social contexts and familiarities.

Given this profile, I wonder if this generation, known for its resilience, resourcefulness, and sense of autonomy, is better set up for longevity than most. Low divorce rates, high fertility rates (resulting in more children to potentially care for them), and low body mass indexes could contribute to this. They are the first cohort to live to later life in large numbers. As mentioned earlier, it is unclear whether younger generations will do as well, given shifts in family formation, parenting practices, and rising rates of obesity.

Keeping all of this in mind, most members of this generation have not lived beyond eighty-five years of age. Thus, while historical events and generational traits matter, these are only part of a life story. Sociohistorical factors must be weighed in combination with individual biographies, including individuals' physical location, socioeconomic status, race, ethnicity, gender, sexual orientation, physical ability, and age. These circumstances shape options and opportunities across the life course.[46] As a result, and despite some similarities, the ways in which the oldest old have actively accomplished age and self-care across their lives vary greatly. For example, the experience of starvation, physical abuse, and psychological torment during the Holocaust may result in lifelong trust issues and health consequences. An ambulatory elder will experience age differently and thus have different needs than a wheelchair-bound elder. Thus, age matters in combination with a variety of other factors.

AGE MATTERS

When you are young, age really matters. Coming-of-age rituals are age-based. School rules are too; age five is old enough for kindergarten. State policies are spelled out by age: work permit and driving permit at sixteen, license and voting at eighteen, and legal alcohol consumption at twenty-one. Even entertainment is organized by age via ratings systems. In a culture with so many age-based norms and rules, we learn to identify by age. Because our lives are organized by age, we learn to self-segregate in this way, a tradition most of us continue throughout our lives without really thinking about it.

As a sociologist of aging and the life course, I see how, in our culture, age does matter—the kind that is chronological, that organizes our lives with age-based milestones, social roles, and, not to be forgotten, discounts. Our age places us in a hierarchy of social privilege, where the "young" (but not too young!) rule. We all play into this age-based game for some semblance of power, always held in contrast to the old, but only for a while. Eventually, the process that we went through in our youth goes backward, down a symbolic "hill" after forty. Then we are reminded to hide our age all over again. Our "middle-aged" friends are dying their hair and using anti-aging beauty products and treatments, all in an effort to be taken seriously again. We are the oldest in the room and deemed "at risk" for health complications and diseases. Meanwhile, the age that we feel ourselves to be, what gerontologists call "subjective age," will always feel in conflict with the raw numbers. And the age others believe us to be, our "perceived age," will not matter when it comes to retirement or claiming Social Security or Medicare benefits, which are tied to chronological age.[47] But these subjective aspects of age make a huge difference when it comes to self-esteem, identity, and social reception.

In our culture, a lifetime is marked by the birth certificate on one end, the death certificate on the other, and all of those Hallmark cards in the middle. Curiously, "aging" is commonly thought to begin in the second half of life. "Development" is what is associated with the early years. What would happen if we shifted our cultural lens and thought about aging as a process that begins at birth, or about development as a process that begins later in life? At the very least, we must consider development as occurring in stages throughout life.[48]

Age, as a system, is generally left out of the short list of intersecting inequalities that shape our lives. This is curious, because it is not all that different from gender, race, and class. Age organizes our lives and stratifies our society. The one difference is that it is temporal. We all pass through the privileges and disadvantages associated with aging; we all get old. How we experience age-based privileges or disadvantages varies, based on other aspects of our social location, and how well we actively "do age" in accordance with societal norms.[49]

Aging is a universal human experience, a bodily process, a social process, and a process that is different for everyone. We remain in collective denial about aging, and in this context of ignorance and disrespect, ageism pervades our culture, our perspectives, and our policies.[50] Pulitzer Prize-winning geriatrician Robert Butler, who coined the term ageism in 1968, explained: "Ageism allows the younger generations to see older people as different than themselves; thus they subtly cease to identify with their elders as human beings."[51] As mentioned earlier, when I first approached them, the majority of study participants were convinced that nobody would want to read about them or people their age. They, too, have learned that their lives do not matter. A good portion of the college students who enrolled in my course on aging say they did so because aging scares them. This is no surprise. Despite what we see in our own families, we tend to expect elders to be nonproductive, dependent, and diseased. We learn and reinforce our culture's age-based expectations and rules throughout our lives, and these cultural scripts overlap with expectations regarding gender, social and physical location, and aging in place.

Age and Gender

Much in the same way that age organizes our lives, gender-specific rules create and maintain difference throughout our lives. Far from being an inherent individual attribute, gender is actively accomplished.[52] Girls and women may learn to "do" gender from an early age in various forms of work, matters related to the home, care giving, personal appearance, relationships, emotions, and health. Boys and men, on the other hand, may learn that masculinity involves nonemotional work, physical work, behavior focused on task completion and mastery, and risk taking. These gendered repertoires continue into old age. Social epidemiologists have shown that gender socialization sets women and men up to behave differently, and this behavior, combined with structural realities, translates into different health outcomes. "Manly" risk-taking behaviors, and many forms of "men's work," can translate into higher mortality rates. Meanwhile, when women care for others, their health worsens. Women's lifelong skill sets can also translate into advantages when it comes to self-care and longevity.[53]

While women are poorer financially, they may be "richer" when it comes to cultivating social skills for self-care, personal comfort, and well-being, such as creating and maintaining networks, asking for help, and health monitoring. These gender repertoires matter in important ways; they provide women with tool kits for self-care throughout their lives and leave men at a disadvantage. So, while women have poorer health and fewer overall economic resources and social advantages than men, they learn and practice daily habits of self-care and living conservatively that may pay off later in life. The benefits of traditionally feminine characteristics are not always easy to see. And yet it is precisely these qualities that can buffer against life's hardships.[54] In other words, those women and men who practice asking for help, attending to their bodies, and building strong relationships across their lives tend to continue these habits in late life and, as a result, experience increased better health, social support, and resilience. Those who are unable to master self-care repertoires late in life may risk losing control over their living environment and care.[55]

Given gendered living practices, it should not be surprising that the majority of the oldest old in America and beyond are predominantly women. Two-thirds of elders over eighty-five are women, and 85 percent of centenarians are women. While they outlive men, elder women are most at risk for serious disability and poverty.[56] Most of these women have cared for and outlived their spouses, leaving few loved ones to care for them. When we met, in this sample of twenty-three women, an astounding eighteen (78 percent) lived alone and cared for themselves. Only one man out of seven, Glenn, lived alone and cared for himself; the rest were couples or living with family members. These individuals are representative of larger gendered patterns; research has shown that single old men have higher remarriage rates and institutionalization rates than single old women. However, this demographic portrait obscures several important points. First, people change; and they can learn self-care practices late in life. Second, men tend to use humor (more so than women) as a coping mechanism for aging, a potentially important factor in health and longevity. Third, many men in this sample are actively involved in caring for others. And finally, the majority of women in this sample who are living autonomously rely on intermittent care from other women.

Social and Physical Location

While gender and age matter, they can only be understood in combination with other social factors like class, race, and sexual orientation, as well as one's physical location, region, and neighborhood. For example, in *Never Say Die*, Susan Jacoby reminds us that lesbians in long term relationships are about the only women as likely to have a partner look after them as to be the caretaker. And childless women must rely on their own resources for care.

In *A Different Shade of Gray*, social scientist Katherine Newman demonstrates how the many stresses associated with social inequality can contribute to middle-aged inner-city residents becoming "old before their time," developing chronic conditions, and living shorter lives. Poor women rarely get a break from caretaking, and this can have a wear-and-tear effect. Most depend entirely on Social Security checks that are quite small, having spent their lives in low wage jobs with no pensions. Location can also constrain opportunities for health and social support, such as living in a rat-infested rental, a high-crime urban neighborhood, or a remote rural community. At the same time, Newman observes how life challenges can reinforce fortitude and resiliency.

Interestingly, a host of social services (meals, transportation, and home care programs) are only available and subsidized for the elder poor, or those who qualify for Medicaid. These programs are the most available in urban locations and are less accessible to the rural poor. Meanwhile, the majority of middle-class elders are left to locate their own resources and pay out-of-pocket for services, spending down their savings. Thus, social location, when added up together, can enable health, social support, and other cumulative advantages over a life, or just the opposite.

Aging in Place

Understanding how the oldest old create support for themselves near the end of life is particularly pressing as the population ages, becomes feminized, and stays at home. Nationwide, the vast majority of the oldest old are aging in their communities.[57] According to *Older Americans 2010*, 7 percent of the oldest old live in community housing with services, and 78 percent live at home. Of all householders in this age group, 73 percent are owners and 27 percent are renters.[58] Almost 40 percent of the oldest old live alone.[59] The majority of elders who need long-term care live at home or reside in community settings, and the percentage of the oldest old currently residing in nursing homes (16 percent) has been declining for several decades.[60]

As population numbers, health care costs, and life spans expand, "aging in place" has become a buzzword for a variety of stakeholders in the United States. State and federal entities as well as health management organizations are invested in reducing costly institutional care for elders.[61] Medicaid funding for the poor, for instance, subsidizes 40 percent of long-term care in the United States. In this changing political context, "home is quickly becoming the context for a widening array of health and human services" with expanded Medicaid (and less frequently, Medicare) coverage for in-home care, decreased hospital stays, and increases in outpatient services. Particularly for the physically frail, the boundaries of hospital and home have blended.[62]

Given the blurring of home and health care, the vast majority of elders state a preference for aging at home, according to forty years of national survey research, including surveys conducted by the American Association of Retired Persons (AARP). Elders cite normalcy, continuity in self-identity, autonomy, and control as reasons for this preference.[63] Many also prefer to die in their own homes. Importantly, informal caregivers like family members still provide 80 percent of care to dependent old persons living at home.[64]

In this context, elders and state entities attach different meanings to aging in place. Many elders associate aging in place with staying at home and being in control of their day-to-day lives; avoiding institutionalization can help to preserve autonomy and dignity. State entities support these initiatives primarily as a cost-saving measure to cut back on health care and hospitalization costs.

Critics argue that aging at home can be extremely isolating, and that home-based health care and transportation can be expensive and difficult to access. Some studies show that isolated elders without clear support networks experience increased vulnerability at home without care. And many elders fear dying alone.

In New York State, aging in place is a key policy initiative as well as the most common way to age. In upstate New York, roughly 80 percent of elders seventy-five years of age and older are already doing so,[65] and a significant proportion of these are women living alone, practicing self-care and playing the role of "solo problem solvers."[66]

New York State aims to be ahead of the curve on the subject of aging in place. Many grassroots and state-funded initiatives on sustainable living, elder care, support services, fall prevention, and co-housing have emerged to support aging at home. A New York State hotline was set up for anyone who wanted information about elder services. And amid controversial discussions about merging or closing state- and county-operated nursing homes, nonprofit Northeast Health demolished their nursing home and started over, moving their institutionalized population into deinstitutionalized home-like care environments. With the help of the Robert Wood Johnson Foundation, they opened the fiftieth Green House in the country, a cutting-edge residential community of small group homes in the Upstate region premised on elder-centered care, autonomy, dignity, and control. In each small group home, complete with twelve private rooms surrounding a common space and walk-in kitchen, a small staff of care workers cater to elder needs regarding food, activities, and care. Here the emphasis is on actively living rather than dying (thus the emphasis on "green").[67]

As our population lives longer and healthier lives, and family members are scattered, the question of how to support elders aging in place is pressing. Today's oldest old are testing the waters, and their lives provide clues as to how to design policy that meets elders' needs for self-sufficiency and support.

THE IMPORTANCE OF A MEANINGFUL LIFE

When policy makers and community leaders focus on providing support for aging, they may address health needs, transportation, and meals, but they tend to miss a big part of the equation: the psychosocial aspects of living a long life. As his ninetieth birthday loomed, my grandfather regularly raised questions about creating a meaningful life in old age. For example, he would say,

> Now Meika, I just don't see it. What is the point of living to ninety, to one hundred? Do the people you interview deal with boredom? How do they fill their lives? I watch my programs. I go for meals, see movies, maybe play some golf. But things are pretty ho-hum.

Gramps is one of the most pragmatic individuals I know, and at eighty-nine, he is healthy and hasn't slowed down a whole lot, but his life has. He has too much time on his hands. He is more alone than ever. He has outlived his siblings, his wife, and the majority of his friends. He sees his three children, four grandchildren, and great-granddaughter only intermittently. Of the eight, only two live near enough to take him to lunch. The young businessmen he has mentored over the years check in once in a while by phone. One lives nearby, and Gramps takes him and his wife out to dinner once a week. He'll talk on the phone, "but only for five to seven minutes, max." He admits he has little patience for phone conversations; as a businessman, his secretary handled most calls. His girlfriend, Linda, whose Alzheimer's disease developed as they dated over the course of a decade, now lives in a dementia-care facility. He manages her care and takes her out to dinner and a movie every weekend.

Knowledge of his past, and the ways in which history intersects with his biography, help me to understand who Gramps is today. He was one of seven children raised by a single mother in Los Angeles, trying to make ends meet during the Depression. He dropped out of school in eighth grade to help the family, taking on odd jobs. Gramps doesn't recall having any hobbies, except for the wonderful rare moments when he could go to the movies to escape into another world. Eventually, Gramps created a successful business, and this success was built on efficiency as well as social networks that my grandmother helped him to build. At home, he had a reputation for punctuality, honking the horn, and getting things done.

As his ninetieth birthday loomed, Gramps found himself out of breath quite often. It seemed that he was still trying to maintain that lifelong momentum, and filling his days by doing what he has always done. He also learned new skills. He learned to use the computer to pay bills and check figures; in this case, box office numbers on movies and cable TV news viewership. He takes care of things around the house. Sometimes he goes in the pool. He eats out at his favorite delis and stocks his fridge with string cheese, gefilte fish, and milk. He files away his health care information. He goes through his mail, reads the paper, and makes lists, as he always has—of his expenses, charities he contributes to, television programs he wants to record, grocery lists. On his calendar, he notes events in the lives of his loved ones and when his children and grandchildren are coming into town. The housekeeper that my grandmother hired many years ago still cleans and does laundry once a week.

Gramps, like many men of his generation, constructed his identity largely around work, and when work ended and he lost his spouse, reinventing himself was a challenge. On the other hand, in many ways, Gramps defies the research on men and old age. He is not interested in remarrying, he has a sizeable social network, and he has a self-care routine that works for now. Driving his car is still his favorite thing to do, in part because that is when time stops, he says. But most of the time, he is at home, where he deals with tasks efficiently, then experiences loneliness and the ticking of the clock. He says he has accomplished all of his life goals. "What is left to live for?" he asks.

Hearing Gramps ask this question makes me deeply sad, although I am proud of all that he has accomplished. He is my only surviving grandparent, and one of my closest friends. I know he wants to continue to contribute, but he can't see how. I have tried many times to answer this question for him, to brainstorm ideas, but the question always comes back. Sometimes, I don't say anything at all. I just listen, hold his hand, and then tell him I love him. I wonder how he'd feel if he lived in a culture that truly respected elders. Then I mentally plan my next trip across the country to see him, and promise myself I will call him weekly, knowing that these things matter. He has always helped to make my life meaningful; it now is my turn to do the same for him.

Interestingly, aging in combination with lifelong pragmatism has prepared my grandfather to embrace the end of life in a way that most have not. Gramps reviews his advance directives and health care proxies with all of us every couple of years, making sure that everyone in the family knows his preference not to be kept alive by artificial means. We don't avoid conversations about death.

Gramps is not alone in asking about creating a meaningful life. Many of us question why we are living at various times in our lives and how to fill our days, but these questions can become magnified in old age, as one experiences time differently and suffers great loss and bodily discomfort. The ways in which my study participants answer these questions are as diverse as the elders themselves. But, if there is one thing that keeps people satisfied with their lives, it would have to be social ties. Most of the participants went out of their way to tell me that living into old age means watching all of your contemporaries die. All were affected deeply by this, and in this context of loss, isolation can be magnified. Moments of connection were re-minders that they were still alive and still contributing.

THE IMPORTANCE OF SOCIAL CAPITAL

In the late nineteenth century, one of the founders of sociology, Emile Durkheim, gathered data on suicide rates across Europe. He found that people with fewer social constraints, bonds, and obligations were more likely to kill themselves. Protestants, who lived the least-demanding religious lives at the time, had higher suicide rates than Catholics, while Jews, with the densest network of social and reli-gious obligation, had the lowest suicide rates. Durkheim concluded that people need social obligation and bonds to provide structure and meaning in their lives.[68] Today, white men aged sixty-five and over are the highest-risk age group for suicide, accounting for almost 16 percent of all suicides, followed by young white men aged twenty to twenty-four. In contrast, women report the highest prevalence of depression.[69] These rates highlight age, gender, and race-based social vulnerabilities.[70]

A vast literature in the social sciences has shown that social net-works can be advantageous across the life course. The value associated with social ties is what sociologists call *social capital.* Like currency, social ties are an investment (of a different type), and their value can accrue over time. Moreover, social capital can be converted into diverse advantages. Researchers have shown that social ties can have profound psychosocial, physiological, and behavioral effects. On a psychosocial level, friendships and social networks can help one to experience increased control over life, access to resources, access to care, and a sense of belonging. In fact, some studies have found that friendship has an even greater effect on health than a spouse or family member. Social networks tend to have a "buffering effect" when it comes to stress, discomfort, and loss. They can also shape how we experience physiological health. Researchers have found connections between social capital and decreased mortality and morbidity. Individual studies show how social networks impact im-munity, heart health, memory loss, recoveries, depression rates, sleep quality, and the experience of pain. Finally, social networks can teach and reinforce health behaviors. As recent studies have shown, just as happiness can be infectious when you surround yourself with people who are content, healthy behaviors can also be contagious. At the same time, social networks can undermine health if they are a source of stress or model unhealthy behaviors like smoking.[71]

The individuals highlighted in this book all nurture, maintain, and value a variety of forms of social capital, and they have done so throughout their lives. In old age, particularly in the context of aging at home (alone), social ties structure their days and give them a reason to continue living. When relationships end, such as through the death of a spouse or loss of work friends in retirement, they lean on others to buffer the blow, ease the transition, and share resources. Many continue to make friends in old age and reconfigure family to include close friends. Interestingly, many choose friends and social groups where complaining about health is kept to a minimum, and abhor the idea of being surrounded by the very sick in care facilities. Visits to doctors can contribute to a sense of health and well-being. The quality of social ties matter, positive or loving relationships enhance health, and strained relationships are problematic for physical and emotional well-being.

I argue that social networks are particularly salient in a context of aging in place. For most, the value of social networks translates into safety nets, a sense of belonging, and decreased isolation. For these study participants, combinations of socioeconomic status, loose intergenerational networks, family connections, and membership in at least one organization added up to social advantages over time. These accumulated social advantages,[72] I believe, contribute to the participants' health and longevity, as well as their ability to teach us how to make connections.

This ethnography examines the wide variety of ways the very old create and maintain social ties in old age. Ruth H. walks with college students, Eddie chats with people at the gym, Julia befriends and hires a homeless woman, Seymour writes for a newsletter, Pauline bakes and shares pies, Johanna hosts a weekly Scrabble game at her home, and Alice counsels friends by phone. By creating or joining groups, reaching out through mail or telephone, or just "hanging out" on a regular basis, these nonagenarians experience a sense of belonging and connectivity that contributes to a sense of routine, health, and well-being. Perhaps most important, social networks allow us perspective and offer a glimpse of the big picture. Knowing that others are feeling lonely puts our own isolation in perspective.

How can one maintain comfort and health, stay at home, and continue to lead a meaningful life? This book answers that question by focusing on these thirty very old individuals and how they approach their daily lives. They reveal their "secrets" to staying at home and maintaining long, meaningful lives. While some lessons for living are familiar, many defy social stereotypes—and even scholarship—on aging.

Instead of approaching old age as a social problem and all old people as dependent, depressed, and disabled, this three-year study views elders as they really are—as agents in their living spaces, neighborhoods, libraries, fitness centers, doctors' offices, and diners. Far from passively experiencing life, elders in this study are actively negotiating aging, ageism, and health across space and time. Over the course of the research, many of the old confront acquired disabilities, loneliness, and loss. Many ask for help, hire and fire, and manage their own care. Many also care for others in important ways. They embrace and critique medical use, self-care technologies, and resources. Many of their day-to-day challenges will be familiar to readers of all ages, and their creative approaches can be important lessons at any stage of life.

The lives of those aged eighty-five and older can be just as exciting, vital, and mundane as those of younger people. At the same time, there is something different about being old; in addition to potential chronic health issues, financial issues, an acute sense of mortality and loss, and other issues that are either unique to old age or accentuated, they must deal with ageism. The oldest old are mostly invisible to us. Each chapter of this book makes visible the everyday life experiences of the oldest old as they actively "do" old age. Like everything we do, this is partly conscious and partly subconscious; much is habit that comes out of a lifetime of doing. In other words, doing old age is largely about doing what one has done all along.

The first half of this book emphasizes self-care regimens. Elders reveal how they stay autonomous and in control, designing their living spaces and daily routines to fit their needs. While loneliness is real, many revel in solitary pleasures and never stop growing and learning. For most, daily living and self-care involves balancing autonomy and dependency. Asking for help and mobilizing resources are central to making it work.

The second half of the book focuses on connections with others, or the various forms of social capital that elders use to maintain health and well-being. Elders reveal creative strategies for finding support and staying engaged in their worlds, by reaching out to peers, social groups, and family members. Building connections not only helps them to cope with aging-related difficulties and loss, but also enables them to keep growing and learning throughout their lives.

LESSON 1

Continue to Do What You Did

Lillian and her second husband, Bernie
(Photo taken by Sidney Albert Albany Jewish Community Center.)

If Lillian were to write her autobiography, it would be about how opera brought her pleasure and romance, two wonderful husbands, and a lifelong passion. In the late 1930s, Lillian fell in love with a fellow student at New York University who took her to *Madame Butterfly*. She says, "That day, [my first husband] detected my interest in opera and the way I responded to the music." That was the beginning. They went to many shows together, and eventually fell in love and married. Opera became something she was good at. She went on to teach classes on how to appreciate opera, and she continues to think about her life as the kind of romantic fantasy upon which opera is premised. Romance has been a guiding theme throughout her life.

When I met Lillian the nonagenarian, she was no longer teaching her "getting to know opera" classes, but she continued to live a life of intimacy and romance with her second husband Bernie, with the help of cable television and lifelong sexual curiosity. She and Bernie sat in matching chairs facing the television, and when I knocked, they called out for me to come in. Lillian was hooked up to an oxygen tank, but she was eager to tell her story. After several hours of talking, she began sharing about sexual intimacy and how it had been important to her in her first marriage and now in her second.

> Bernie and I enjoy spending time together and a little bit of sex. It is very satisfactory, by the way. I find that people our age don't talk about that because we're of the generation where we didn't talk about that. . . . Right Bernie? But it always has been a wonderful experience for me. Frankly, I'll be honest. Many times I think I'm just the luckiest girl in the world. . . . Bernie and I love each other very much. And you know, we watch romance movies every night on cable.

Lillian loves to talk about her first night in Bernie's bed, and how that night confirmed for her that her lifelong needs and desires would be met.

> Bernie said, "I want you to move in with me." And as I heard that, all the little hairs on my neck went up because it was lot of change for me—selling my house and all. Anyways, he said at one point, "I can't offer you much in the way of physical things, a couple of hugs, a couple of kisses." So anyway, I still remember that first night that I was in his bed. And I suddenly realized to myself, I'm lying here like I'm a virgin on my wedding night. What is it going to be? How is it going to be? And I thought, This is ridiculous. Anyway, he comes in and Bernie was, well, very, very good in bed. I said, "You know, you sold yourself short, Bernie. That's a lot more than a couple of hugs and kisses." So we've always had a very nice relationship that way.

Even when she discusses health concerns, Lillian's stories emphasize intimacy and togetherness and stoke Bernie's ego.

> Last night I was in bed, and Bernie said, "Check your Nitro." And I saw that I had four. I always have [Nitroglycerine pills] with me wherever I am. Bernie said, "Maybe you should get some more," and I said "I'll be fine." Well, I woke up and took one, and you know, two dropped out of the container! So now I was down to only one. Well, it got to me. I couldn't sleep, and then I felt terrible. But I had to wake up Bernie and ask him to get my Nitro and he did. And I apologized and said I felt horrible, and he wasn't mad at all. I thought, "[Bernie] saved my life!" Mark my words, I'll never question Bernie being over-prepared again. I understand it! (In the background Bernie adds in, "Remember Lillian, this is on tape!" and laughs.)

More than anything, Lillian tells a story about a life of romance and intimacy, and she continues to work hard to actively accomplish what she knows will make her happy in old age. In this way, Lillian exemplifies how individuals work at continuity across the life course in order to lead meaningful lives.

LIFELONG THEMES AND AGELESS SELVES

A question anthropologist Sharon Kaufman likes to ask when doing a life history interview is this: "If you were to write your autobiography, what would the chapters be?" The answer to this question highlights guiding themes across a life, whether that theme is education, family, creativity, or even loss. As I sat and listened to Lillian's life story, I saw how the chapters in her life—dating, marriages, opera, and familial closeness—added up to a life of continuity and meaning. Despite her health issues, Lillian had an upbeat personality, and she continued to refine and contribute to her personal story of romance and intimacy. It was central to her quality of life: she knew what she lived for.

The overarching story we tell about our lives matters enormously when it comes to how we construct our days, even in old age. In her book, *The Ageless Self*, Sharon Kaufman reminds us that we all work at continuity across the life course, using guiding themes that ground us and help us to construct meaning.[1] An ageless sense of self can also help to transcend the change that results from the physical and mental manifestations of old age. Thus, how one actively ages today may be very much linked to how one has lived in the past, contributing to a sense of continuity as well as agelessness.

Continuity theory, similar to personality theory in psychology, stresses a sense of consistency and coherence over time.[2] We are not static beings, of course, but experience life's pleasures in different ways over time. The oldest old reveal both continuity and change— and here a life course perspective helps to illuminate how life events and social structures push individuals in new and varied directions. Glen H. Elder Jr's classic text, *Children of the Great Depression*, was one of the first studies of children who grew to be elders that placed life development in the context of larger social changes, while acknowledging that the effects of the Great Depression varied by a number of factors, including gender, birth cohort, and class. Elder's study paved the way for understanding the life course and appreciating the uniqueness of each life.

Using a life course perspective, one can see how at least five overlapping factors have shaped Lillian's life, specifically: (1) sociohistorical events and contexts, such as a thriving arts scene in New York City, where she came of age; (2) situational imperatives, such as aging and gender socialization that may reinforce emotional and physical dependencies; (3) interpersonal networks (in this case, linked to education); (4) personal agency, or the ways in which people act, react, and make choices (in this case, an embrace of sexual enjoyment early in life); and (5) life stage, or how timing matters in terms of meanings and consequences.[3]

Lillian's stories serve as a reminder that social location matters in shaping life stories and guiding themes. Lillian's location in New York City, and being a young Jewish, heterosexual, upper-middle class college student in the 1930s, were factors that shaped her opportunities, her interests, her level of confidence, and her future decisions. In many ways, Lillian's emphasis on romance, intimacy, and stroking her second husband's ego fit with gender and class expectations, particularly for her generation. At the same time, Lillian defied gender expectations for her era. She emphasized romance and intimacy in these stories, actively cutting against stereotypes of the sexless old in stating that she desires and derives pleasure in sex, and always has.

Lillian's accumulation of healthy, satisfying sexual relationships, coupled with location, leisure activities, and educational work, have reinforced their importance in her life.[4] While some of these elements have fallen into place over time, Lillian has also had to work to maintain romance and intimacy, particularly in times of challenge, after the death of her first husband, and, more recently, in the context of emerging health concerns. Health status and medical side-effects can shape potential for sexual intimacy,[5] and in Lillian's case, being connected to an oxygen tank at all times, having problems hearing, and "not feeling so hot" limit her options for sexual expression. On the other hand, Lillian makes sure that hearing loss and breathing problems do not interfere with romantic traditions, by emphasizing physical proximity and rituals with Bernie. They sit side-by-side in matching recliners, and Lillian asks Bernie to choose a movie for them to watch every night.

The rest of this chapter identifies a key guiding theme across the lives of eight study participants. By emphasizing key defining traits, we can see the threads of continuity running through their lives and into old age. Like all of us, the oldest old continue to work at defining themselves through the stories they tell about their lives, as well as through their daily actions. At the same time, each is defined by their unique life circumstances and social locations. As elders negotiate life circumstances, guiding themes emerge and provide a sense of tradition, continuity, and meaning in their day-to-day lives. In trying times, these defining themes can provide solace and comfort.

Juana's Baseball

It is easy to see how baseball structures Juana's life and invests it with meaning. Just walk into her living space. On one side of Juana's living room is a wall of framed pictures featuring New York Yankees players Jorge Posada and Derek Jeter. On the other side are shelves covered in bobblehead dolls and autographed balls. Like roughly half of her age group, Juana is serious about a hobby.

Juana's love of baseball stretches back to her childhood in Puerto Rico, where she played ball with her siblings and her mother. She remembers watching Babe Ruth or "Bambino." In her late twenties she was a "Madrina," or godmother, for a minor league softball team in Puerto Rico. She enjoyed being a mother figure for the players and representing the team at opening ceremonies. After coming to the United States in her forties, she played recreationally with her sister and other family members in Connecticut. Her position was second base, her sister (two years older than Juana) was on first. She laughs as she recalls, "The rule was, you never say 'out' to mothers! Only to the children."

Juana is a diminutive woman with thin salt and pepper hair pulled back in a small ponytail. She laughs easily and walks confidently, without assistance. She is most comfortable speaking her native Spanish. Juana worked for years in plastics factories in Puerto Rico, and in 1965, she moved to Brooklyn to follow her now-adult children. Juana worked in a factory not too far from Yankee Stadium, and despite her busy life "growing" seven children by herself, Juana says, "I have always made time for the Yankees. Siempre. I would never miss a game." She has followed the team for sixty years.

Today, Juana's daily routine is much the same. She still leads a busy life, cooking for her children, tending her herb garden, cleaning her home, sewing, and walking to the post office, the dollar store, and the pharmacy. In the evenings she watches baseball.

> At night, I watch the weather and then I watch the Yankees. When the Yankees are playing in California, and it starts at ten, I cannot sleep. I have to watch the game. When they finish the game I will go to sleep.

Juana says she also loves football and basketball, but becomes animated when talking about baseball and the Yankees. She and her daughter Miriam have matching Posada jerseys. She feels a kinship with Posada, who grew up in Puerto Rico, and she is certain that he does not use steroids. She tells a story about when she met Posada at her daughter's workplace (raising funds for disabilities), and she joked with him about his autograph. Her daughter says she whoops and hollers when she watches the games, but Juana does not hesitate to change the channel when the Yankees play poorly.

Ruth L.'s Music

Ruth L. was initially hesitant to meet with me. Over the phone she asked many questions about my marriage, my ethnicity, and my cultural background, revealing the characteristics that were important to her. When she found out I had Russian Jewish roots on my mother's side, she agreed to speak with me in person. She met me on her porch, wearing a house dress and Velcro wrist guards and pushing a simple aluminum walker. Her white hair was pinned up with a handful of bobby pins. That was the first of many visits and the beginning of a close friendship.

Ruth L. is well known in her community for singing "Yiddishe Mama" at local synagogues on Jewish Remembrance Day, to commemorate lost families and the six million lost in the Holocaust. She also has a reputation for being difficult, as we will see in future chapters. Ruth L. says she lives to take care of the dead, to remember her family. She prays to them every day. She remembers all of their names, five children on each side. She was the youngest of three girls, and then there were nieces, nephews, and cousins. No pictures remain, but she remembers. Song is a key part of her memory rituals, both public and private, and on those yearly public occasions, she says her singing brings tears to all, including the rabbis.

Growing up in Warsaw, Poland, Ruth L. would stand on a chair and sing with her parents and siblings. Passersby would come to the window to hear this musical family. When she turned sixteen, someone wanted to take Ruth L. to audition for the opera, but "the glamorous life" was not for her. Family was her biggest pleasure. Yet, music remained central to her life, helping her to cope with life's challenges, to learn a new language in America, to preserve and share her Orthodox Jewish culture and the memory of her family, and to create intimacy with others.

Today, singing in Russian or Yiddish allows Ruth L. to express nostalgia and longing, as well as insist on cultural recognition and pride. Sometimes Ruth L. will serenade friends, to thank them for their good deeds. For example, one day Ruth L. offered, "You want me to sing you a love song in Russian? I will sing just a little bit because you are so nice."

When I ask Ruth L. about music in her life now, she says she keeps a radio near her bed, as she has for years. When she wakes up early, she stays in bed and listens to classical music for a while before starting her day. Music and the radio have always been central to her life at home.

I had a small radio when I was first here [in the United States]. I would listen to the songs and that way I could pick up some English.

I was home with my sons, and so we would listen to the songs. I remember my favorite—"Que sera sera, whatever will be will be, the future is not ours to. . . ." I lived by this song. It was a long song about a girl who asks her mother, "Will I be pretty? Will I have children?" and what comes for her. I lived by this song. And I still do.

In the three years I have known Ruth L., I have heard her sing "Que Sera Sera" several times when things seemed hopeless, or there were no answers. At the doctor's office, I overheard her tell the receptionist that she finds most people cranky. They both agreed on this, and together, at Ruth L.'s request, they sang another of her favorites, Sofia Loren's song from *Showboat*—"Presto Presto, Do Your Very Best-O."

On another more panicked occasion, I was thankful that Ruth L. was able to use song to calm herself and others. I had taken her with me to a Hanukkah party at the local Jewish Community Center. I helped both Ruth L. and my baby daughter into the car, and then my daughter inadvertently locked both of them in the car together (and me out) by pressing buttons on the key remote. The whole episode lasted minutes, but felt like a lifetime. To calm herself and the baby while they waited to be rescued, Ruth L. sang songs, just as she did so long ago with the children in the concentration camps.

Olga's Service

Olga is always on the move, taking care of business. She walks to the grocery store (even in below-freezing temperatures), volunteers in two locations, makes soup, and hems pants. She is so busy it is difficult to make an appointment to see her. When I finally was able to find her in her apartment, she was wearing glasses, a teddy bear sweatshirt, black slacks, and black comfort shoes; she said she hadn't purchased new shoes in decades. I brought her favorite splurge: a McDonald's hot apple pie, and she thanked me profusely.

Olga grew up on a farm in central New York, the eldest of seven kids. While her mother tended the stove day and night and ran the farm, Olga was part housekeeper and part farm laborer, doing everything from washing dishes to making beds, to picking corn and potatoes and cooking for the family. She looks back with fondness, "We had all that we needed there on the farm." Later, married, with two young children and an eighth grade education, she took a WPA job serving soup and sandwiches and worked her way up to a waitressing position at a local diner, where she worked for twenty-five years. She loved those years working in the diner, meeting and making friends with all kinds of people, and, as she says, "furthering [her] education" in an informal way.

When we met, Olga was still serving food and people, volunteering for a hot meal program operated by the County Office for Aging, located one floor down from her apartment in a HUD-subsidized senior apartment complex, and for a church-run thrift shop. Olga is one of 30 percent of individuals in her age group who actively volunteer. After completing her morning housekeeping routine, including making soup with many of the ingredients she had on the farm, she dons her shower cap, apron, and plastic gloves and heads downstairs to work from 10:00 a.m. to 1:00 p.m., setting up chairs, disinfecting tables, heating and serving food, and greeting people. Olga jokes that she might retire next year, at age ninety-seven. But, she points out, she'll still be on call. "[Volunteering] just comes so naturally, you know? So why not help out? It's a good feeling. As long as I can help, sure I will."

Meanwhile, Olga makes a point to assist others in her senior apartment complex. She hems pants for three dollars each, makes soups that she can share with a neighbor, reminds people about bingo, and takes cookies to those she hasn't seen for a while. Serving others makes her feel like she is contributing. For all of these reasons, she loves where she lives and works. "There is so much sadness in the world. And I feel needed here, you know?"

Eddie the Greeter

Eddie has a grin that seems to stretch from ear to ear. He worked for thirty-two years as an elevator operator in the state capitol buildings in Albany, New York. He quickly earned a reputation for being the friendly greeter at the capitol. He remembers holding the doors open for Governors Rockefeller, Carey, and Cuomo. These days, Eddie greets the early morning crowd two days a week at a local community center, where he puts on his exercise clothes, complete with crew socks pulled up high, and perfects his exercise routine. Talking and joking with anyone and everyone, he paces the perimeter of the gym, flailing his arms like a chicken, then like a helicopter, and whistling. He says it does wonders for his circulation. The next minute he'll wave to someone across the room—"Hey there, where you been? Tell me, how do you spell your last name?" And "Hey babe, how are you holding up?" During our interview, Eddie reminds me that he likes to ask the questions, and that he'd prefer to interview me. After all, that's how his life has been.

His friends and admirers call Eddie "the celebrity," referring to his "standing room only" 90th birthday party held in the gym and thrown by his morning workout friends. A local news article emphasized how he cares for others, quoting one of Eddie's friends as saying, "He's got a special way of lifting the spirits of those he's around." Ever since that celebration, Eddie wears their gift when he works out: a blue tank top with his Italian name, Enrico, in big white letters.

After chatting it up in the locker room with the guys, Eddie emerges at 8:00 a.m., stopping to kiss an old friend. "Hey doll, how's that leg of yours?" She turns to me, "He kisses all the ladies at church." He chimes in, "Isn't that what I'm supposed to do? Ha ha ha." Someone nearby says, "That guy is an Albany institution." Others nod their heads. He greets another, "There's Marilyn Monroe!" And then he gets serious, turning to ask one woman how she's doing since her husband passed away. He listens hard and remembers details. Those from the area all know him—they know him from Sunday mass, or from the many odd jobs he's done since the age of seven, or from his days as a bellhop and then an elevator operator. Eddie, like roughly 30 percent of those aged eighty-five and older, left high school well before graduating to help the family make ends meet. After he greets everyone, he waves to me, shouting "Bye babe!" and whistles a tune as he walks out the door. By starting the day connecting with others and helping people to feel good, Eddie can benefit from being known, and can continue to play his lifelong role as a vibrant community-builder.

Emma's Babies

Emma, an African American octogenarian who laughs easily, welcomes me into her tidy apartment and says she needs to show me something. She picks up a stuffed Elmo doll in the corner of her apartment and explains, "I saw a child snugglin' with this doll in Rite Aid and I *had* to have it. *Lord*, it was too adorable. Listen to it go!" And with that, she pushes the button and it giggles along with her.

Emma is wearing an oversized pink gingham blouse with butterflies on it, pink pants, dangly pearl earrings, and white plastic Croc shoe knockoffs. She is animated as we talk, exclaiming things like "Good Lord, child!" when I ask if she has grandchildren.

Most of Emma's life has been spent with children. Growing up in North Carolina, she took care of local kids and later had ten of her own. She is one of only 4 percent of individuals in her age group who is divorced, and she did it twice. In the context of a difficult childhood and two abusive marriages, children, especially babies, represented innocence and hope, as well as companionship.

> I got [to Albany, New York] in '52, thirty-two years old, with seven kids. My husband pushed me out the door—he had been drinking— and oh, honey, that was enough. But I was crazy about my kids. I always loved babies. If there was a baby in the church, I'd be there, and if Mama knew someone who wanted to go uptown to go shopping, she'd say "Shoog will take care of your babies." And I did. I played with them and then I said "Let's lay down on the bed and take a nap." They were my company 'cuz I didn't have none.

Take one look at Emma's small apartment and you know she has a thing for children. Amidst biblical sayings and images, the living room is filled with stuffed animals and framed pictures of family, especially her "grands," as she calls them. She says she stopped counting a long time ago but guesses there are at least thirty grandchildren, scattered around the country. "I can't have them here with me but I can have them here and look at 'em!" In the corner, two dolls face the wall. She says they are playing hide and seek. In the bedroom doorway, a large Aunt Jemima doll with long braids welcomes her in. She lifts up the doll's bonnet, "Look here, honeychild, I went to the dollar store and got her some hair and braided it. She needed something, you know?" Emma is still caring for children in her own way.

Hy's Education and Activism

Hy is giving me a tour of his upscale retirement community. He is medium height with light-colored hair and glasses. He moves easily through the halls, pointing out the workout facilities and the dining room. A woman coming out of the salon says to Hy, "It would be prudent to meet soon"—and it is clear that something is afoot. There's a movement brewing about governance in the community. Hy explains that the residents want to be part of major decisions, rather than being told what is happening. They want a say. An activist his whole adult life, Hy has taken a leadership role in this effort in natural stride. He leaves the impression that he is easygoing and unassuming.

Back in his apartment, Hy points to his study. He says he makes a point of staying on top of the latest research in history. No longer teaching in a university, he volunteers to teach and lead discussions at a senior center and in a continuing education program for retirees. His recent discussion session on the topic of "What Makes a Historical Event" was a huge success.

Education has been central to Hy's life since childhood. As a first-generation immigrant born to poor Russian parents, Hy was the first of his family to attend college. It was his 97-year-old grandmother who made the biggest impression when he was growing up. She wanted him to pursue whatever he wanted and encouraged him to leave the voluntary immigrant ghetto where he grew up, and experience the world. He went on to earn a PhD in history and teach at several colleges. He is one of only 14 percent in his age group to have an advanced degree. The teaching award he received while on faculty at a black college during the early civil rights movement is his proudest achievement. Later, he helped in efforts to diversify and expand a small community college into a large public university.

To this day, Hy continues to do a variety of educational, activist, and community-oriented work. He and his second wife chose to move to this community to be near friends. Yet Hy always makes an effort to introduce himself to new residents, mostly retired faculty. He also spends much of his time away from his apartment, facilitating discussions and working with advocacy groups like Amnesty International and AARP. When describing his current daily routine, Hy emphasizes the educational work he continues to do.

I was told that retirement can be traumatic, that you move from work to no work, but really, my way of life hasn't changed. It has been a smooth transition. I do all the things I did before—I read, I write, I don't get paid for it, but it's most of what I did before. I teach and lead discussions. I lead a moderate life—with food, and I exercise a lot. So basic health is important here, but also attitude . . .

Hy epitomizes continuity in his commitment to education. Although he retired decades ago, Hy still spends a significant amount of time on the university campus he helped to transform. In 2006, Hy helped to advocate for, design, and implement an Emeritus Center at SUNY Albany. This space allowed retired faculty like Hy to continue to utilize the university campus as a center for community and learning. On a cold winter day, Hy gave me a tour of the Emeritus Center. He pointed to a schedule of guest speakers and films, the five new computers paid for by the university, and the comfy chairs. He is proud of this accomplishment, particularly the scholarly community he has been able to build through this space.

Ann's Walks

Ann is Irish-American, tall and lean, with blue eyes and a full head of reddish-brown hair. Her clothing is fashionably casual—capri pants and fitted button-down shirts. She is quiet and gracious, and has a low husky voice that sometimes makes her self-conscious. She says she hopes it sounds like the famous throaty-voiced actress of the 1950s, Tallulah Bankhead. In between comments, a low murmur (almost a hum) emanates from her mouth, and when she walks, she shuffles her feet carefully.

Exercise has always been important to Ann, who was "robust" as a child. Years ago, Ann watched her father and her aunt walk to work. Later, as a social worker, she joined "a parade of folks" every morning, walking several miles to work from uptown to downtown Albany. After she married, she and her husband began a regular walking routine in their suburban neighborhood that included a stop at Ella's café, where they would sit and eat something before walking back to the house.

> You have to understand that my mother and sister were slim, and I was not fat, but I was robust. So I was always watching my food. When my husband died, I lost quite a bit of weight, and I have been trying to stay thin ever since. I am a diet freak, I attend exercise classes, and I walk everywhere.

Now widowed for seven years, Ann walks to Ella's on her own, where the owner greets her by name. To avoid taking up a table, Ann sits at the counter in the front window and has a cup of coffee. The other route she likes takes her past Stewart's mini-market, where she can pick up milk and eggs. Snow and rain do not stop her. "Even on bad weather days there's a moment when it isn't raining, so that's when I go," she says.

She also takes a daily trip down two short flights of stairs to the basement of her apartment building to drop off her garbage and recycling. Lately, she finds she can be out of breath when she returns, but that just reminds her to appreciate living on the ground floor. She says she would never ask anyone to help her with this. "I can be a real bug about diet and exercise. It is a lifelong habit, and it also helps me to sleep."

Ann is anomalous among her age group about exercise. According to the Centers for Disease Control and Prevention, only 11 percent of individuals aged eighty-five and over report engaging in regular physical activity, which has been found to improve mobility and overall quality of life.[6] At the same time, such activity is risky, especially for women in late life. Falls are common, and that is why Ann's lifelong walking routine has begun to worry her friends. I was in the locker room when Ann got in trouble, again, with her friends from the hydroslimnastics class. She was caught walking in bitterly cold weather. Someone in the class pulled over and picked her up. They offer her regular rides to class; most are worried about her slipping on the ice. Ann responds that she doesn't mind the walk from where the bus drops her off. "I guess I come from a long line of walkers," she says.

Seymour the Technogenarian

The cochlear implant is not quite hidden in the short wavy grey hair just above Seymour's ear. Seymour has been deaf since the age of eighteen as the result of a genetic disorder.[7] Given his disability, this short, broad-shouldered man learned to rely on and refine his remaining senses, with a special emphasis on the tactile. As a "mechanically inclined" young man who grew up playing ball in the streets of Harlem, Seymour gravitated toward machines and words.

> I made a good life despite the handicap. I had no formal training to be a linotype operator, but it's one of those things. If you couldn't do anything else you could play with words. I was a premium operator, and

they called me a "combination man" because I could do a combination of skills. So people cooperated with me—they depended on me, and me them. So we just worked together—it was mostly the same stuff every day. And then everything went from typeset to computers, so when I was fifty-five or sixty, I had to adapt. So that's how I learned computers.

After fifty years as a linotype operator for newspapers and print outlets, as well as an airplane mechanic during and after World War II, Seymour was set up to be a lifelong technogenarian, or an elder who has embraced technology to open up opportunities for communication and connection.[8]

In old age, Seymour continues to structure his days through technology and type—in this case, his keyboard, e-mail, and the written word. As an up-to-date "techie," Seymour is uncharacteristic for his age group. He writes a monthly column for a local Florida publication, and he uses Skype (a way to communicate through his computer screen) with family members, including a daughter at NASA. His reputation among his friends is "the fix-it guy" who helps out when he can. When he is away from these tools, Seymour can feel lost—like the time his apartment was flooded and he was unable to access a computer, or even at his own birthday party where everyone was talking with each other, but not with him.

On his annual visits to Florida with his second wife Bernice, Seymour observes most of his peers playing cards, watching movies, joining clubs, and engaging in "endless conversation." More than 60 percent of individuals in his age group have problems with hearing, but Seymour's hearing handicap is severe. Knowing that these moments and observations make him feel "bad" about his disability, Seymour structures his day to include the experiences that bring him physical and mental satisfaction, including reading, interacting with virtual communities, and exercising.

CONTINUITY ACROSS LIVES

By continuing to do what they have always done, the contemporary lives of Lillian, Juana, Ruth L., Olga, Eddie, Emma, Hy, Ann, and Seymour remain focused, grounded, and satisfying. They all have regular routines, and these rituals are invested with meaning. As anthropologist

Barbara Myerhoff reminds us in her classic text *Number Our Days*, ritual—whether religious or not—manifests personal beliefs and values. Beyond this, ritual can be deeply therapeutic.

These elders show us that lifelong routines are not static and unchanging, nor are they passive. As we saw with Lillian, bodies and life circumstances are always in flux. Continuity, therefore, requires real effort and some stubborn resilience. Anthropologist Sharon Kaufman would say that these individuals use their life themes and formed identities to navigate new life circumstances and experiences.[9] Each story emphasizes not only lifelong continuity and autonomy, but also adaptability in the face of changing circumstances. Thus, Ruth L. uses music to soothe and console herself in a variety of challenging situations. Eddie and Olga are officially retired from paid work, yet they manage the continuation of their working identities into old age. And Ann finds value in her lifelong walking regimen despite weather hurdles and others' fears that she might fall.

If continuity is not possible, elders sometimes experience a sense of disruption and loss. For Eddie, a week without visiting the gym can feel particularly lonely. Olga feels a similar sense of emptiness when she does not volunteer. Most find ways to fill the void. Seymour still misses the hearing life he had as a child, and to counter self-pity, he generally avoids social groups and spends more time communicating through e-mail. Emma can't have her "grands" around, so she creates other opportunities for caretaking. For Ruth L., the experience of singing with her musical family is something she can never get back, so she sings by herself and holds on to the memories.

All of these elders have had a lifetime to construct and reconstruct their life stories, and to become attached to their own unique guiding themes. In contrast, at the age of twenty, many of my college students are in the early stages of "finding" themselves. A college essay is one opportunity to engage in life review. Having to declare a major is another opportunity. As graduation looms and they prepare themselves for post-college lives, many in their twenties look back over their two decades of living for clues that might point to what comes next. The sense of possibility involved in building a life that one desires, within social constraints, can be inspiring as well as humbling in its seeming enormity. When they are matched with elder learning partners in my class, students come to understand the cumulative consequences of small and big decisions and life events across the course of one elder's life. In a big-picture way, the significance of a life course perspective is illuminated. At the same time, they come to see how, at twenty, they are already creating unique pathways.

This chapter has focused on a single thread or theme that runs through the multifaceted fabric of each elder's life. And yet, as we saw with Lillian, each elder's life story is complex and constantly in dialogue with their social world. All of these stories relate to other themes in this book. All involve social ties in some way, even for Ann, whose walking is first and foremost about autonomy and control, the subject of Lesson 5 ("Ask for Help and Mobilize Resources"). Emma's photo-filled walls and Juana's baseball-themed living space reveal how meaningful and important one's living environment can be, the subject of Lesson 2 ("(Re)Design Your Living Space"). Ruth L.'s relationship with music is both about connecting, as well as enabling solitary pleasure, the subject of Lesson 3 ("Take Time for Self"). Hy's life of education reveals that growing and learning in a group environment can continue into old age, further discussed in Lesson 6 ("Get Connected with Peers"). Eddie's social life at the gym reminds us of the importance of a sense of belonging and purpose, as well as humor, the subject of Lesson 7 ("Resort to Tomfoolery"). Seymour's regular submissions to a local newsletter and repair work as a favor to friends reveal the importance of contributing throughout one's life, further discussed in Lesson 8 ("Care for Others"). And Lesson 11 ("Insist on Hugs") emphasizes the importance of physical touch in old age, as Lillian exemplifies in the beginning of this chapter.

As we have seen, lifelong themes are woven into daily or weekly routines, such as Lillian's nightly movies, Ruth L.'s morning music, Eddie's morning gym routine, Olga's midday volunteer work, and Ann's daily walks. Daily routines are crucial for continuity and self-care. They structure days, weeks, and months, add a sense of purpose to a life, and enable self-care. In many ways, the concept of daily routine structured my conversations with elders. Asking about daily practices became a barometer for measuring shifting circumstances, bodies, and living environments, and a way to visualize how elders learn and practice flexibility on a daily basis, as they plan and redesign their everyday practices and spaces. The next lesson specifically discusses the social significance of place and design.

LESSON 2
(Re)Design Your Living Space

Florence and her command center

On warm days, Florence leaves the front door of her suburban ranch-style home open so that the mail carrier can walk in and hand her the mail. When I approached her front door for the first time, I saw and heard Florence through the screen, waving me in. "Come in, hon."

I walked into a large living room and greeted a tall, bookish-looking nonagenarian, who was sitting in her recliner, the spot where she spends the better part of each day, wearing comfortable clothing and sensible shoes. She was in the most agreeable place she could be, and rather than haphazardly making do, Florence had designed a user-friendly space that kept her occupied and connected, and met her changing health needs.

Florence surrounds herself with the essentials of her life. Pictures of her husband and family surround her on all sides. On a side table to her right sit a lamp, a transistor radio, and telephone. A cane leans against the table. Slightly below that (perched on an ottoman) are two plastic containers, one that holds mail and a calendar, and one that she calls her "medicine cubby" for about ten prescription bottles and a large bottle of Rolaids. To her left sits her walker, which doubles as a storage shelf, complete with flashlight, checkbook, and a lifeline alert necklace draped over the side.[1] And on the floor next to her recliner are a blanket, a pillow, and her purse. This small area symbolizes relative self-sufficiency for Florence.

> I'm content to sit here [in the recliner]. My back aches most of the time. And I have everything here that I need. I've got my addresses, my checks, letters to answer. My TV remote. My chair remote. See, my legs are up like they are supposed to . . .

Because Florence values rest and relaxation over busyness, she is content to concentrate her life around her reclining chair, her family pictures, her cubbies, and her television. By contracting most of her daily activities into a small space, she has set up a central command center from which she can manage phone calls, deliveries, medical needs, and entertainment options.[2]

My visit with Florence helped me to recognize that elders, like all of us, are interior designers. As their needs shift, they create comfortable, user-friendly spaces and systems to meet their needs.

PLACE MATTERS

Place matters, and most of us confront at least three important questions about place: Where should I live? How can I maximize location? And how do I create a living space that works for me?

All of the oldest old in this study designed a physical place to age comfortably. Such adaptation fits with German developmental psychologist Paul B. Baltes' theory of selection, optimization, and compensation (SOC), which emphasizes how elders alter and adapt their environment to fit their current needs.[3] As we will see, elders shape the places they inhabit, just as locations shape bodies and selves.[4]

This chapter focuses on eight households, including one group-home care community, to examine how elder occupants have adapted their home spaces to meet their needs with personalized features designed for functional independence. This first section provides an overview of each household and how locations and outside environments can contribute to or constrain elder well-being.

Margaret and Rose both recently moved into compact one-bedroom or studio apartments in HUD-subsidized senior housing complexes. For Rose, taking care of a home had become difficult for practical and financial reasons. The complex where she now lives is in a downtown area with businesses and bus lines within close walking distance. Margaret moved to be near loved ones. In contrast to Rose's community, Margaret's complex is in a rural area without public transportation. Both have learned to organize and maximize limited space indoors, as well as maximize outside resources and access community in new ways.

Ruth H., Ruth L., and Mary and Bill all have occupied large family homes for at least fifty years, and they want to stay. Ruth H.'s home is located in a rural village of several thousand people, Ruth L. lives in a suburban neighborhood, and Mary and Bill live in a three-story row house in a downtown area. Most of them have closed off certain rooms and floors and focused on central pivot points, as Florence did. They made their homes accessible, installing ramps, handrails, and chair glides for stairways. Their modifications accentuate ease of use, comfort, and convenience and allow them to use familiar spaces differently at this stage of their lives.

Pauline and Juana have spent the last few decades in compact two-story homes in increasingly impoverished inner-city neighborhoods. Pauline, who worries about her location, spends most of her time on the ground floor in her favorite chair. The curtains are drawn for privacy. She ambles into the kitchen several times a day and climbs the stairs only to go to bed. Juana occupies the second floor of a two-story home; her daughter lives on the first floor.

During the day, when she runs errands for food, she is respected in her neighborhood; and she is safe in bed before she hears gunshots.

Finally, Fred and Christine have each recently moved from shared rooms in a crowded nursing home into group-care Green Houses they now consider "home." Built to update and replace older nursing facilities, Green Houses integrate "universal design" principles with the latest care technologies around an elder-centered vision.[5] Christine can wheel her chair into the bathroom or use an overhead lift, with assistance, to get to the toilet. She can also help to prepare a meal by using wheelchair-accessible counters. Both she and Fred are free to spread out and personalize their private spaces. Each lives with eleven other elders in a shared ranch-style home composed of a large living room, den, spa, dining room, and walk-in kitchen. As full-time residents, their homes are theirs to claim and to make their own. And their location in a secure residential care community, with a team of nurses and therapists nearby, enables them to meet all of their health, safety, and transportation needs.

Beyond an indoor space that emphasizes well-being, social and geographic location—or "extended home space"—can also be crucial for all of these elders. The right location can help to remedy loneliness and provide a social safety net. When she was feeling up to it, Ruth L. sat on her porch to watch the comings and goings of a changing residential community. For her, this was a way to feel connected to the community and its history.

> There is movement on the street, but not a lot. Not like it used to be. It used to be full of children and families who would come together on the street or on the steps. Many Jewish families. No more. People stay in their houses.

Through her porch-sitting, Ruth L. was able to meet a new neighbor family who became an important emergency contact. Location can also enable access to key resources such as groceries and transportation. Mary's proximity to a downtown resale shop inspired her to do some spring cleaning.

> Have you seen that tea kettle in the window? That was mine from way back. I walked over and told [the shop owner] I have no need for this anymore . . .

Mary's downtown location in a commercial-residential district also allows her access to an intergenerational community whose members take turns bringing her and her husband weekly meals. Mary and Bill reciprocate by hosting their neighbors at the local university club every few months for Friday-night suppers. Similarly, Ruth H., who lives in a tight-knit rural village just a block from the farmers market, explains why she does not want to move:

> This is the best place for a widow. You are taken care of. I've given up all travel. I can't drive that far. What other place could I be so content to stay in the rest of my life? It is so beautiful and wonderful people. . . . And I know people are looking out for me.

For Ruth L., Mary, and Ruth H., location translates into safety, convenience, and crucial connections to community. In stark contrast to Mary and Bill's close downtown community in a mostly white, historic preservation district, Pauline's clapboard home, located several miles away, is in an impoverished neighborhood, a few doors from a now-empty crack house. Like Ruth L, Pauline has watched her neighborhood change over the past thirty-five years. It has become increasingly poor and crime-ridden, with many vacant buildings and a majority of poor African American residents. Although Pauline hears sirens less often this year than last, she still does not feel safe where she lives. However, she owns her home and cannot imagine moving.

> I have a few neighbors—but I don't know their names. The houses [just around the corner] burned down. They were dope dens—and it was a blessing in disguise that they burned. People have moved on. But this was a neighborhood with sirens, and gunshots. Sometimes you thought *all* the police were there, with so many lights and sirens. It was just awful.

Despite the poverty and crime in the neighborhood, Pauline is able to take advantage of exercise classes and health services offered in community centers just blocks away, as long as she can get a ride.

In old age, location can translate into preventative health care, security, connectedness, and general quality of life. In Pauline's case, location is much more nuanced; it can mean increased isolation and danger as well as access to limited but crucial resources.

HOME AS A SOCIAL CONSTRUCT

Moving indoors now, design can literally mean the difference between falling or maintaining health and balance. In the following vignettes, ten very old individuals actively organize their living spaces to emphasize continuity, comfort, and convenience. In so doing, they expose "home" as a social construct, both literally and figuratively. Margaret, Rose, Ruth H., Mary and Bill, Ruth L., Pauline, Juana, Christine, and Fred have carefully thought about and planned their living spaces, and this has had real ramifications for them. They remain comfortable, healthy, safe, and perhaps most important, at home.

Margaret: Making Things Handy

> I like to get up and move around in my apartment. Even if I don't do a whole lot, I know I'm walking around. I walk around and do my dishes all the time. And sometimes when I'm doing things I like to listen to hymns, and some of the old good music.

Margaret is sitting in her yellow chair, wearing lipstick, a necklace, a blue velour long-sleeved blouse, and matching slacks. She spends her days in a tidy one-bedroom apartment. Over the course of a day, she moves from her reading chair, to the kitchen counter to prepare food, to the kitchen table to eat, and back to her reading chair. In general, she likes the movement back and forth; she appreciates the exercise. But she has arthritis in the shoulder, so cabinets are too high to reach, and she cannot stand for long without her legs feeling weak. Margaret keeps things "handy" to make it easy on herself—her pills and a cutting board on her kitchen table, a music player on a nearby TV table. She has designed each of these stops to structure her day and maximize self-efficacy and accessibility.

> I used to do a hot meal at night, and all those pots and pans, well, it was a lot of preparation and clean-up. Now I don't have much clean-up. I have soup and crackers or a sandwich. I'm not standing at the stove anymore. And if I need to prepare something, I sit at the table and work. I spread out the newspaper and the wax paper if things might get gooey or oozey, and then I can clean it up real easily afterwards.

Like Florence, Margaret has organized a central pivot around her reading chair, for the more sedentary periods of her day, to be comfortable and efficient. A phone and lifeline remote monitor sit on a table next to her chair, and reading materials are in an organizer by her side. In the kitchen, Margaret has stacked several bowls and dishes in the corner near the sink, for easy access. Her coffee machine and toaster, which are used daily, are out on the counter and ready to go. And if she needs something up high, she has a "pincher" for grabbing out-of-the-way items. Margaret also stages two walkers, one new fancy red one that "turns on a dime" with wheels, brakes, and a basket[6] by the front door of her apartment, for use when she goes out, and one older hand-me-down walker by her bed for use at night when she is "groggy" and needs stability.

For some, downscaling may seem like a reduction in living standards, but elders like Florence and Margaret describe the benefits in terms of simplicity, efficiency, and comfort.

Rose: Creating a Cozy Nest

Greeting cards from many occasions decorate Rose's door, located just around the corner from the elevator. I knock, and Rose greets me with a joyous "hello!" and a broad smile, accentuated against her dark skin. She is wearing a smock-like, button-down work shirt, polyester pants, and slippers. Her thick curled brown hair could be a wig. She ushers me in, offering me meatballs and ginger ale and saying I can sit anywhere I like. Her presence is nonjudgmental and reassuring; she murmurs "mmmhmmm" regularly as we talk.

Rose moved into her apartment when she could no longer maintain her family house in a nearby rural area of New York. Her memories moved with her, and her apartment is filled with photos and piles of papers. While initially she didn't want to move into this low-income senior apartment complex, she says, "It turns out this was the best place for me. They take care of everything—like electric! It is my nest, and I never want to leave."

Rose has managed to create meaningful spaces by turning her tiny studio into a one-bedroom apartment with the use of a wall/shelving unit.

When they asked me to move to another apartment several years ago, I said I would not go without my partition there. So they said fine, and me and my partition moved together! Now this [partition, with built-in shelving] is where I display my most prized possessions—pictures of my adopted children and my late "great" husband. And behind the partition I have a sweet little bedroom in there.

Rose persevered to literally build a space that works for her, and she works hard to organize it. She navigates several piles of newspapers quickly and easily, pulling out a newspaper article featuring her attendance at an Obama inauguration party at her senior complex. "The inauguration of a black president was the most beautiful thing I have ever witnessed," she remembers. Then she points to a picture of the Obama family on her wall, "My goodness, isn't that the most perfect family? And color has nothing to do with anything." Rose has created a space that reminds her of family and a newfound national pride. While Florence's and Margaret's design work emphasizes bodily comfort and convenience, Rose's organization and decoration accentuate privacy, memory, and a personal commitment to staying positive.

Florence, Margaret, and Rose all honed their technique of concentrating essential tools of life into a "command center." While some might see stacks of paper, cubbies, or dishes as clutter, others would see maximized space, tidy piles, and rich layering, evidence that these elders have created home spaces that are an extension of themselves and what they deem important.

Ruth H.: Making the Family House Hers

Ruth H. is like a female Mr. Rogers. She has the relaxed familiarity of a teacher; she is tall, slender, loves to wear cardigan sweaters, and epitomizes what it means to be neighborly. She lives in a large Victorian home in a small rural village where she is friendly with a significant portion of the three thousand residents, many of whom she has known for years.

On a brief tour of her house, I got a sense of how Ruth H. structures her days and weeks, how she keeps busy despite going "stir crazy" in the winter, and what she valued in old age. Above all, Ruth H. values staying at home and being independent. To do this, she closed off the upstairs, and only uses the downstairs rooms. The biggest change came when she moved her bedroom downstairs, and built a handicap-accessible bathroom.

> The question for my own parents was, "Are you going to stay here or go to a nursing home?" . . . And then my daughter was here once, and I was saying, "I don't know quite what to do." I had a stair elevator that was my mother's if I had problems going upstairs. But the shower was in the bath tub. And I was a little worried about, as I got older, stepping into that. And she said, "Make the playroom into a bedroom, make Tim's room into a bathroom and make my room into a walk-in closet, and there you are." And that's what I did. So, I live down here. And of course it's um . . . a handicap bathroom. I didn't need it then, but now I'm thankful, with grab bars and things. So the answer was, "I'll stay here," in this huge house with fifteen rooms.

After moving downstairs, Ruth H. capitalized on the expansive space, circulating through every room, every day. She uses the living room for social visits and weekly discussion group meetings. The den she uses for "brain stimulation," like computer work and reading. (At the entrance to the den, a sign reads "I'm not unorganized, I'm just flexible.") The kitchen space allows for "creative expression." Sometimes Ruth H. uses the stairs for exercise. Most important, Ruth H. associates her house with learning how to be an independent woman after raising children and caring for her parents in this space.

> Here, I'm me. It took me a long time to become me because I was my husband's wife for many years. When my parents moved here, I was their daughter. When all those three died off, I was an orphan, then a widow. Now, I'm Me! And I like having all this space.

Three years later, Ruth H. continues to adapt and claim the space as her own, decorating the walls, adding lighting and safety features, and staying connected while remaining independent. Maintaining this large old home is not stress-free. When I arrived, workers were in the basement attending to a small flood. She had just replaced her furnace and concluded, "I'm a whole lot poorer, but I am warmer now. I was making do with small heaters." Now Ruth H. was rubbing her head, concerned about all of her home maintenance expenses, but then reminding herself, "I say it all the time. I'm CEO of this corporation and it is a lot to care for. *And* I have to care for this little old lady who is a handful."

Several years after we first met, Ruth H. now seems to spend more time in the chair in her sitting room, reading and talking on the phone. We sit together in this corner facing the large front windows, talking. At age ninety-seven, she hosts visitors in this space, continues to work in the den, and loves to cook. In her corner, she has created a minimized version of Florence's command center, but for a more mobile person. A half-eaten peanut butter sandwich sits beside her, a dictionary nearby, and a cloth purse is draped over the side of the chair, with her cordless phone in it. The purse is always in the same place when she is seated, to minimize confusion. When Ruth H. moves, the phone purse travels with her, including when she does "laps" in the hallway for exercise.

New wall hangings and nightlights provide evidence that Ruth H. is still taken care of by her family and community; they also exemplify how Ruth H. embraces change as she ages. New, colorful paintings of global children by her daughter adorn the walls in the dining room and living room. As Ruth H. points each one out to me, she proudly recounts the stories behind the paintings. In the dim kitchen, new stained-glass nightlights, made by a friend and caretaker, glowed in the outlets. Despite sedentary periods, Ruth H. has continued to adapt and modify her space according to her needs.

Mary and Bill: Upstairs, Downstairs

Mary and Bill still climb the flights of stairs inside and outside their three-story downtown brownstone. They use canes to steady themselves on the outside stairs and then, once inside, Bill uses a mechanical chair lift to reach the floor they inhabit. Mary and Bill have been in this home for sixty years, since the days when Bill had his dental practice on the ground floor. They do not want to live anywhere else.

Like any large home, it takes work to keep it comfortable. At some point, the dining room chairs got to be too hard on their bodies and the window areas were too cold. Mary, whose mother was a seamstress, used her sewing skills to sew pads for the chairs and heavy curtains to keep the heat inside. Meanwhile, Bill, with the help of his hired helper, Ray, places plastic sheeting on the windows to keep out the winter cold.

Mary and Bill occupy separate floors of the brownstone much of the day, a routine that is reinforced by lifelong habits, gendered division of labor, and differences in mobility. Upstairs, Mary has set up a sewing room where she can lay out everything on a long table and work mostly while seated. Downstairs, in Bill's old dental office, he has a computer where he can play solitaire and access jokes. They enjoy their upstairs, downstairs rituals and separate spaces.

> BILL: I have my computer and everything down there on the first floor and Mary has the top floor with her sewing equipment.
>
> MARY: It just became like that a long time ago. When we retired, he would be downstairs working on his computer and I would be upstairs sewing and enjoying that.

Most days, after lunch Mary and Bill will head to their respective floors for afternoon activities. Downstairs, Bill will generally take a nap, play computer games, and work with Ray. Upstairs, Mary will sew, work on the computer, clean, write letters, read, or get organized. When happy hour arrives, both convene on the second floor. By designing, occupying, and maintaining separate intentional spaces, Mary and Bill are able to lead independent meaningful lives while also taking care of each other.

Ruth L.: Design to Enhance Mobility

On a tour of the main level of her large home, ninety-five-year-old Ruth L., the music-loving Holocaust survivor we met in Lesson 1, described her self-designed mobility and safety system. Her self-reliance tool kit includes a variety of technologies, each with a particular purpose. Her electric scooter is for use outside on the sidewalks, in nice weather; however, Ruth needs someone to take it down a few stairs, so it typically sits covered in her dark sitting room. Her indoor walker moves with her, but not everywhere. Because she inhabits a compact area on the ground floor, she relies on counters and walls for leverage when navigating halls and the kitchen. When she needs to leave the house, she must walk a distance to the back door, and relies on walker #1 to get there. She leaves one walker at the top of the back staircase, and at the bottom stands walker #2, which goes with Ruth L. when she must leave the house for doctors' appointments.

In the winter, Ruth L. keeps a bucket of rock salt near the back door and scatters it, to avoid falling on icy concrete. A few steps on the salt with the help of the walker and she can reach the car waiting to drive her to her appointment. Having two walkers is "absolutely necessary"—"another pair of legs" without which Ruth L. believes she would fall. Finally, Ruth L. says she would never leave the house without enabling her home security system, including a variety of locks and a security alarm; these assuage her fears and assure her that everything will be the same when she returns.

Several years ago, it seemed that Ruth L. had perfected her own system to enable mobility, independence, and security, and she was proud of this. She never depended completely on any one element, but always had a back-up in place. Because Ruth L. asked for and accepted little assistance with her daily life and care, this system was crucial for supporting her aging in place and made her role as designer and implementer of it all the more evident. Eventually Ruth L. will be forced to accept some assistance, though many aspects of her mobility routine remain in place.

Pauline: A Safe Haven

Much like Ruth L., Pauline needs assistance in her later years. But the period from adulthood to her mid-eighties was about independent living. I met Pauline at an end-of-the-year party for her senior exercise group. She was wearing a safari hat over her curly black-grey hair, a sweater and slacks, and nice-looking flats. Without fanfare, she presented a wrapped gift of bath soaps to the instructor and thanked her warmly for a wonderful class.

Pauline exudes Southern charm. In her thirties, she moved from South Carolina to New York and worked her way up from a job as a chambermaid at a Catskills resort to a well-paying three-year stint at the armory, where she trained others to operate twelve different machines, and everyone called her "Ma." After years of renting a room at the YMCA, she eventually saved enough to purchase a home in Albany, a city known as a transportation hub. From there, Pauline traveled frequently to see her sister in the air force and her family in South Carolina. She never married.

As mentioned previously, Pauline (now in her mid-eighties) says her neighborhood of thirty-five years looks different. She no longer knows her neighbors by name, and she keeps the curtains drawn for privacy. The police presence and gunshots she has heard in the past continue to put her on alert. Yet, once she passes through her Astroturf-covered entryway, Pauline's safe haven hasn't changed a whole lot. The television is in the corner. Magazines are spread out on the coffee table for guests. Family photos line the walls. The oven, where she has baked countless sweet potato pies, and the bathtub, where she has soaked for years, remain central to her life.

As Pauline's bodily discomfort increases, she occupies her living space differently. Because she has arthritis "from the tippy toes to the neck," she longs for comfort. When not in her exercise class or at church, she spends much of the day in a recliner, like Florence. Pauline keeps her chair locked in the "eject" position so she can get in and out without trouble. She keeps the cordless phone with her at all times, spending hours talking with pharmacies and doctors' offices. At last count, she takes twelve pills a day.

When she ventures into the kitchen to unload the dishwasher, it doesn't take long before the pain is so unbearable that she needs to sit down again. Because of this, her interest in meals and pie-baking has waned, except when she hosts distant relatives at holiday time. Then, she'll do her famous home cooking.

Juana: A Shrine to Baseball and a Place to Stay Busy

Unlike Pauline, Juana has no complaints about health. At her last annual exam, Juana's doctor declared that she was healthy enough to live to 150, and Juana responded with excitement. In general, she says her age does not weigh on her, and, unlike others, she does not feel any stress. She likes to joke around. She says her secret is eating rice and beans for every meal, and resting. In many ways, Juana personifies what social epidemiologists call the "Latino health paradox." In health and longevity studies, Latinos seem to have better health outcomes than social indicators would predict. Juana, having grown up impoverished in Puerto Rico, and then raising seven children on her own while working factory jobs, is a case in point.

Perhaps it is Juana's active lifestyle, enabled by her physical proximity to family, shopping, and her bilingual Catholic community that contribute significantly to her good health and well-being. At ninety-one, Juana walks confidently without a cane. Aside from tripping over the recycling can once, she has no problems with stairs. She insists on cleaning her own home and rarely asks for help for anything other than occasional transportation.

Juana's living space, the second story and the attic of a house shared with her daughter Miriam, enables her to do what she has always done. As we learned in Lesson 1, Juana devotes her living room to baseball. This is where she watches the Yankees on television, as well as basketball and football. If the games run late into the night, Juana watches from her bed in the attic. The rest of Juana's living space is organized to enable all of the household duties she has always done: cooking, washing and ironing clothes, and sewing. Her favorite part of her daily routine is a siesta after taking care of these tasks. Afterwards, her home space extends beyond her second floor into her daughter's ground-floor apartment, her garden, the surrounding neighborhood, and her Catholic community, all experienced as places where she feels comfortable.

Christine and Fred: Living and Growing in Green Houses

Unlike the other elders aging in houses and apartments, Christine and Fred, who each had lived alone in apartments for many years, now require assistance with at least three activities of daily living (ADL), such as dressing, walking, and bathing. Because of this, they live in a care environment where they can maintain semi-independent lives, while receiving assistance when needed. Christine is a soft-spoken, shy Irish woman. She has been in a wheelchair since a fall dislocated her hip and a botched surgery left one leg longer than the other. Fred is quiet and slim, a slightly disabled former postman who ended up in the rehab floor of the nursing home while recovering from a major operation. Today, both nonagenarians spend their days living in a "de-institutionalized" group-home care environment. As the number of nursing home residents declines, Green Houses have emerged as a new ethical, elder-centered model of care envisioned by a doctor-gerontologist team.

Christine and Fred live in the fiftieth Green House development in the nation, and both say that this new living environment has changed their outlook and saved their lives.

Green Houses emphasize living and growing. Here, as in elders' individual homes, place follows vision. Spaces are communal (the dining room table is designed for fourteen), accessible (with everything from bathrooms to kitchen counters designed for walkers and wheelchairs), personalizable, and comfortable (in the living room, the fireplace is always going, and the chairs and couches are designed for comfort and ease of use). Activity centers around the lives of the elders—there are twelve residents per house, and each individual occupies his or her own private rooms (each with its own bathroom), and they decide when to get up and go to bed, choose activities to take part in, design the house menu, and make the house a home. At any given time, two or three certified nursing assistants trained in culinary arts, cleaning, nursing, and elder empowerment are on hand, preparing meals in the large walk-in kitchen and attending to elders' calls. Each elder wears a necklace that, with a push of a button, can call for assistance. Nurses and therapists also circulate through each house throughout the day, but importantly, the houses do not have nursing stations. Unlike nursing homes, these settings are centered around elders, not medicine or rules.

The Green House exemplifies how "place" matters. While nursing homes across the nation, with their outdated hospital-like institutional feel, lack of privacy, and stringent rules, can't fill rooms, Green Houses have waiting lists. Why? Because Green Houses are envisioned as the next best thing to aging at home, in a neighborhood, with added benefits like social networks, personalized care and housekeeping, universal design, and transportation.

Christine's and Fred's homes are part of a neighborhood of sixteen differently colored ranch-style houses. Between 2007 and 2010, I watched with them as Green Houses arose out of the debris of their recently demolished high-rise nursing home. Each house has a screened-in porch with comfortable chairs in front, and a side yard shared with the house next door. Mail is delivered in the mailbox, and you ring a doorbell to get in. On sunny days, Fred and his fellow resident and friend Alice sit on their enclosed porch, doing crosswords and watching the comings and goings. Inside, residents have chosen the interior design style and wall decorations, and have designed their own rooms to fit their needs and represent their interests.

Christine, shy and increasingly disabled, spends a good deal of time in her room, emerging for meals and once in a while for exercise classes and activities. Sitting in her wheelchair, bundled in handmade crocheted blankets, she is surrounded by pictures and memorabilia. An Irish prayer is posted above her bed. Sun streams through her large window, lighting a saint figurine from behind. After years of working as a bookkeeper in New York City, operating comptometers (the precursor to the computer) for corporations like Chase Manhattan, Christine has lost much of the use of her arms, hands, and fingers. When someone presses play on her cassette player, she cries with delight, and sings along to her Celtic music. Other times she watches her soaps, talks on the phone, or follows the local news. She says the Green House model of care saved her life—at the nursing home, she was not eating or sleeping and cried herself to sleep. Now she gets food and Irish tea made for her, uses special eating implements that she can grip, and when her blanket falls off her legs, someone is there to help. From her bed, she can reach the toilet with the help of a state-of-the-art ceiling lift (and an aide's help). She stays warm and comfortable and surrounded by people she sees regularly, and appreciates. She says, "I have lost my shyness in this place." At age ninety-two, Christine has become a local celebrity, interviewed by local television media about her appreciation for the personalized care she now receives.

Fred, age ninety-six, is constantly amazed at how "modern" everything is in the house, and how great the food tastes. He participates in residence council meetings and numerous activities. Fred's favorites include evening bocce (his idea) and trivia. He walks the length of the house four times every morning to get exercise. He gets his crossword puzzles photocopied by staff at 200 percent so he can read them, and lays perfectly sharpened pencils out on his desk. He delights in team-trivia competitions with local schoolchildren, and proudly opens his dresser to show off his snack collection. He needs help tying his shoes and getting his hernia brace on in the morning, and it troubles him that nobody cares if the mail sits in the box all day. As he shakes your hand, he points that he has a bad right arm and shoulder, "from carrying that mail bag for all those years." But mostly, Fred takes care of his own needs.

By definition, aging in place requires a home space that can enable self-care and ensure comfort, convenience, and connection.[7] These examples show how the oldest old can be designers and location maximizers, literally constructing "home." As such, they are engaged in a dynamic, reciprocal relationship with these living spaces, investing them with significant meaning and ensuring continuity, ease, and safety.[8] We see how these elders set up their living spaces to enable their daily routines, complete with exercise, food preparation, memorializing, resting, bathing, and connecting with others. They create living spaces that enable comfortable aging. Indoor spaces are also used as staging space for entering the outdoors. Despite these best efforts, changing bodies and communities and new experiences with familiar spaces can make the outdoors daunting. For example, with limited mobility, the steps leading up to Pauline's and Ruth L.'s front doors, as well as their lack of trust in neighbors, can deter both from leaving the house on their own. To cope, Pauline closes her curtains, calls taxis, and waits for rides, and then uses the handrail on her stairs for balance. When the weather is good, Ruth L. feels safe enough to sit on her screened-in porch and watch for her ride, but must hold onto a walker for stability.

Despite our growing societal passion for aging in place, very few studies emphasize elders as space organizers and designers. If anything, we tend to hear more about elders creating problematic cluttered living environments. But Rose's piles of papers allow her to continually review memories and reinforce a newfound sense of pride in her country. Florence's cubby command center allows her to take pressure off of her aching back and feet while greeting those who come to the door and continuing with familiar activities. And making things handy enables Margaret to care for herself without a fear of falling associated with standing for too long.

Beyond organizing their things, elders emphasize accessibility in other ways. Ruth H. installed a handicapped bathroom that is close to her bedroom and favorite place to sit, and thus easy to access. Margaret focuses on the appliances and utensils she can still use. Fred created a pantry in his room so that he could access snacks between meals. Importantly, each adapt and innovate in small ways while preventing radical reorganization of their living spaces.[9] As such, all are actively creating *and* maintaining familiar, meaningful, and healthy spaces.

A growing literature emphasizes the importance of location when it comes to aging in place. For example, sociologist Eric Klinenberg has argued that location and neighborhoods matter when it comes to health, safety, and civic engagement. His *Heat Wave* study exposes the large number of elders who died alone in their residences during the Chicago heat wave of 1995. A "geography of vulnerability," enhanced by social neglect, was partly to blame for those isolated in their homes, according to Klinenberg. Many residents did not feel safe in their neighborhoods, and their fear kept them indoors even in desperate times.[10]

Much like those living in poor, neglected neighborhoods in Chicago, Pauline and Juana live in a run-down, high-crime area of Albany, New York. Decades ago, they purchased homes in this area out of financial necessity and a sense of community with others from similar backgrounds. Since then, they went from knowing their neighbors to feeling a loss of community. The neighborhood now has many signs of neglect, from numerous abandoned buildings to poorly maintained streets. A local legislator told me the saddest thing he has seen is the elders who do not venture out of their homes because of fear. Moving may not be financially feasible. And in their isolation, these elders may not be aware of senior transportation services, meal delivery services, or elder exercise programs. Thus, location can either enhance a sense of connection, or contribute to increased isolation.

Despite living in the same neighborhood, Pauline and Juana experience their shared environment differently. Pauline feels unsafe in her crime-ridden neighborhood and rarely goes outside. Limited in her mobility, she accepts a weekly ride to a free, low-impact exercise class and a local senior center to attend church. Only a few blocks away, Juana feels secure and finds the location convenient, although her daughter shares Pauline's feelings of insecurity and vulnerability. In contrast to Pauline, Juana is a visible presence in the neighborhood, walking to pick up mail and prescriptions, and gardening. When she walks in the daytime, she does not know the men on the streets, but they call her "Mama" and treat her with respect. She says she does not fear for her life because the violence is at nighttime, when she is in bed. Juana finds her location enabling, while Pauline feels increasingly isolated.

The experiences of Pauline and Juana contrast directly with elders like Mary and Bill, whose mostly white, downtown neighborhood of historic row houses located less than a mile away has increased in value over the past fifty years. Mary and Bill do not bemoan the changes in their neighborhood; they appreciate what they see as an ideal environment for aging (except for the icy stoop and sidewalk in winter), where their intergenerational neighborhood actively looks after them. In their case, location as well as socioeconomic status enables good health and well-being.

Rose is perhaps the most constrained in terms of space and financial resources. Her "cozy" apartment and location are enabling. Rent is determined on a sliding scale, and as one of very few African American woman in her nineties living in the complex, she is particularly visible. People tend to look after her, including neighbors on her hall and in the downstairs office.

In his research on "Blue Zones," the areas of the world where inhabitants have unusually long life spans, Dan Buettner and his team ask how place and environment contribute to longer and better lives. They found that these individuals live in environments that encourage physical and social activity and discourage overeating.[11] Many elders in this chapter exemplify this phenomenon; for example, Ruth H. and Fred do "laps" around their large living spaces, and Margaret's and Ruth L.'s kitchen arrangements emphasize small meals.

For those with the good health and resources to decide on where to live in old age, there are more options than ever. Close-knit senior and intergenerational communities clustered around a common space, like Green Houses or co-housing communities like Ecovillage at Ithaca, are on the rise.[12] Age-segregated retirement communities, such as the state and federally subsidized senior apartment complex in which Margaret resides, offer limited activities, a state-run hot meal program, and limited transportation.

Scholars who specialize in aging and housing estimate that only 6 percent of homeowners over sixty-five will live in a retirement or senior housing community, followed by less than 5 percent in a nursing home environment.[13] Despite this, developers are hoping to attract aging baby boomers. One of the first U.S. senior retirement communities, Sun City in Arizona, with a mostly white, well-educated, high-income population, has been recently upgraded to appeal to singles, touting Internet cafes and continuing education classes.[14] Two individuals discussed in Lesson 1, Hy and Lillian, chose to downsize and move into full-service senior retirement communities near their previous homes to avoid the stress associated with home ownership, and find a peer community. Beyond enjoying an environment that has been designed with elders in mind, both Hy and Lillian and their partners have personalized their apartment spaces in meaningful and practical ways. Hy turned one room into a personal study, and his second wife uses the other room as a jewelry workshop. Lillian and Bernie have room for side-by-side recliners and a dining room table they can use to easily access and organize their numerous medicines.

The majority of Americans want to, or must, because of financial reasons, stay in their current communities after they retire. Designers, builders, and urban planners are being trained and certified in "aging in place" designations on how to build or renovate to create an enabling environment.[15] Communities and city planners across the nation are rushing to emulate the successes of places like Sun City, to retain and recruit retirees by offering an array of opportunities and services. In New York's capital, where I conducted portions of this research, town hall meetings on supporting aging in place occur regularly. New state-supported programs for in-home health care have long waiting lists. Elders can take advantage of free exercise classes, friendly home visitor programs, continuing education, senior transportation, and meal services. One hour north is wealthy Saratoga Springs, an increasingly popular destination for retirees that emphasizes walkability and well-being. Three hours east in Boston, the Beacon Hill Project is a model neighborhood where well-off homeowners have pooled resources for access to maintenance and delivery services. Two hours west, elders enjoy the perks of living in a college community. However, outside of this village, in rural upstate New York, resources and options are scarce. In the next chapter, we will see how elders utilize local resources, when they exist, or create their own in the interest of community and self-care.

We can also learn from other countries how to support aging in place. In Spain, public housing for seniors is often situated as close as possible to areas of commerce and health services.[16] One Israeli program for the elderly meets needs that are not otherwise addressed in the community by pooling existing resources to provide a benefits package that includes medical services, an emergency call switchboard, a "neighborhood facilitator," and social activities.[17]

The elders in this chapter, representing a spectrum of ability, mobility, and busyness, exemplify how home is a social construct. On their own and with the help of others, they are doing what developers and gerontologists advocate: designing spaces for universal convenience and accessibility. They adapt living spaces to fit their needs. They also extend their home spaces, utilizing area resources, businesses, neighbors, and sidewalks to meet their needs. In sum, many of the principles and systems that elders have integrated into their own homes and beyond have been institutionalized as "best practices" in new cutting-edge care environments like Green Houses.

While livable spaces and places may be particularly crucial in old age—especially to enable exercise, comfort, a healthy diet, self-care, and avert falls—they also are vitally important across the life course. In our mobile, contemporary world, individuals and families seek livable communities that are safe, walkable, accessible, and emphasize convenience. Neighborhood grocery stores serve those without an automobile. Curb cuts and ramps enable walkers, wheelchairs, and strollers. Indoors, "universal" design is also crucial. Grab bars, low countertops, and "command centers" make life easier for people of all ages and body types.[18]

While this lesson emphasized place and space in terms of an individual's current living environment, the next lesson explores the importance of historical time and place. The oldest old who came of age in America have been shaped by the historical events of their lifetime. As we will see, many members of the Greatest Generation approach life with an ethic of restraint derived from experiences of economic and social hardship, and this influences their willingness to depend on others, as well as their approaches to self-care.

LESSON 3
Live in Moderation

Johanna makes lunch

A few days after her 101st birthday, I visited Johanna in her small house in Schenectady. Johanna stands slightly hunched, her longish white hair clipped in a ponytail. She has a gravelly voice that gets high-pitched when she's intrigued by something. Otherwise, her tone is matter-of-fact. Nearby sits a picture of Johanna in her thirties, newly married, with her husband the professional violin-player. The picture reveals a smiling, slim, dark-haired woman wearing shorts and a sailor top. When she sees me looking at this, she says she still wants her legs to look good, and it bothers her when her ankles get swollen. "Can you believe I'm still vain?" she asks with a chuckle.

The birthday celebrations were continuing, and she was enjoying this. She said her friends made her feel like she had "accomplished something," living so long. But she argued with them, asserting that living a long life isn't any great achievement.

JOHANNA: People want to honor me just because I'm old! I didn't do anything! Except to last! I'm just an ordinary person who has lasted. People want to know my secret. But what choice do we have? We have to keep going. So we do.

MEIKA: But you are an inspiration for other reasons as well.

JOHANNA: Maybe because I'm independent. They see so many of their friends who are not independent, and I think it frightens them.

As we talked, Johanna came to recognize that maybe she was not so ordinary. She was one of five elder participants who could track longevity in her genes. On the other hand, she felt that genetics wasn't the only factor contributing to her long life. Lifestyle also mattered. She insisted on retaining her independence in late life. She also stayed alert, made the right decisions (e.g., who to marry), and had no problems making friends and asking for help. Finally, she believed that taking it easy and living in moderation contributed to her long life:

JOHANNA: I think if you're not too . . . what's the word I want? Too grasping for life at an early age. You should take things easier, slower. If you live in moderation you have a better chance of reaching old age than if you overdo it. . . . But that's not much fun though.

MEIKA: Didn't you have a fun life?

JOHANNA: I wouldn't say I did. (pause) Well, I enjoyed lots of things, but it had it's share of problems and challenges. (pause) The challenges keep you alert.

Johanna's outlook on life resonated with many of her peers. Living in moderation is a common theme for many members of the Greatest Generation who lived through the Depression era. For some, it is not a choice, it is their current financial reality. Financially stressed or not, an ethic of restraint emerges in many aspects of daily life, including diet, medicine, consumption, attitudes, daily pacing, and humility. Even the causes the oldest old support sometimes fit with an ethic of conservation. Johanna, an ardent environmentalist, was well aware that recklessness not only hurt individual lives, but the planet as well.

AN ETHOS OF RESTRAINT

Johanna got me thinking that her generation was particularly well suited for longevity. The wisdom these elders gained from adversity early in life prepared them for adaptability across the life course, and into old age. Hardship at a young age fostered industriousness and resilience. One study of rural Canadian women aging at home revealed that after lives of economic hardship, disruption of family life, and fears and uncertainties associated with the Great Depression and world wars of the twentieth century, they had developed resilience through frugality, reliance on social supports, and acceptance of hardship.[1] Many years later, they depended on those hard-earned skills to weather the challenges of aging and in some cases disability. As Johanna pointed out, these challenges kept them alert, but moderated their potential for fun and joy.

The Longevity Project[2] found only two traits that correlate with long life: prudence and persistence. This chapter captures how a lifelong spirit of conservation and prudence pervades the lives of many elders aged eighty-five and older, in terms of diet (Ruth H., Ann, and Julia), medicine (Alice, Mary, and Ruth H.), finance and consumption (Rose and Olga), industry (Mary), and humility (Glenn).

Ruth H., Ann, and Julia: Balanced Meals and Caloric Moderation

Many elders participating in this study have dietary rules that they live by in old age. Eddie, for example, skips some meals and believes in drinking wine for good health. Margaret consumes a hot meal in the middle of the day, followed with a light supper (soup or sandwich) in the evening. Alice tries to save time and money and maximize nutrition with her slow cooker.

Taken together, this is not a crowd interested in supersized meals. Quite the contrary, and this probably has much to do with the historical events that shaped their lives. Ruth H. remembers cooking for large groups during periods of wartime rationing:

> It was wartime and the students kept coming to talk to [my husband]. I don't know how I did it because I would have as many as ten people for lunch and our food was rationed. Meals probably weren't that good. I remember one time I served cold macaroni and cheese. And then I used to get red tomatoes, green tomatoes, and salami and fry them all. That was a good wartime meal. . . . Everyone had a victory garden for vegetables during the war.

Today Ruth H., the nonagenarian who occupies a large Victorian home, still loves experimenting in the kitchen with fresh vegetables, which were scarce in her childhood. Her dinners generally involve mixed vegetables from the farmer's market with a protein, like chicken or fish. To her, this is a healthful diet. Her friends worry that a fat-free diet may be limiting, but Ruth H. doesn't want it any other way.

Like Ruth H., Ann, the lifelong walker, also believes in an everything-in-moderation approach when it comes to food and caloric intake. Ann says she has "life habits" associated with balanced meals and limiting food and alcohol. Though she doesn't deny herself things, she does limit serving sizes and emphasizes nutrition and balance. While food rations may be typical for someone of Ann's generation, they were pronounced for Ann, who always longed to be slender like her sister and mother.

> ANN: I am sort of a bug about well-balanced meals. In the mornings I have raisin bran, sometimes with sliced banana. And for lunch I have a grilled cheese sandwich with milk. I have milk—not coffee—at home. And for dinner I'm a big fan of the crock-pot—stew, goulash, and a pork and apple dinner. I have a salad with that.
>
> MEIKA: Any dessert?
>
> ANN: I got so much candy at Christmas time (laughs) that I still ration myself and just have two or three pieces of

candy. I enjoy that, but I consider it kind of wicked to do. I can't wait till all the candy is gone. I guess it is a life habit. . . . A waitress told me that people who order a cocktail before dinner never order just one, so I'm strict with myself. I believe living alone, you shouldn't drink alone, so when my son comes, he makes me a screwdriver, which is vodka and orange juice. And I never drink more than one drink.

In contrast to Ann and Ruth H., Julia, a medium-sized stocky woman who played softball in college and says she suffers from a "bad heart," favors efficiency. For her, moderation allows for convenience and good health, as well as longevity. She explains that she has lived into her nineties partly because of her diet. "I have a good diet. I usually just open a can or a frozen meal, like chicken soup." By keeping meals simple like this, Julia spends limited time on her feet and achieves a balanced diet. She also is able to share mealtime with her friend Mo (See Lesson 10 for more on Julia's friendship with Mo.), who usually brings along a frozen meal.

For Ann, Ruth H., and Julia, small balanced meals are expressions of lifelong continuity central to living active and efficient lives. A generational effect is evident here. The Centers for Disease Control and Prevention have found that the diets of Americans seventy-five years and older are superior in quality to the diets of their younger counterparts in all areas except total vegetables.[3] As the ethic of caloric restriction disappears in the United States, demographers wonder whether upcoming generations may live shorter lives than their parents (contradicting the decades-old trend), because of diabetes and obesity reaching epidemic proportions. On the other end of the spectrum, contemporary caloric restriction (CR) movements preach dramatically minimizing food intake to improve health and longevity beyond what many of the oldest old practice.[4] Ann, Ruth H. and Julia are among those who try to take a middle ground here, using their ethos of restraint to emphasize nutrition and limit portion size, excessive fat, sugar, and alcohol.[5] This type of caloric restriction is particularly important in later life as physical activity levels and calorie burning declines significantly, especially among the bed- or chair-bound.

The oldest old grew up in a time when a doctor was an expert, not to be questioned. They also came of age in a time when medicine was simpler. They have watched as more and more life events fall under the medical umbrella, and aging itself is now treated as a medical problem.[6] The benefits from health care access, medical technologies, and treatments are many, but elders may also view some aspects of medical care and life extension as excessive. In fact, research studies by the Dartmouth Atlas medical research group have shown that many Americans reject aggressive treatments and do not want to extend their lives.[7]

Day to day, many of the oldest old make frequent visits to a range of medical specialists. Some appreciate these visits, the opportunity to "get out," and the relationships they have with their doctors. Others resent the time they spend in doctors' offices. Most are ambivalent. While most elders agree with their current doctors' health recommendations, they also proceed with caution, especially when it comes to new or unfamiliar procedures. As we will see in Lesson 5 ("Ask for Help; Mobilize Resources"), Ruth L. has assembled a medical team that she trusts, and this helps her to feel good about their recommendations. Below, Alice and Mary are concerned with what they perceive as the overuse of medical technologies. A sense of caution helps them to weigh the costs and benefits of new treatments and procedures, such as life extension, eye surgeries, biopsies, and preventative tests.

> ALICE: I talk with [a friend] about old age and what they do
> to old people—medically I mean—these newfangled
> medical things. She told me she saw someone in the
> hospital, eighty-three, and she was in pain, and they were
> giving her something so she could live five months. We
> both agree, we don't want any part of that. We'd rather be
> comfortable. To me, the eye [injections] are worth doing.
> I can try that again, and see if it works. So far not. But that
> other stuff—I won't take it. It is for the doctors, not for us.
> Their pride. That's why I'm not going to a nursing home. I
> need to be in control—that's the big thing.

MARY: Recently I have been having TIAs (mini-strokes). They come on quickly and then disappear. Even though I feel fine afterward, I go to the emergency room to be checked. Each time I am subjected to a full day of tests, and sometimes they keep me overnight to observe. This is frustrating, because I know I am fine and really I just want to be home. Then last week my gynecologist suggested a precautionary measure—a biopsy—to make sure I didn't have ovarian cancer. Was this really necessary? I don't know. I didn't really want to go, but [my daughter] wouldn't let me pass on it. Afterward I was very uncomfortable and had heavy bleeding for weeks. It reminded me of the surgery I had—that created more stress on my body, in new places. I just don't know about all of this.

Although Mary's daughter is concerned about her mother's health and wants her to take all precautionary health measures, Mary (who is married to Bill) wants to avoid stress associated with time spent in doctor's offices, in the hospital, and recovering from procedures. Mary and Alice point out that sometimes the practice of medicine can create health issues, instead of remedy them. Similarly, Ruth H. is cautious about prescription medication and its side effects, and prefers to seek out a homeopathic doctor's advice over the phone.

I have been taking something for pain in my wrist, but I don't like drugs. My doctor knows that I think they are a mixed blessing. They have side effects. And natural healing is more viable. So I have a homeopathic doctor in Albuquerque. I've been calling him on the phone for twenty-five years. So if I have a cold, he'll send me a remedy. That helps.

Despite what we might expect, the oldest old negotiate medicine in their daily lives, making decisions about use and non-use of medical services. These nonagenarians assess medicine in terms of perceived necessity. They wonder: Are these medical procedures really needed? Are doctors to be trusted in what seems to be an increasingly out-of-balance health care system, one that favors treatment and life extension over quality of life? A spirit of cautiousness and a greater investment in personal comfort causes them to critically weigh which medical and end-of-life decisions are right for them, in a more complex spectrum of acquiescence than we might imagine.[8] Then again, unlike the baby boomers, who were socialized to believe that they could protest or change anything from war to sagging skin, the Greatest Generation has a greater sense of acceptance and equanimity. Although these traits have been maligned by some observers as passive, it may serve individuals well as they deal with the inevitable biological processes of senescence.

Declining potentially life-extending procedures or preventative tests may not always contribute to longevity. Then again, if medical visits and tests create anxiety, opting out can enable personal comfort and improve quality of life. In this case, comfortable aging and a sense of balance and control may make more sense to Alice, Mary, and Ruth H. than a form of successful aging that prioritizes medical solutions and life extension.

Olga and Rose: Living With Less

The only treat Olga rarely splurges on is a McDonald's apple pie. Other than that, she delights in what she has, an attitude learned from growing up on a farm in central New York, where everyone had be resourceful. She was one of seven children who shared one bicycle without tires and wore underwear made from cloth salt bags. "We were just happy to have it!" she says with pride.

> We always had what we needed, but not much extra. . . . I remember we had pancakes for breakfast growing up. A truck would come at six in the morning for us to pick peas and I would jump on the truck with a pancake in my hand. (laughter) It all comes back—that feeling of being independent and doing all these crazy things—it was normal for me, and we were happy with nothing. . . . I used to pick blackberries out in the field. They were wild but, oh, they were great. I'd sell them for twenty-five cents a quart so I could pay my dentist bill and have my teeth cleaned for eight dollars. Now, I pay $125 to have them cleaned twice a year. And I still have my teeth—I've done something right there!

Today, Olga insists on walking to get her groceries, even in the ice and snow. And when she goes, she says she gets more than she needs so that she never goes hungry. In her small apartment, Olga proudly points out her "pantry"—a cardboard box on the floor of her small kitchen, full of canned and boxed grocery items that could last her through the winter.

> Did you see the pantry I have there? All the grocery items? I have what I need, and extra. If you buy one thing of corn you have to buy two because you're going to have to get up and go buy another tomorrow...

On that cold January day, Olga told me her freezer was full of soups that she had made. She lived on soup on the farm, and she's still making it, with much of the same fresh produce that she loves, like potatoes and broccoli. She explained that she lets it cool and then puts soup into baggies in the freezer. "When you open up my freezer you have to be careful of your feet (laughs) because I am so packed. Sometimes I exchange with Fran across the hall."

Leftovers and freebies are a particular joy for Olga, who was taught never to waste. She explains, "They serve milk for everybody at the [state-subsidized] lunch downstairs, where I work as a [volunteer] waitress. And if there's anything left over, you can have it. . . . Imagine all the food we took home when the snow storm hit!" Similarly, at her weekly church dinner, Olga spotted something that was going to be thrown out and stopped this just in time. "They had a ham bone there the other day and I said don't you dare throw that out! I made a nice split pea soup for my grandson."

Being resourceful when it comes to food and health costs, as well as housing costs, is a point of pride for Olga, who has been doing this throughout her life, and particularly after her husband's death thirty years ago. Every year, Olga collects financial evidence showing that she is still living below the poverty line, and presents it to her apartment manager, in order to keep her rent low.

> You think a little differently when you get older, about money. With just two in my family—and my daughter has cancer—it is me or her. I've got a lot of little envelopes all ready. Just in case. . . . I want to leave that for her. There's a lot to think about. Last week I went to [the housing director's] office—hate to do it—but I did—it took five minutes. I got all my paperwork and went over there. It's all regarding rent, so she has to know your means. . . . I pay $185 a month, and this is the best place in the world.

Taking odd jobs, advocating for discounts, collecting and storing food, and saving money all fit with Olga's lifelong ethic of living with little and making the most of what she has. Rose also shares this ethic, and finds herself frustrated when it may not be shared by others.

Like Olga, Rose, who currently occupies a "cozy" studio apartment, grew up with limited means on a farm in South Carolina. She moved to New York to live with her aunt and attend high school, and then returned home to help her family financially.

> ROSE: After high school I wanted to go back to New York and finish my college, but I stayed to help Mama and make some money. Things were tight—my stepdad was a farmer and that didn't make much. So I didn't finish college, but I helped Mama.
>
> MEIKA: How did you make money?
>
> ROSE: Oh, I always loved kids. I was a babysitter! But I don't think I'd want to be a babysitter now. Those babies will tell you what to do! (laughs) Today they want so much. We didn't have so much. We just got a few toys and fruit for the holidays and we were happy.

Today, as a parent, a grandparent, and a wise elder at her church, Rose tries to teach young people the value of saving money, a difficult lesson to learn for some in today's immediate-gratification and credit-based society.

> The young people—we try to teach them, don't spend your last dollar. It is hard to get a dollar when you don't have one. You know, I always had a bank account. It don't mean you always have money, but you don't have to borrow. You borrow from yourself. This is an advantage, but you can't get them to see that. Young people don't understand this and then they come back to you. . . . They will break you if you let them. So I'm hard on them sometimes. I say instead of spending on yourself, *save*, so everybody can have something and make it useful.

The lessons that Olga and Rose learned about frugality, conservation, and resourcefulness, growing up working-class on American farms, continue to pervade their daily approaches to living. Both live with little and approach their days with gratitude. Yet they each worry about their families and future generations. Olga puts aside money for family members with health concerns, and Rose sternly deals with those whose material needs she deems excessive. Both hope that children today can learn to be happy with less.

Mary: Use What You Have and Make What You Need

Mary (wife to Bill) grew up in a working class Polish immigrant community, where men and women worked long hours in factories making gloves, rugs, brooms, and buttons. She describes living a frugal life in "the flats," with a coal stove for cooking and heating, and mostly loving it. On the other hand, sometimes being resourceful was a challenge.

> We were told to wear our long underwear, and you know, we washed once a week, so after the second or third day the ribbon would wear out and we'd have to fold it over and secure it and I just hated it. It was supposed to keep you warm, but it was so awkward. American-born kids didn't have this and you know, richer kids, so they laughed at it.

As a child of first-generation immigrants who was taught never to "sit back," she learned the value of hard work and resourcefulness. When her mother died, Mary was left, at age twelve, as the only girl in the household with three brothers. She felt she had to drop out of school to help out around the house. As a teenager, her hard work in caring for an employer's home earned her a ticket to college.

Mary will tell you that her good fortune came from "pure luck" and her faith. Yet she still lives by the values she was taught as a child. Unlike Johanna, Mary has a hard time taking it easy and slowing down. But she does follow an ethic of restraint when it comes to being resourceful. As we learned in Lesson 2 ("(Re)Design your Living Space"), Mary uses her sewing machine to care for her husband and extended family.

> I've never been able to sit down. I go up to my sewing machine, and then I find something else that is even more pressing, so I don't do the thing I wanted to do. Like I did the drapes and the slipcovers. And I do hems—for my grandson and granddaughter and son-in-law. You

know, my mother sewed. She made all of our clothing and made her own wedding dress and the bridesmaids' dresses.

As we talk, Mary is reminded of more household projects she'd like to complete. She looks at the coffee table in front of us. "You know, I used to do furniture refinishing, and this one needs it. If I had more time, I'd strip this and just get it done."

Mary's approach to life involves industry, economy, and resourcefulness, and Glenn is not so different. He built his family home and continues to fill his days tending to this space. Days are filled with activities and to-do lists. When asked about their lives, both Mary and Glenn are self-effacing and modest. While Mary associates her life achievements with luck and faith, Glenn insists that he is simply an ordinary man, while humming a bar from *My Fair Lady*. Like many members of the Greatest Generation, Glenn and others channel their ethos of self-restraint into their self-presentation.

Glenn: Avoiding Risk and Practicing Humility

Glenn is a white-haired, unassuming, friendly Dane who drives a Volkswagen Beetle. Like Johanna, Glenn emphasizes that he has never been a risk taker, "climbing mountains or doing daring feats." Instead, he has just "happened" to be in places where important events occurred, like doing translation and wartime intelligence work in Hiroshima. He explained that he was "duped" into going to war; he was drafted because he wasn't carrying a full load in college, and then when they learned of his language skills, he was sent to the translation department.

> I didn't do anything very interesting or exciting in my life. I just happened to be at places where interesting things happened. Okay, take an example: Hiroshima. I just survived and looked back on it, and that was an interesting time and I was not the one waving the flag, not the one charging up the hill . . . just a job to be done and somebody said you do it. And after all, I was *assigned* to the war, I didn't volunteer.

Glenn's conservative approach is linked to his humble persona. When I tell Glenn that he is a role model when it comes to caring for others and for his children, Glenn agrees that he has wonderful children, but gives much of the credit to his first wife. As for his caretaking, he is surprised that other men would not care for their wives. And then he admonishes me to scale back what I'm writing about him—or take it out. He worries that the story I will tell is overly positive, and it will come off as bragging, which he insists is pointless and one-sided. "For example, I didn't do anything bad, but I may have done things differently in life."

MODERATION AND LONGEVITY

There is no denying that history and generation can shape a population in terms of shared challenges, outlook, and resilience, as evidenced by many of the stories in this chapter. Persevering through hardship was a life lesson for this generation, a lesson that pervades much of what they do now, and a message many would like to pass along to future generations to consider. For many it is their secret to living a long life.

In the final sentences of *Children of the Great Depression*, life course scholar Glen H. Elder Jr. looks to the future:

> For children of the Depression generations and especially for their children, some disciplines practiced in the '30s—frugality, conservation, and so forth—are likely to become imperatives in the years ahead.

Elder may be pointing to the need to scale back in the context of a culture of abundance, a damaged ecosystem, and a widening gap between the rich and poor. In other words, excess and waste can be tremendously risky to societal health. The very old individuals highlighted in this chapter would alert us to the risks of abundance when it comes to individual health as well.

For those who came of age in the United States, their ethos of personal restraint and humility cannot be separated from an ethic that stressed service—to home and country—and took focus off of the individual. Mary's reluctance, at the age of ninety-two, to "sit back," and her regular use of the sewing machine to care for her home and family, reflect an ethos of interdependence, industry, and resourcefulness. She was not alone; as family income declined in the 1930s, American households produced more goods and services to meet their own needs, particularly among the working class.[9] Further, food rationing and financial conservation that Ruth H., Ann, and Rose experienced as young adults is still evident in their daily lives. A similar spirit of conservation and caution is evident in Alice's, Mary's, and Ruth H.'s approaches to medicine. For these individuals, who were in their early to mid-teens when the stock market crashed in 1929, family economic losses translated into new realities when it came to labor, education, work, and marriage.[10]

Lore, who grew up in Germany and Amsterdam and arrived in the United States in her twenties (mid-1930s) is an important contrast to many of her peers who came of age in the United States. Lore says her father made fur-lined coats when she was a girl, paid for Lore to attend top schools, and to marry and leave Europe before World War II. Lore's father then immigrated to Canada and went on to make a fortune in the pickle business. This "pickle money," as she calls it, allowed Lore to travel the world on her own and eventually pursue ceramics in New York City.

For the oldest old who did grow up in the United States, practicality is subjective and can result in a range of actions that may appear excessively conservative, or not. In relation to health care services, we saw how Alice, Mary, and Ruth H., three highly educated individuals, expressed concerns about overuse of medication in society, but occupied a middle ground when it came to the services they used. Pauline and Fred, whom we met in Lesson 2, are in a more extreme position, having opted out of surgery several times, despite experiencing increased disability. Both told me they figured they would die soon, so they decided that there was no need for elective surgery. Often I hear elders express concern over investing in their own health care and comfort in old age. Looking back years later, Pauline and Fred regret these decisions, as those surgeries may have enabled a level of bodily comfort that they currently miss. On the other hand, Lillian and Florence take a large variety of prescription and over-the-counter medications. When asked about this, Lillian checked the list in her purse to confirm that she was currently taking eleven medications (all arrayed on her dining room table), and Florence pointed to the ten bottles in her medicine caddy. Well above the national average, this number of medications could be perceived as risky or excessive. Lillian and Florence questioned the need for so many medications, but accepted that these medications were deemed necessary by their doctors.[11] Here we see how, despite having the same health care coverage, educational and socioeconomic background might affect practical decision-making. Fred and Pauline, with working-class roots and high school educations, opted out of medical procedures. (Gender and race may also contribute to reluctance to pursue medical procedures, or a general wariness about medical authority.) While Lillian and Florence, with middle-class backgrounds, college educations, and general trust in (or acceptance of) medicine, followed doctor's orders when it came to using an array of prescription medications. Clearly there is no single "correct" approach here. All, I would argue, were viewing their own health situation with practicality and prudence, but their sense of what constituted a practical health approach differed based on social location.[12]

History is not the only factor in shaping these lives; social location matters too. Ethnic background, socioeconomic status, immigrant status, geographic location, access to education and health care, and degree of social connectedness all contribute to who these elders have become, and the obstacles they confronted throughout their lives. While Mary and Ruth H. are both white, Mary's status as a working-class Polish immigrant meant growing up with homemade underwear and taking jobs at an early age. In stark contrast, Ruth H. had a black "mammy" who took care of her as a child growing up in the South. Similarly, Lore and Johanna are both ethnically Jewish, but have experienced anti-Semitism differently across their lives. Lore arrived in Queens in the 1930s with access to financial resources, but locked in a loveless marriage to an engineer. Johanna, in contrast, came of age in New York during the Depression with a libertine father. In the context of anti-Semitism, she had to lie about her religious background to get a job and could never invite her work friends to her home. She eventually married (a Jewish violinist) for love and became a teacher, and she and her husband struggled to make ends meet.

Sociologists have explored how the cumulative effects of social location can shape experiences over the course of a life. For instance, even with comparable salaries, whites tend to be wealthier due to inheritance. Whites also tend to be healthier and live longer. Katherine Newman's research on inner city middle-aged individuals reveals that structural inequality can contribute to members of minority groups becoming "old before their time."[13] Rose and Pauline, who have survived into old age as African American women, defy this "weathering hypothesis" in important ways, revealing the intersecting and multidimensional aspects of social location.

Gender is also a factor in mortality and morbidity. For centuries, women could not avoid the high risk of death associated with childbirth. Today, even though women in industrialized countries experience high levels of stress and disease throughout their lives, on average they outlive men by ten years. Social epidemiologists, who study the many social and environmental contributors to mortality and morbidity, believe this gender gap has formed largely due to changing risk factors. While violence against women continues to be a serious problem in the industrialized world (contributing to women's mortality and morbidity rates), the risk of dying in childbirth has decreased significantly with advances in medicine, and girls and women now monitor their health from adolescence on. In contrast, men are more often exposed to occupational hazards (e.g., serving in the military), and more likely to engage in risky health-related behaviors such as smoking, drug abuse, and dangerous sexual activities, all of which make them more vulnerable to disease.[14]

In an era of supersized meals, working longer hours, living on credit, and little personal balance, the lives and experiences of the oldest old remind us of a different approach to living, a commonsense preventative health approach that emphasizes moderation in all things: from food, to spending, to materialism. The goal is to live comfortably, never excessively.[15] It remains to be seen whether future generations will be as well prepared for living long lives.

At the beginning of this chapter, Johanna advocates "taking it easier, slower." On the other hand, she and others warn that this approach may moderate one's ability to enjoy life. While this may be true, it is also true that the elders who take it easy do experience pleasure. As the next chapter discusses, solitary time can be, for many elders, time well spent, allowing them to maintain meaningful, creative, healthy, and even joyful lives.

Take Time for Self

Shana in her flower garden

S hana is able to achieve personal fulfillment through reaching out to others and also into the earth, two themes that go back through generations of her family. For most of her life she has run an "informal B&B," opening her home to international visitors and to her large extended family. These days, she spends equal time tending to her garden. She longs to know more about her Russian Jewish ancestors, who were farmers, and insists that taking care of her garden helps her to appreciate life and the seasons and allows her to reach out to neighbors by sharing plants, flowers, and produce. Most important, she believes that gardening has enhanced her health.

> ... To be in the garden, that is my pleasure. Even in the winter, I look to see what is budding and what is dying and what's going on. This spring I had a white rhododendron outside of my bedroom and it was just beautiful, with white flowers. I have to go and see if anything is coming up now. . . . Oh, I think when you are gardening you can never have mental illness. It is so grounding. And you don't mind being alone.

Shana cared for her mother and father and her children in this home. After years of caretaking, she feels a newfound freedom.

> Now I do what I darn please. I garden. I read. I went to the library yesterday. I take pleasure in being alone. I'm not lonely at all. I used to play bridge—I was on the team in college—now I don't want do that anymore. Now I do things for myself.

For Shana, dying in or near the garden would not be a bad way to go. She says, "They can drag me out of here with my [gardening] boots on."

After decades of caring for family and spouses, Shana, living alone, has learned to slow down, breathe, and live "in the moment." In between family and medical visits, she makes time for solitary pleasures like reading and gardening. These solitary activities help her cultivate a sense of peacefulness and, ironically, keep her engaged in the community and in a spirit of continuous learning. Little discoveries, like a plant blossoming out of season, are evidence of growing and learning in old age.

DOWNSHIFTING, WHILE GROWING INTO ONESELF

This chapter emphasizes elders "doing things for themselves," which is somewhat out of place in a book that focuses on the importance of social networks for support and meaning. As we will see in the next six chapters, immersion in social worlds can enable a crucial safety net, serve as a buffer in a time of change or loss, and can help to enhance health and quality of life. And while many of the elders in this book enjoy time spent with others, most are solitary the greater part of their days. The majority live alone, and those who don't, like married couple Mary and Bill, purposely divide up the day to maximize alone-time. This chapter emphasizes solitary activities, beyond simply passing the time, that contribute to a sense of well-being through creativity, personal challenge, escape, sensory gratification, peacefulness, healing, and reflection.

In their research on the oldest old across the globe, Dan Buettner's research team found that most long-living elders made time during their days and weeks to unwind with friends and families, in nature, in spiritual practice, or through meditation. Throughout their lives, they worked hard and also set aside time for rest and relaxation. In old age, they welcomed the natural slowing down of their bodies and their lives. This ability to downshift correlated with significant health benefits associated with stress reduction and higher quality of life.

For Shana, a nonagenarian who is generally in her garden or hosting family or guests, "taking it easy" is something she feels she has earned after years of caretaking and over-commitment. Shana grew up in a small town where her father owned the local department store. After he died young, Shana's mother moved to the city and opened her own business, a children's shop, to pay the bills. Shana came of age helping her parents in their respective stores, and then caring for them (alongside her own children) when they grew ill.

After years of nonstop activity, Shana appreciates the opportunity to scale back her activities and focus on herself and what she loves to do. A daily routine that involves reading the paper every morning, gardening, and resting, is what Shana believes keeps her mentally healthy and physically strong. While being busy wins esteem in our society,[1] Shana's life experiences reveal that slowing down can add richness and a sense of balance to life.

Ruby is also downshifting. Ruby has lived in the same small-town neighborhood for over fifty years; twenty-five of those years alone. She recently experienced a stroke, but it doesn't seem to have affected her. Most warm and sunny days, Ruby can be found sitting for hours on her screened-in porch, watching the comings and goings on her block. Next to her sits her eyeglasses, a book, and a small cup and paper for catching wasps inside the screen and sending them outside, her "nonlethal method for controlling insects." This small collection of tools helps to ensure comfort, a humane approach to all forms of life, engagement with her community, and access to fictional worlds (especially during quiet times in the neighborhood). As a former math and literature major in college and a longtime community member, Ruby finds her regular routine familiar and comforting.

> I like sitting here and observing my neighborhood. Everyone knows you here—the garbage man, the postman. . . . The block used to have twenty kids when we moved in in the '40s, but now it has fewer. People have gotten old on the block! Still, it is interesting. (pointing next door) He's a bachelor . . . so he doesn't really eat meals in, and he's zooming in and out at all times of the day and night.

A neighbor walks by and shouts hello to Ruby. A cat slinks by. Then silence. Sitting with Ruby, enjoying the warm day and feeling the breeze, you can understand why Ruby chooses to spend her time here. Watching the neighborhood where she has lived for more than half a century enables her to reflect on her past and present, interact with old friends, and maintain a state of peaceful contemplation.

Old age can be a time to grow into oneself.[2] This is just what Shana and Ruby are doing as they take the time to engage not only with their environment, but also with their own life stories. Shana's and Ruby's daily satisfactions are linked to activities and environments that they associate with contentedness and growth at other stages in their lives. Likewise, for all of us, accumulated experiences contribute to how we constitute pleasure and satisfaction across our lives.

As spare time becomes more plentiful in old age, one's sense of the passage of time shifts. Whereas some associate this shift with frustration and boredom, others come to embrace a sense of peacefulness and the opportunity to live in the present, and to appreciate simplicity. Seymour, the technogenarian we met in Lesson 1, describes a new frame of mind in an e-mail:

> I find that I am not nearly as interested in the future as I was. The here and now of my everyday life has become very important. Like I have been frequently told, but never really believed; live for today, etc. I find I am no longer interested in what will happen ten years from

now. In a way, I also do not take too seriously the daily negative happenings that plague a lot of us old timers. In a word, my life is suddenly different . . . and simpler. I do not know if that is bad or good.

Living one day at a time is a common strategy for dealing with the unpredictability of later life.[3] This new relationship with time, coupled with an acute sense of mortality, leaves elders like Seymour feeling conflicted. He explained that a focus on goal attainment and achieving happiness do not make as much sense for him in this stage of life. Life circumstances have pushed him into a more nuanced position, where contemplation, simplicity, and living in the moment make more sense. He wonders whether this is a good thing. Seymour is not sure how to feel about this shift in priorities; it is so different from how he used to approach his life as a high achiever. He is not alone; this question resonated with many other study participants, as well as my own Gramps.

Seymour makes a good point: appreciating the little things, living in the moment, and slowing down get short shrift in a fast-paced world that obligates individuals to a certain pace and productivity level. This pressure exists even for elders, in the context of popular "productive aging" admonitions). Yet this extreme cultural context makes downshifting and taking time for self all the more necessary as a counterbalance. As Shana says, without social obligations, she can finally focus on what she darn well pleases. Taking time for self can be liberating.

The seven subsections in this chapter are based on the most common solitary activities in which the oldest old engage, including growing in faith, consuming media, immersion in books, playing games, caring for the body, embracing creativity, and taking time to reflect and heal. Many of these are overlapping categories. When Alice sees something on television that intrigues her, she finds a book on that subject. When Ann takes care of her body, she actively heals childhood psychological wounds. All of these activities hold potential for personal growth, meaning, and well-being.

Margaret and Rose: Growing in Faith

Research shows that faith, like humor, can be a great help in coping with challenges. We can expect that, as people age, they may turn to faith to make sense of their lives and to cope with loss and age-based challenges. Margaret and Rose go beyond this, revealing how faith can help one to understand and celebrate the positive things in life, including natural beauty and social justice.

On a sunny, crisp April morning, Margaret, who organized her second-floor apartment to make things handy in Lesson 2, sits in her favorite chair, looking out the window. She was a youth group leader in her church as a young woman, but it wasn't until recently that her faith grew to encompass an appreciation for nature.

> I love that we have a bit of nature here—we're not staring at brick. I have my tree there and I have been watching it. It got a red tint and I knew it was going to be spring, and then little red leaves appeared! And I love the birds. When I turn on the TV in the summer and the A/C, I think the birds like it. They seem to like the noise and they come and make lots of noise in the trees. . . . The sun shines in here in the afternoon and I watch the birds. . . . As a child, I wasn't much into nature, but I think my love of nature has grown with my appreciation for God. I think of how wonderful he must be to create such beauty. And to give this to us to enjoy.

On days like these, Margaret will sometimes leave the building just to sit and "enjoy the air." She takes her walker down one floor to sit outside on a bench. She takes her word-game book and appreciates all that is calm and beautiful. Having retired at age eighty-eight, she is now able to take the time to appreciate nature and her new location.

Similarly, for Rose, who created a "cozy" studio apartment in an urban complex, being thankful for every single day is the centerpiece of her faith. Inauguration Day on January 20, 2009, was a day like no other for Rose. After she watched Barack Obama take the oath of office on the television in the common room of her high-rise subsidized senior apartment complex, she told the local newspaper, "It's a new day." The picture in the paper caught her clapping her hands in joy. Later, Rose said, with her blue eyes sparkling. "I'm so glad God let me live to see this day."

For Rose, Barack Obama's election provided hope that racism was on its way out. In her words, it proved that "color has nothing to do with anything." Rose explained that the "color line" had been a problem in her life. She and her husband, both African American, had adopted a white baby, and had grown attached to her. They were crushed when the agency decided to move the child to a white household.

> They wouldn't let me keep her. She wasn't but three years old when they wanted to place her in a white home. In that day, a white child in a black household didn't happen, so that's why they did it. Even if we were family. . . . We got used to the heartbreak, and we stayed in touch with her all these years.

Faith became even more of a grounding force in Rose's life, on a personal as well as a community level. At ninety-three, Rose sings in her church choir and does "missionary work"—visiting the sick in their homes and hospitals, blessing people, and "singing softly to lift their spirits." Outside of her congregational involvement, Rose has a personal set of beliefs and rituals that have evolved out of her own life experiences. She tells me that her mother's version of faith was to make peace with everyone. She says she has a similar missionary spirit, recognizing that everyone has troubles, and that she can help to lift spirits. She says she doesn't believe in gossip, and she prays for those in trouble, including her own family members. Like Margaret, Rose delights in flowers and sunlight, signs of a new day. As our conversation comes to a close, Rose says she feels stiff from sitting. "Sitting does wear on you, and the system does slow down the older you get. But I'm glad I'm still here, and I'm still moving! Thank the Lord."

Not all elders embrace religion. Some remain staunchly agnostic or atheistic and find secular means of spiritual gratification. Others eschew the spiritual altogether, and like Alice and Florence, focus on other means of self-discovery.

Alice, Florence, and Margaret: Consuming Media

Many consider television-watching a passive activity, limited in self-expression, creativity, or growth potential. For others, watching, reading, or listening to the news is a way to feel connected to the world and to other people. As we saw in Lesson 1, for Lillian and her second husband, Bernie, television (movie) time represents a special part of the day. Cable television programming is something to look forward to, and Lillian associates this time with romance and companionship. For those living alone, like Alice, Florence, and Margaret, they may use media on their own, but they use it to stay engaged in their communities, to grow and learn, and to structure their days.

Alice depends on public television programming and local radio to learn new things and keep up with local and national news. She says she never misses listening to the city mayor on a weekly radio program. And she regularly tunes in to a national interview show to keep up with the latest in politics, business, and entertainment. Sometimes, watching these shows spurs her to action. She points to a book on her TV table, explaining:

> I saw the Poet Laureate on *Charlie Rose* [interview show], so I got this book out to get more information on her. Very interesting poetry!

More recently, because of her vision handicap, Alice can no longer read books or focus on television. Instead, she fills the gap with books on tape. She shows me her machine designed for the blind:

> This is quite an interesting gadget. You put the cartridge in here. I have been listening to Emily Post's biography. I thought you'd find it interesting. She really was ahead of her time . . .

Just as Alice depends on auditory stimulation to stay challenged and connected, Florence is content to pass time watching old movies and reminiscing while sitting in her recliner. Florence has fond memories of receiving free passes to the local movie theater from a neighbor's father. She enjoyed following the actors, and developing a relationship with them as a fan and an audience member.

> Years ago, you knew the actors, and you followed them. Now there's a different one every time you look; you don't really get to know them. And every movie or show has violence and killing, and they all seem to copy each other. There's nothing good on, really.

Far from "zoning out," Florence actively seeks out the movies and actors that meant something to her growing up. Like many in her generation, she is disgusted with the quality of television programming today, and sees these classics as a refuge from violent programming. On the other hand, she grows frustrated with the reruns.

When asked if she ever feels lonely, Florence replies, "I'm not lonely, I have television." She still feels connected to many of the movie stars of her era, as well as the storylines of the films. She tells me she has seen *Casablanca* ten times; it's her favorite because the actors were good and "It was a nice story with no killing. The romance was the best part." She quotes, "Frankly, darlin' . . ." and we laugh.[4]

Margaret shares Florence's frustration with inappropriate television programming. While she spends roughly four hours a day watching television, she begins each day with the newspaper. This, coupled with watching sports, game shows, and soap operas, brings enjoyment and information and helps Margaret structure her day, pass the time, and connect with others.

> I think it is important for old people to keep up with the news. Then you're in the know when you're talking with people. So I can talk sports because I keep up with that. I actually talk sports with three men in church! I enjoy watching the ballgames at night. I also happen to be someone who is watching a couple of soaps. You get involved in the story lines. But I am getting disgusted with them. It is nothing but sex. I'm a religious person and I just don't go for that—this person going to bed with this person. . . . I'm thinking I'll give it up. But that will be hard. Those two-and-a-half hours occupied my afternoons and then before you knew it, it was suppertime.

In the daily lives of long-living elders, communications technologies are about more than simply passing the time. They can provide a respite from loneliness and boredom, and stimulate the mind. Most important, elders like Alice, Ann, and Margaret use them to maintain control and connectedness, and continue education and self-discovery.

Ruth L. and Glenn: Immersion in Books

For Ruth L. and Glenn, immersion in a book can help one to remember, or to forget, as needed—and to travel beyond their limited worlds.

Ruth L., the music lover who grew up in an Orthodox Jewish family in Poland, barely survived her years in concentration camps, and now wonders why she is still alive over sixty years later. She has devoted herself to keeping alive the memory of her family members killed in the Holocaust. Having no photos or mementos, all Ruth L.

can do is repeat their names, honoring them daily in the private ritual of prayer and, if she is up to it, participating in services at her synagogue (such as Yom Heshovah or National Day of Remembrance). Despite her efforts, Ruth L. wants very much to forget. For this reason, immersion in a book is one of her only pleasures in old age.

> I do not want to be alive, but that English soldier told me I am immortal when I was barely alive at the end of the war. And look at me now, I'm still here, so he must have been right. I wish I were not alive, but I am. So. What to do? I will read and that will help me pass the time. I found a book that I want to read for hours. It is so beautifully written. So I sit for fifteen to twenty minutes and read, turning the pages, as long as I can do before I have to lay down, and I'm already over a hundred pages, . . . Without my reading apparatus I would be dead.

Ruth L. reads in small pockets of time, bound by periods of rest. The act of reading takes a physical toll on weak eyes and arthritic hands so her reading machine helps her to manage these physical challenges. In her day-to-day life, Ruth L. has, in her words, lost her trust in humanity and is ready to leave this world. Escaping into books, Ruth L. enters a loving world where characters are honorable and trustworthy. She gravitates to stories that emphasize her lifelong values associated with work, family, religion, and marriage. One favorite is *The Horse Whisperer.* Ruth L. explains, "You have to have a big heart to write this book. This is a man who is a husband and full of love. He is absolutely marvelous, this writer. I really wish I hadn't finished, it is such a lovely book. . . . But, I will go to something else." For Ruth L., books allow her to leave her world and suspend her past and current suffering, so that she can *feel* again.

While Ruth L. uses books to escape traumatic memories, to pass the time, order her days, and create the imaginative space in which to feel deep emotions, Glenn, the modest war veteran, has other motivations.

Glenn's love of reading is exemplified in his own life stories, many of which involve books. The story of how he built his house begins with a book: *How to Build Your Dream House for $3500.* He is mentioned by name in two books about Iwo Jima, detailing his service in the U.S. Army. He is most proud of the historical account currently being written about his mother-in-law, a Norwegian homesteader.

Glenn's living room table is filled with books on a variety of subjects, from the making of the atomic bomb to historical fiction. He explains:

> Some people want to take a nap, but no naps for me. Anyhow, I do read a lot, and I have gotten to the point where I read books I enjoyed when they first came out. For instance, there was an author about fifty years ago, Irving Shaw, who wrote a number of interesting books. . . . I'm reading one now called *Two Weeks in Another Town*, about a film star living in Rome . . . and I have been to Rome three or four times, so I say "Ah, I was there!" and it is like a bit of nostalgia.

Unlike Ruth L., Glenn does not have to strain while reading, especially since he doesn't have to use his ears, one of which is "no good." He can take his hearing aid out and relax. Besides using books to relax, revisit his memories, and travel back in time, Glenn also depends on reading to get up-to-date, and to learn new things:

> I'm one who delights in the little things. I'll be washing dishes and then I'll wonder about something and go to the encyclopedia and forget all about the dishes. I have gaps in my knowledge, very large ones, and I really enjoy figuring things out.

Lately, Glenn has taken to reading in order to connect with new friends and understand what they do. He says, "I have been reading about the making of the bomb. One reason for that is Tuesday morning at eight-thirty, four of us meet at the diner, and one of them is a chemistry professor at SUNY, and he and I get along very fine."

Mary and Bill: Playing Games

Many participants in this study delight in solitary puzzles and games, everything from word searches, to solitaire, to crosswords. (See Lesson 6 for more on gaming with others.) Researchers have found that regular participation in "cognitively stimulating leisure activities" may help to prevent Alzheimer's and other declines in mental function.[5] Following these findings, "brain fitness" is all the rage. However, brain stimulation is not limited solely to activities requiring a computer, or a pencil and the daily newspaper. Throughout this chapter and the book as a whole, the oldest old practice mental stimulation in their gardens, their kitchens, in social groups, and even while watching television. Interestingly, this body of scholarship on mental health and fitness does not discuss how continuity across the life course might drive and reinforce participation in such activities, nor does it acknowledge how they can go beyond "leisure" to foster cognitive problem-solving and memory abilities required for day-to-day living.

For many elders who have enjoyed playing mentally stimulating games in the past, successful completion of brainteasers reassures them of mental health now and in the future, and this contributes to a sense of confidence in being able to continue to care for themselves. Mary and Bill exemplify this; both have spent years playing solitaire card games. Recently they have discovered that playing on the computer can be more challenging and allow for more personal growth. This excites each of them. Below, we discuss why they both prefer the computer version:

MEIKA: So you're saying it's easier on the computer?

MARY: More difficult. On the regular cards, I think you get bored because once you've gone through all the cards, you can't play anymore, whereas with the computer you have the chance to at least play the same game over and try to figure out what you did wrong, and quite often I get it the second time if I didn't get it the first. It's a challenge, it really is, much more so than playing with the regular cards.

MEIKA: So you can start over, same game?

MARY: Right, yeah. They ask you, they give you a choice, do you want to quit this game, do you want a new game, or do you want to restart this one, or what do you want to do? I usually say restart.

MEIKA: Do you do that, Bill?

BILL: I do, oh yes.

MARY: Otherwise you don't gain anything.

MEIKA: You learn in the process.

BILL: And when you win one they shoot rockets, "boom, boom, boom," all over the screen. It's exciting.

Mary and Bill each have their own computers: Mary upstairs, Bill downstairs. Both gravitated toward the computer version of this game because it enables them to learn from their mistakes, refine their problem-solving skills, and avoid boredom. A victory in solitaire gives both Bill and Mary a sense of confidence; they take satisfaction in knowing they have the mental capacity for problem-solving, skills they have honed and refined throughout their adult lives, through education (Mary) and medical practice (Bill).

Margaret, Ann, and Emma: Caring for Self and Body

When it comes to maintaining health, confidence, and a sense of self-efficacy, Margaret swears by cosmetics, Ann relies on exercise and fashion, and Emma loves her baths. Sociologist Julia Twigg calls this embodied carework that women tend to perform and receive throughout their lives "bodywork."[6] Just as they were when they were younger, for many old women, signs of external fitness, beauty, and youthfulness, as well as the internalized confidence associated with attractiveness, are crucial to their sense of self. Laura Hurd Clarke and Melanie Griffin argue that some forms of self-initiated beauty-based bodywork can be a response to sexism and ageism and a sense of invisibility.[7] Margaret and Ann reveal how social pressures and perceptions associated with body image do not go away for women in old age, particularly when it comes to weight and facial attractiveness.[8] In fact, for some, lifelong bodily dissatisfaction can be more pronounced in old age.[9] These women continue to engage in lifelong body projects for themselves, as well as others.[10] Margaret and Ann see attractiveness and fitness as marks of distinction and respectability for their age group.[11] [12] In contrast, Emma sees body care as central to comfort and feeling good.

After retiring from Avon at age eighty-eight, Margaret still uses the lotions and cosmetics she sold for many years. "Keeping herself up" is associated with confidence, youthfulness, and a sense of continuity. Perhaps most important, makeup helps her stand out as someone who, at age ninety-seven, still cares about the way she looks; in an age-based society, she believes, this means she is taken more seriously by her doctors and peers.

You may be surprised that I wear makeup, because most people my age when they get this age don't bother. But going to the Avon customers, I would always try to look nice and I would put makeup on. Now, I would have no eyebrows at all if I didn't use an eyebrow pencil! I have been taken for much younger by doctors and everybody else, and I think it's because I use makeup and keep myself up. I used to use blush, but I don't even need it anymore—I still have color. Just a little lipstick and eyebrow pencil.

While Ann, the regular walker we met in Lesson 1, rarely uses cosmetics, staying fit, active, and looking good have been key lifelong themes. Like many white women in particular, Ann has come to believe her appearance is central to her self-worth and her value in society, and that thinness is an important ideal.[13] Her husband's death in 2003 marked a turning point in her life, when Ann saw an opportunity to achieve this ideal. She began to focus on bodywork and self-care, and to derive pride and pleasure from shedding the negative labels (like looking "stocky") she associates with her youth. Today, Ann proudly tells of winning a trophy for swimming the most laps at the YMCA, being the oldest person in her water aerobics class, and being the only one who walks to class from the bus stop. Ann does have her concerns—she bemoans that she is getting shorter with age, but she is thrilled that capri pants are in style, and she wears these daily. As a woman, Ann attaches her sense of self-worth to her body. Self-care might seem entirely individualistic, but it is accomplished in a social context of daily interaction and perception.

Unlike Margaret and Ann, Emma's self-care routine focuses on bathing. She has time for this form of self-care now that her childcare responsibilities are over:

After all that time taking care of the kids—and that was hard work, let me tell you—now I can do what I want. Uh huh. I like to take a bath with the Epsom salts. They say it is good for the joints. I ordered a beautiful [shower] curtain from a catalog. I put the water up to here and then put the salt in my water and oh, it make you feel so good! Lord have mercy!

Emma, the African American nonagenarian who married three times, delights in children, and had ten of her own, admits, "I never knew what it was to be on my own." Now, in old age, she lives alone in a small apartment and experiences a certain level of liberation and luxury being able to care for herself for the first time. At the same time, she needs this type of self-care more than ever because she suffers from painful rheumatoid arthritis.

Ann, Margaret, and Emma all focus on different forms of body-work to feel good about themselves and their bodies in old age, and to gather daily strength and confidence. While they all take part in embodied care rituals, the rituals differ based on social location and life experience. Of the three, Emma is the youngest, but the one with the most health concerns, a material reality that cannot be separated from her lifelong experiences with poverty and prejudice. For her, bathing and bodywork are about achieving comfort in old age. In contrast, Margaret's and Ann's health and lifelong experiences, inseparable from middle class white feminine ideals, emphasize youthfulness, good health, and respect in the context of aging and ageism.

Lore, Vivien, and Ruth H.: Embracing Creativity

Geriatric psychiatrist Gene Cohen emphasizes the impulse and the need to be creative across the life course.[14] He highlights neuroscience research that reveals that brain cells are not fully developed in childhood, but are constantly made and produced throughout one's life, contrary to what we might expect. He argues that creative expression allows one's brain to adapt and remain vital. In addition, age-related social psychological shifts, such as loss of inhibition, can enable creative intelligence in old age. Cohen's research highlights famous elders like the painter Grandma Moses who began a new chapter in late life, and argues that creativity can lead to positive health outcomes. In this section, Ruth H., Lore, and Vivian reveal how creative expression can go hand in hand with establishing meaningful lives and healing the self.

German immigrant Lore sits sketching at the dining room table. She sketches the flowers in the vase, the pear tree outside the window, and the "marvelous" Mr. and Mrs. Itzhak Perlman from the Arts and Entertainment page of the *New York Times*. In her sketchbook you can also find her many attempts to capture one-minute poses struck by nude models in her art class. Art has always been a creative outlet for Lore, who has had a life she describes in one word—miserable. When asked, she angrily expounds on a difficult childhood growing up Jewish in Germany, where nobody believed in her, and ending up in a loveless arranged marriage in order to escape Europe.

Lore lives with her granddaughter in her suburban home, and we page through her sketchbook together there. She provides some answers to my questions, yet they come in the form of a fluid and wandering narrative, some of it undecipherable. In our second interview session, Lore is more focused and coherent while talking about her art. Her narrative is colored with memories that cross into Russia and Switzerland, reflecting the perspective of a well-traveled German immigrant who still loves to travel in her mind. When we get to her figure drawings (the "minutes"), she describes her approach: first sketch, then take them home and "improve" them with color and texture:

> LORE: I saw the violinist Perlman. Do you know him? He is marvelous. His wife is wonderful—as a wife of such a man who travels, it is difficult, And they went to Russia, wonderful. . . . And there's a painting of this tree.
>
> MEIKA: What kind of tree?
>
> LORE: A pear tree that you could sell to the dentist. . . . These are from the minutes. They pose one minute doing one gesture and then I fill them out when I come home.
>
> MEIKA: With watercolors?
>
> LORE: With anything I have. For instance I went very often to Switzerland and they have wonderful things. . . . colorful pencils. . . . These [minutes] are much too fast for me. But I use them. That's why I take them home and improve them, see. . . . And I took [recycled paper tickets] and pasted them in. Whatever I have, I use.

At the age of ninety-four, Lore had her first public showing of her paper art,[15] which she had hidden for years in diaries, drawers, and sketchbooks. What started as sketches were made vibrant with watercolors and found objects (pieces of packaging, receipts, cards, and tickets). The result is a collage-like blend of figure, color, shapes, and found paper materials that seem to tell a mysterious personal story. One clown-like figure is called "Einstein," and a woman in silhouette is inscribed with the words "Mad Mother."

On opening night of her gallery show, Lore sat in a wheelchair wearing a tiara, a gift from a friend who told her she had permission to be queen for the day. She beamed and clutched the hands of friends (including the deli manager at her local grocery store), who congratulated her. Afterwards, when asked about the show and the news coverage she received, Lore said, "I don't take it too seriously. They called me great grandmother. . . . I liked this. . . . Did you have a mother? Where is your mother?" Lore has always been the one to ask the questions, and she has a knack for changing the subject.

In contrast to Lore, Vivien delights in the moment. You can see this in her choice of dress, as she always wears colorful scarves, and she exudes curiosity about all things. Vivien lives in a small house in a rural village. Nurses visit her regularly. At eighty-nine, this Juilliard graduate still composes, teaches, and plays piano for others, even as the early stages of dementia have set in. When we spoke over the phone, Vivian explained why she was busy doing informal research on Chinese music. In her women's research club, the annual theme of "Researching China" sparked her interest in learning about Chinese music. She explains:

> I have been busy researching Chinese harmonies and scales, and playing for kids. I was going to do a piece for [the research club], but we didn't get to it. It was a piece I had written based on my research. I called it the "Chinese Temple Gong" piece.

Vivien swears the key to longevity is curiosity. "I find that a good interest in a number of things keeps you alive. . . ." For Vivien and Lore, curiosity and creative expression not only define who they are, but also have potential health benefits as they begin to show signs of dementia.

While Lore expresses her creativity through drawing and painting, and Vivien through piano composition and playing, Ruth H. enjoys the inventiveness of food preparation. As a former wife and mother of three, Ruth H. always had to cook. She learned to cook on a wood stove, and she smiles as she remembers her husband frequently calling out, "Are you burning garbage or making food?" Now she has time to enjoy preparing meals with fresh vegetables on an electric stove. She describes how cooking for herself is a creative process that can be novel, suspenseful, and rewarding.

> Cooking is a completely creative thing. With fresh vegetables and chicken and fish, and there's so much you can do with those things! It is the process, the fun, and looking forward to eating it. Sometimes it turns out great, sometimes not.

Rather than hire someone to cook her meals, Ruth H. prefers to ask her aide to chop vegetables so she can continue to innovate in the kitchen, something she looks forward to each day. Taking time for this creative ritual may be particularly liberating in the context of her daily healing process.

Ruth H. and Christine: Reflecting and Healing

Ruth H. and Christine remind us that it is never too late to invest in one's mental health. Both are still working to process and reclaim their personal stories, their bodies, and their histories through memory work, art therapy, and letter-writing. Applied gerontologists have shown that these forms of narrative therapy or storytelling may be particularly well suited for the elderly.[16] Robert Butler, the first director of the National Institute of Aging, emphasized the therapeutic role of life review, allowing one to balance logic and emotion and create perspective. For Ruth H. and Christine, taking time to delve deeply into their pain is a solitary endeavor that helps them to know themselves, to heal psychological wounds, and to contribute to a sense of well-being in their final years. They show that positive healing and personal growth can come from looking deep into one's psyche and life history, even when it is painful.

Ruth H.'s husband never knew that Ruth H. had been sexually abused, and neither did she. Years after Ruth H. was widowed, at the age of seventy-eight, she started dating a man she met on an Elder Hostel trip. She said, "I would have liked to hug this man, but I didn't. I didn't feel anything. I loved—loved from my head, but didn't feel anything." So she started to think back on her marriage and her relationships prior to that, and how familiar this felt—"not feeling anything" other than in her head. At the age of eighty-seven, Ruth H. sought out a therapist to help her piece things together. Her therapist helped her to realize that she had been sexually abused as a child by an uncle who would masturbate and sexually experiment on her. Ruth H. remembered imitating what she saw her uncle doing and being severely reprimanded. Later, she was warned throughout her life not to let men make a fool out of her. She says, "I was a preacher's daughter studying theology, after all." These accumulated experiences, she came to understand, led her to be "repressed down there" for many years. Ruth H. started the healing process, and opened up to a group of close friends about her past in an intimate healing ceremony that involved honesty, music, and ritual.

Today, Ruth H.'s healing work continues mostly on her own. One therapist suggested that she walk back through life events with her child-self, whom she calls Dorothia, to understand how she responded to sexual abuse as a child. Practicing this imaginative memory work is both challenging and enlightening, difficult and joyful. For example, she says, "I was there when Dorothia experienced her first shower. We did not have showers when I was a child. So when she came out of the shower and was giggling, she really opened up to me!" To see and experience the world through the eyes of a child version of herself is to connect with her past, and to put life in perspective. Ruth H. says that her child-self is amazed at modern technology and the expansion of opportunities for women. Meanwhile, the elder Ruth H. continues her passion for expression in a variety of other arenas, including reading, writing, as well as food preparation.

Christine, the shy wheelchair-bound Irish immigrant we met in Lesson 2, is also healing. In her case, recent institutional care created great personal hardship. Eight months before her death, Christine asked if I could help her write a letter to her family in England and Ireland. She had been battling illness and severe arthritis, which made writing and talking on the phone difficult. Instead, she composed a letter in her head that made sense of the last several years of her life. She told me that it would make her feel good to let her extended family know that she was okay. I told her that next time I visited she could talk into my recorder, and I'd be happy to type up her words and send the letters to her family members. She agreed, and we made a date to do the recording.

When I arrived, Christine was prepared. Without hesitation, she dictated a letter into the tape recorder, beginning this way:

Dear Family,

I want to tell you how I love being here. At first when I came here I was very lonely and very unhappy. I thought it was a big ugly place, cold as ice. I thought it was God punishing me for whatever sins I committed in the past. But soon our Green Houses were built and I changed altogether after that.

Christine's letter told of great pain (when she was living in a nursing home), followed by the personal growth, newfound friendship, and serenity she found in her new living environment, the Green House. She spoke of the nurses who cared for her there, the good food made with her desires in mind, and the new friends she met. She cried as she spoke into the recorder, and ended this way:

So you see, I'm very happy here. I hope I stay here a long time. I'll be very happy if I do. Love to all of you. I can't write too much—if I do, it is scrawly and scribbly and you can't read it, so I'm hoping you'll let the others know and your mom, too.

I imagine that for Christine, putting her thoughts on paper was a way to heal, a way to reclaim the years before her death as happy and positive. The letter was also a way to thank the people and institutions that provided support, to assure faraway family members that she was in good hands, and to say goodbye as she prepared for death. Some would say she achieved the ultimate goal of reminiscence, the experience of gratitude.[17] Meanwhile, she awaited word that her family received the letters. Five months later, on her ninety-second birthday, she received a surprise visit from her niece and nephew. They had all received the letters, and had come to visit and exchange stories and memories. Two days before Christine passed away, she smiled as she told me all about their visit. She was able to see them one last time.

HOME ALONE, BUT NOT NECESSARILY LONELY

At the beginning of this chapter, we met Shana and then Ruby, both of whom engage in solitary activities that bring them a sense of continuity, well-being, and contentedness. Their experiences, along with those of the others profiled in this chapter, suggest that the oldest old have not lost the capacity to grow and learn. They reveal how the ability to live in the moment can sometimes improve with age. They provide evidence that loneliness does not have to be synonymous with old age.

Dr. William Thomas, a gerontologist and founder of the Green House model, lists loneliness, sadness, and boredom among the "plagues of old age." However, the National Council on Aging found that those aged eighteen to twenty-four were more lonely than the oldest old.[18] And two more recent studies found that the oldest old are generally happier now than when they were teenagers.[19] This is not to say that elders do not complain of loneliness, depression, and boredom—quite the contrary. But putting this in perspective reminds us the problems we tend to associate with aging are shared across the life course, and are perhaps more episodic or situational than age-specific.

Shana, Ruby, and others evade loneliness and boredom by arranging their days and environments to maximize what positive psychologist Mihaly Csikszentmihalyi called "flow."[20] Activities like gardening and watching the neighborhood that engage them fully, challenge them, draw on their strengths, and allow them to lose self-consciousness, can lead to a state of flow.[21] Thus, gardening is "grounding" for Shana because it engages her fully, leading to a state where she doesn't mind being alone. This, coupled with the sensory pleasures of being outside, reaching into the earth, and smelling her flowers, makes Shana's days happy and healthy. Similarly, Ruby loses a sense of time as she engages in the immediate scene around her porch, learning new things about her longtime neighborhood, and enjoying the sensory pleasures of turning the pages of her book, while hearing the sounds of children playing and feeling the breeze. For both Shana and Ruby, sunshine and the seasons are central to experiencing pleasure.

Gene Cohen's research is rare in its recognition of how a sense of control, mastery, and satisfaction associated with creative expression can contribute to individuals' mental and psychological health.[22] He points out that research on aging and even dementia must stretch beyond a consideration of signs and symptoms to also emphasize skills, strengths, and satisfactions. Focusing on activities and actions that result in a satisfying feeling, like Lore's painting or Christine's letter-writing, emphasizes the multilayered realities (beyond feelings of isolation or depression) of old age, and may help us to better understand contentedness and health across the life course. While vital engagement with social networks is well researched and linked to positive health outcomes, recognition of solitary activities that contribute to well-being is limited.[23]

Ironically, solitary activities can be unexpectedly connective. Consider the social dimensions that undergird Shana's and Ruby's daily routines. Shana gives seedlings, flowers, and vegetables from her garden to her neighbors, and as she ages, she relies on family to assist her in caring for her garden. And in connecting with the earth, Shana is connecting with family history and ancestral ritual. Ruby's observation time takes place in a dynamic social scene and involves greeting neighborhood acquaintances. While connecting with new and familiar people as well as family memories, Ruby also engages with fictional social worlds as she reads. Many other examples of solitary active ties in this chapter feed into vital engagement with social worlds whether fictional or real, ancestral or contemporary. Through her solitary appreciation of televised baseball, Margaret solidifies the social bonds she enjoys within her church, while reflecting on nature fosters a sense of religious continuity throughout her life. And in the (mostly) solitary act of letter-writing, Christine connects with family abroad and attempts to heal herself. Even Ruth L., who generally avoids interaction, immerses herself in fictional worlds in order to escape her own. And Lore, who describes her life as miserable, finds meaningful connections through art.

The oldest old remind us that opportunities for personal satisfaction and liberation do not disappear in late life.[24] They can be found, in part, in solitary activities that enable personal growth—everything from reading, to creative cooking, to immersing oneself in the outdoors. Many elders who lose their spouses can experience a new freedom that comes from being alone, or, as Gloria Steinem has said, living for oneself, without explanation.[25] Particularly for widows like Shana, who have a break after decades of caretaking responsibilities, this is a chance to live selfishly without guilt. Some elders use this as an opportunity to take on new projects and hobbies. Many others return to lifelong patterns that emphasizes continuity in their lives. In this way, Shana links her love of gardening to that of her parents and ancestors. Lore's art show at age ninety-four was the culmination of a form of art therapy that she has practiced independently throughout her adult life. Glenn continues his life of learning through books. Ruth H. cooks. But while they continue on familiar paths, each is actively learning, growing, and adapting in new ways.[26]

Despite stereotypes to the contrary, this chapter also reveals how the oldest old (especially old women) use and rely on new and mundane technologies to create and sustain meaningful lives. Gardening tools, pots and pans, magnification machines for reading, televisions, computers, and radios are only a handful of the many everyday tools that elders employ for health and well-being.[27]

The oldest old also remind us of the sensory dimensions of life and living. (See Lesson 11, "Insist on Hugs," for more on the importance of sensory gratification in old age.) This is particularly clear where hearing, sight, or mobility loss force elders like Alice, Lore, and Christine to adapt and increasingly rely on a range of tactile activities to experience their worlds, achieve satisfaction, and continue their life work. Even without physical impairment or other difficulties, aging-related changes push elders into new or altered sensory experiences, such as Margaret's new appreciation for signs of nature, Ann's intensified interest in exercise and self-care, and Mary's and Bill's migration to computer solitaire.

Two recent memoirs take up the theme of lifelong pleasure (continuous and adaptive, and mostly outside of marriage) for nonagenarian single women. Diana Athill, in her Costa Prize-winning memoir, *Somewhere Towards The End*, discusses the disappearance of what used to be the most important thing in her life, her sexuality—and how a host of other pleasures have filled this void into her nineties—including reading, writing, gardening, and friendships with young people. In addition, Lily Koppel's *Red Leather Diary* features the sexy, exploratory teenage diaries of nonagenarian Florence Howitt coming of age in New York City in the 1930s. This book concludes with a discussion of Florence's everyday life, living independently in Florida where she continues to engage in creative self-expression through the arts.

Solitary time comes with its own set of challenges. Growing into ourselves can be painful; memories can be raw. For Ruth L., who survived the Holocaust, and Lore, who survived a loveless and perhaps abusive marriage, the memory of living with the trauma remains deeply painful years later. Ruth L. lives to escape into fictional worlds. Lore uses painting and art to process and vent her anger. Ruth H. and Christine try to find closure on past abuses that continue to haunt them. Others deeply miss their spouses, family members, and friends, and find that the grieving never ends.

Likewise, bodily obstacles to pleasure are real. Sensory handicaps mute the potential for various forms of pleasure, such as the effects of worsening eyesight on Alice's enjoyment of dance and particular television programming. Physical weakness or poor health can put an end to solitary gratification (at least in the short term), like when Shana fell while gardening, or when Ruby sustained a stroke while alone in her house. Finally, for those who depend on brain stimulation to "test" their mental health, when the test goes wrong, the personal satisfaction is over.

Sometimes the very activities that bring us enjoyment can also bring frustration or worse. While Margaret enjoys her TV time, she is disgusted with the sexualized and violent programming that she encounters. Florence loves old movies, but admits that she has seen them all, and the repetition is frustrating. For Ruth L., reading can take a physical toll. The difficulties of loneliness and boredom, which are real and painful, underscore the importance of social connections so as not to sink into depression or despair. The rest of this book focuses on the importance of social contact to that end.

So far, this book has emphasized elders' autonomy when it comes to creating continuity, designing living spaces to fit their needs, living in moderation, caring for and growing into themselves. By choosing comfort over an ethic of "productivity" or "busy-ness," they redefine what successful aging can look like. Yet autonomy is not the whole story. Perhaps ironically, while the oldest old may live alone and emphasize independence, many are only able to be autonomous *because* they ask for help. They, like all of us, balance dependence with independence. Because I rarely visit when elders are actively receiving assistance, I do not see how they lean on others. But I can usually find evidence of others' care, such as Ruth H.'s new light fixtures (made for her by a friend and caretaker) or newly fixed computer, fresh fruit in Ruth L.'s kitchen, furniture occupying new spaces in Margaret's apartment, Bill talking about his "helper," or even a lift in Ruth L.'s spirit. All of this is evidence that elders are creatively coordinating their own care and balancing autonomy and dependence. The next chapter emphasizes the complement to independent self-care, or "asking for help," a crucial aspect of aging in place.

LESSON 5
Ask for Help; Mobilize Resources

Alice navigates the outdoors

D espite various health-related setbacks, Alice, a tall and witty former director of libraries, has always remained in control, coordinating her own care. When I met Alice in the summer of 2007, it was clear that she had thought long and hard about how she would continue to live alone and make it work. She is a pro at mobilizing social and technological resources for her health and well-being. After spending a lifetime helping others, she knew nobody could do it alone. She was realistic and practical, and yet tenacious about protecting her independence. I learned from Alice that the key to protecting autonomy is asking for assistance when you really need it.

At that time she was ninety, living near other nonagenarian friends in a condominium community. They had joint birthday parties and got together for holidays and walks. Like Alice, many of them were living alone, and in some cases, were sharing resources. Sitting in her living room, Alice walked me through the series of decisions she had made to maximize her potential for living independently: moving into the condo, keeping her car, purchasing support services, hiring help, and calling for rides.

There's a handful of us ninety-somethings here. We're all very proud of living on our own. Of course, some of us have died since last year. But we all think that independence is important. And of course with the condo they take care of all of the outside stuff—painting and snow removal and gardening. So that is partly why we are here. One problem is the transportation, but I have a whole system for making it work. My older friends, most of them can't drive. One of them shouldn't. (laughing). But some of my younger friends are wonderful, and they'll call me up and take me to the doctors. I try not to depend on them too much because the town has a system—they'll take you to appointments. The other thing is Umbrella. You join for a nominal fee—and then retired folks from various occupations— plumbers, carpenters, handymen, whatever you need, you can get. They have gotten me a very nice person who will drive me around in my 1984 Rabbit.... I have a neighbor who just lost her husband... and twice now we have called this lady from Umbrella and she takes us out. Last week we went on a picnic down on the river. She will take us grocery shopping, too. It is a great service. They screen the people so you have a little security there. And then besides my cleaning lady,

I have one of these contraptions—it connects with St. Peter's hospital. It works very well. I wear this pendant around my neck. If I press the button they will talk to you and see what you want. . . . They can hear you on the speakerphone. They can call an ambulance or a loved one. And if they don't hear from me, I hear it squawk my name— "AAALICE MURPHYYYY" at 7 or 8 in the morning. I think I pay $40 a month and it is worth it.

Of all of the nonagenarians I spoke with, Alice seemed to have the clearest plan for mobilizing services for home maintenance, transportation, health emergencies, errands, and cleaning. Alice also had creative approaches to maintaining her health and nutrition and communicating with the outside world. To maximize time and resources, stay healthy and connected, Alice depended on and appreciated a range of organizations and "contraptions" to achieve these goals.

On a drive to the grocery store in 2008, Alice told me about her new, exciting project to save money, time, and eat healthfully, with help from her "beautiful crock-pot." She would purchase relatively inexpensive vegetables, legumes, and grains and prepare the ingredients early in the day in order to have a healthy hot meal for dinner. This slow cooker approach not only saved money (she was down to $70 a month on groceries), but also gave her the time and energy for taking care of taxes and finances, and to fill out paperwork like health care proxies and advance directives. Alice let her doctors know her desires: she did not want to go to a nursing home, and she did not want to be on life support.

Alice always thought ahead and anticipated her needs. As I got to know Alice over several years, I came to understand why. First of all, planning and management was what she did, and did well, for much of her life. She had worked her way up from librarian to director of libraries for the state university system, where she managed staffing, equipment, and a whole lot of logistics. Thus, not only her gender, but also her past work experience mattered when it came to mobilizing care for herself. Also, she had lived alone for most of her life (she was married for only ten years when her husband passed away), and had significant practice living independently. She had no children or living relatives upon whom she could depend. Finally, Alice understood the big picture, having served on the board that founded and operated the first elder care center in her region. This "home for the aged and the helpless," or women who couldn't quite afford to live on their own in the era before social security, had been a big part of Alice's life. Each board member adopted a particular elder and checked in on her, and Alice came to care for many over the years. Covering all bases, she had put her own name on the list for an assisted living facility, but she wasn't at all interested in that option and preferred to take care of herself.

Alice's story reveals how one can retain control, dignity, and independence, while also asking for help. It is important to note that Alice's resources and her ability to leverage these services cannot be separated from her circumstances. Not having relatives living close by forced her to ask for favors from friends and to purchase services. Her location in a resource-rich urban area means she can turn to local, state-supported, and national organizations for assistance. Her middle-class status enabled her to purchase crucial resources (housing, medical care and coverage, and transportation), and borrow others (reading machine, walker). Lifelong informal intergenerational networks translated into resources in old age. Finally, her social connections, elder care experiences, and status as a former professional enabled her to locate, understand, and navigate a potentially confusing array of services.

ELDERS COORDINATING THEIR OWN CARE

We tend to think of elders, particularly the oldest old, as passive recipients of formal and informal care. Indeed, for some elders, surrendering responsibility, or adapting to someone else's view of their needs, can be comforting, or it may be their only option. But research tends to assume elder dependence, and focuses on the actions of care providers, not elders themselves, when it comes to care arrangements.[1] Alice and the others highlighted in this chapter tend to be more representative of most elders living at home, who are constantly balancing their own autonomy and dependence. In other words, they are their own care providers.

Alice does what many middle-class adults do; outsourcing the things she cannot take care of herself, devoting her energy to self-care, and managing a "whole system of care." Beyond depending on people and a walker, Alice uses a variety of technological "gadgets" to maintain autonomy and dependence. This list has shifted over the years, from her slow cooker, remote monitoring device, and computer to, more recently, a magnifying reaching machine, talking watch and calculator, large-digit telephone, and books-on-tape player.

In considering how elders capitalize on professional and personal networks to meet their needs, it is important to remember that they are not the only ones leaning on others to meet daily needs. In my household, our system of care relies on a mix of paid and nonpaid child caregivers, home maintenance specialists (such as plumbers), and food delivery services (milk and eggs from a local farm).

As we have seen in other chapters, elders tend to turn to informal systems of kin, friends, and neighbors first, before approaching formal support systems (see Lessons 8 and 10 for more on informal care). Elder reliance on informal networks is also borne out in the literature on aging. Alice's case is typical in some ways. She held out for as long as possible before moving into a condo, where many services are included, enlisting home maintenance workers and emergency monitoring systems, and she only accepted home health care from a distant family member when it was required for recuperation and discharge from the hospital. Alice is atypical in that she's more willing to research, consider, and try formal service providers like Umbrella, possibly because of her gender, occupational experience, educational status, and lack of kin.[2]

How do the oldest old envision the "big picture" when it comes to well-being and household support? How do they create personalized "systems" of care, as Alice does, to enhance support and comfort? What types of formal and informal services do elders rely on? And how do elders coordinate and mobilize these resources? This chapter addresses these questions in the context of study participants' shifting individual needs and social services over time. As the oldest old come to identify activities of daily living that are becoming challenging, how and where do they ask for help? As both government-funded and not-for-profit organizations expand their elder-based services, how do potential elder clients become aware of and call upon these services?

The stories in this chapter are success stories, models for how one goes about locating and mobilizing resources and asking for help. Frustrations do emerge along the way though. Because elders tend to rely on informal care providers first, they sometimes place an undue burden on family and friends, and this can take a toll. Navigating formal care services can be frustrating and discouraging too. For example, Ruth L. was looking for transportation to take her to a doctor's appointment, and I offered to help her locate a service that could assist her. She needed someone who could meet her at her door and help her navigate her three steps with her walker. Calling around, I realized that these door-to-door services did exist, but because she was not on Medicaid, elder taxi services, or ambulettes, were extremely expensive (more than $100 for a ten-minute drive). Regular taxis and nonprofit bus drivers could not commit to helping a frail elder for liability reasons. At another point, when Ruth L. was mostly bedbound, she wanted kosher meals delivered. Meals on Wheels delivers six hundred daily meals to seniors in her county, but did not offer a vegetarian meal, much less a kosher one.[3] So for transportation and meals, Ruth L. went back to relying on informal systems (friends and family) to meet these needs.

Researchers have found that a sense of control can contribute to health and contentedness. In his book *The Happiness Hypothesis,* Jonathan Haidt reports on a famous experiment on two floors of a nursing home. One floor got plants in their rooms and a movie screening every week, and nurses took care of the plants and made decisions about movies. The other floor's residents chose the plants themselves and took responsibility for watering them, and decided which night was movie night. Over a year later, the residents on the floor with increased control were happier, more active, and more alert (as rated by nurses and residents) than those on the floor where decisions were made for them. The empowered floor also had better health and half as many deaths. This study reveals how a sense of power or control can foster health and well-being. Changing an institution's environment to increase a sense of control among workers, students, patients, and users was one of the most effective ways to increase their sense of engagement, energy, happiness.[4]

The oldest old in this chapter emphasize the importance of having autonomy and control over day-to-day life as a way of maintaining dignity. Perhaps ironically, elders like Alice have found that asking for help is a means of retaining control. In other words, asking for assistance does not preclude autonomy. Elders aging in place have the ability to hire, fire, and direct home health care aides, for example. Many say that loss of control would constitute loss of self, a reduction of dignity. One benefit of living a long life is learning from the mistakes of others. For example, many of these elders have watched friends or have themselves succumbed to exploitation or identity theft. They tell these stories with great concern about others who might be preying on their perceived vulnerability.[5] For example, one elder received a phone call from someone who claimed to be her grandson's best friend, asking for money to get her grandson out of jail. She had no way of knowing if this was a scam or not, but out of concern, she wired the money. These stories and a general culture of fear contribute to elders' desire to retain control.[6]

In the following vignettes, Johanna, Margaret, Ruth H, Mary and Bill, Diva, and Ruth L. reveal the who, what, when, and how of asking others for help while retaining control. Like Alice, each identifies and cultivates a personalized support system that involves a mix of paid and unpaid assistance. These systems emerge after identifying at least one physical limitation or need (e.g., inability to shower independently, or need for new furniture). Then they go about finding resources to fill the gaps. Over the years, the systems shift and expand to fit changing needs.

Johanna: Enlisting a Granddaughter, Aides, and a Personal Shopper

At age 101, Johanna, who advocates living in moderation and asking for help, is still coordinating her own care. Friends and family members are central to making sure her needs are met. Johanna's closest family member, her granddaughter, lives three hours away, but her local support network is strong. Johanna says she has never had problems making friends, and maybe this is because she is willing to ask for favors. She asks her neighbor to pick up prescriptions. She requests that friends drive her to visit her sister in a care facility three hours away. And she doesn't mind when friends from the synagogue bring her food.

When I show Johanna the list of ten lessons I have gathered over the course of the research, she goes straight to "Ask for Help." "People can always say no; that's their prerogative," she reminds me. "But it is important to ask for help."

Johanna and I talk as she makes herself a cheese melt using a small toaster oven. I ask her if she prepares all of her meals, and she responds:

"If I stand and cook for any period of time my back hurts, so my aides, who do everything, they cook. They make tasty simple things. I like my vegetables."

Johanna describes how her aides come every day for a few hours, at the insistence of her family. She didn't feel she needed it, and worried about the cost, but because this made her family feel secure, she has accepted it. It's November, and she's looking forward to Thanksgiving. "My family will all come here, and they make the food. I don't do a thing. It is wonderful."

Johanna continues to make dinner for herself once in a while, but since more people are taking care of food preparation for her, she asks them to use her own recipes. Johanna has retained some control over the ultimate outcome:

> When my granddaughter comes, I stay out of the kitchen, it's hers. I don't want to cook for anyone anymore. Tonight I'm cooking for myself, I'm doing fish. One of the women who comes on Wednesday and Friday does cooking. She follows my recipes, so it is good, and I have leftovers from that.

While Johanna continues to perform most daily activities and self-care routines on her own, she is able to skip some tasks that require standing, like laundry and food preparation, with the help of her aides. "I have a wide group of helpers—I couldn't stay at home otherwise," she says. Johanna also wants me to know that asking for help goes beyond meeting daily needs, to enhancing quality of life. She borrows books from friends, and asks people to visit, or to take her to lunch.

Asking for help does not mean a loss of independence for Johanna; it means just the opposite. In order to continue to live alone and eventually die at home as she would like, she knows she has to lean on others. She learned this when her husband was dying at home after fifty-two years of marriage. At that time, Johanna insisted that he not be moved to a nursing home. Despite the hard work involved in caring for him, she is proud of that decision.

On one visit, Johanna proudly points out two new pieces of furniture in her small living room, where she sits for much of the day.

JOHANNA: I got new furniture. The swivel chair and the couch over there (she points it out while sitting at the kitchen table). The other furniture was tearing and of course lots of people would have lived with it, but it bothered me. I didn't like it. And I didn't think . . . having it reupholstered . . . I thought that I might even die before it was finished! (laughter) So I decided to go out and buy. I called up my friend Dan who used to be my neighbor; we have the same birthday. He has many vacation days, so he was able to take a day off. He also has a wheelchair, so he picked me up, took me to the store and wheeled me around, and I bought the furniture.

MEIKA: It was that easy?

JOHANNA: That's right, I didn't make a big deal of it, you know? I knew exactly what I wanted. Someone said that store had good stuff and so we went.

With her support network, coordination abilities, and "can-do" attitude, Johanna identifies particular needs and then mobilizes resources to fill those needs; her success gives her confidence to do it again. This enables Johanna to enhance her comfort and her environment in old age, just as she has done throughout her life, emphasizing autonomy and control above all else.

Margaret: Embracing Familial Care, Hiring an Aide, and Taking Care of the Little Things

After years of caring for children and grandchildren, Margaret is now able to embrace the care provided for her. Several years ago, after retiring from Avon at age eighty-eight, she moved into an apartment in a senior housing complex to be closer to family. While her location ensures independent living, its proximity to family also means accepting their care.

I think this location maybe has brought me closer to my family, because they're looking after me more. When I was down there, I was helping them. I used to babysit their children when they were young and things like that. I was helping them all the time—even in the cooking line. I taught my granddaughter how to make gravy and little insignificant things like that, and now, they're looking after me. They even made my gravy at the holidays! I think it's nice that they think enough of me to do these things for me.

Like Johanna, Margaret loves to cook but avoids standing on her feet for too long. As a result, she has come to accept the next best thing: food prepared by others using her own recipes. This passing down of recipes has manifold effects. It is a way to meet elders' needs as well as to honor them and their family legacies, and is gratifying for granddaughters, mothers, and grandmothers alike.

Margaret's closeness with family and her Christian faith have enabled her to prepare them for her death as well as plan memorial celebrations.

[My family] has a folder with my favorite hymn and bible verse, and the health care proxy. I must have done all of that before I moved [to this apartment] in 2002 and before the heart attack. Some people really don't want to talk about that stuff; they are superstitious. But I say, "I know where I'm going, and things should be light and happy because of this."

While Margaret welcomes and enjoys familial care in the form of food preparation, visits, excursions, regular phone calls, favors, and future planning, there may be times when family involvement and protectionist tendencies are less welcome. When I spoke with Margaret by phone during a snowstorm, she told me that this was the first year she wasn't in Florida during the winter, and she missed it. When asked why she wasn't making the trip, she explained: the year before, she had been made to walk a great distance in the airport and felt the effects for some time. To avoid such things, she said, the family thought it best that she stay in New York for the winter. She honored their wishes, but wondered if this really was the best decision for her in the context of seasonal loneliness and limited mobility, as she watched the snow come down outside her window.

Beyond depending on familial care, Margaret has hired a home health care aide to help her twice a week with showering and personal care, as well as light household cleaning. After interviewing several potential employees, she specifically requested Donna, who could come at 7:30 a.m. so that she could be "showered and dressed and have the day." Here, she describes the process of choosing and entering into a "steady" relationship with Donna:

I asked [Donna, my aide] to be steady because we hit it off very well and she just goes about her business. It's wonderful because some of [the aides] I didn't like at all. And we work it out together—she had a son who went to college and she had to go down with him and view colleges, and last week she had another son who had hurt his hand and had to have surgery, and then we adjust and change days and what have you.

As we talked, Donna was just finishing up her morning routine in Margaret's apartment. Margaret addressed her with great respect and warmth, using terms of endearment like "hon" and "dear." Margaret clearly appreciates Donna's help, and cannot say enough positive things about the County Office of Aging that has paid for this care since she was hospitalized for a stroke. Yet, Margaret actively avoids becoming dependent on Donna for everything:

MEIKA: Are there certain things you leave for [Donna] to take care of?

MARGARET: Oh, yes. I can't change the water in the humidifier, to fill it. I found I've weakened a lot in old age. I can't lift the heavy things. Trash. I don't have to do much because she's here twice a week and I don't get things dirty or anything. The only thing I keep clean is the toilet bowl and I do my dishes and everything. Outside of that, it's not too much I do in the way of housekeeping. But as soon as I eat, I do my dishes. I like to move around and take care of the little things. [A neighbor of mine] would get a sink full of dishes and just wait for her aide to come and do them. Pretty soon she came to be dependent on help for everything. . . . That's why I said those people who sit in a rocking chair and don't get up, they're doing themselves more harm than good.

Like the others, Margaret has struck a balance between autonomy and dependency. In Lesson 2, we learned how Margaret has designed her living space to enable comfort as well as movement. Here, we see how she has designed a system of care that involves outsourcing the big things. Taking care of small meals, coffee-making, and limited cleaning responsibilities herself keeps her moving and engaged in her space and life. Knowing her limits at age ninety-seven keeps her comfortable in her physically weakened condition.

Ruth H.: Friends and Volunteers for Calling, Chopping, and Walking

While Ruth H., the self-described "CEO" of her large Victorian home, is independent in many ways, she depends upon innumerable informal support systems. Many formal services like transportation are unavailable or difficult to locate in her rural county. Luckily, at ninety-six, Ruth H. has had practice throughout her life making things happen on a grassroots level. She uses these life-long skills to coordinate her own care. Over the past few years in particular, with the help of friends, she has formalized previously informal care arrangements to meet her changing needs. Her reliance on regular phone check-ins, help around the house, and walking partners enables Ruth H. not only to stay in her home, but also to continue to maintain her routines and healthy habits.

For example, Ruth H. has her own phone-calling network with friends in her village. Every morning at 8:00 a.m., Joanne calls Carol, and then Carol calls Ruth H. If someone does not answer, the next step is to make a visit. All three have keys to each others' homes. Ruth H., the eldest by several decades, admits that this network has saved her life several times.

> The other day, my phone wasn't working very well, so I didn't hear it. Carol came over to see what was wrong with me, but I got [an amplified] ringer now so I can hear that. Once before (pause) I fell in the night and I couldn't reach the phone and they came over and got me to the hospital. I had broken something or other. So . . . I couldn't reach the phone to call anybody. Since they didn't hear from me, Carol came over. That's good security for all of us.

Ruth H.'s calling network is entirely voluntary, made up of close friends who stand in for family (see Lesson 10 on redefining family).

Beyond this, Ruth H. recently decided to pay an hourly wage to an old friend who can, among other things, enable her to continue to do the things she loves to do—like cooking with fresh vegetables. Rather than outsourcing the cooking (as Johanna does), Ruth H. prefers to outsource the food preparation:

> I feel so sorry for old people who live on frozen dinners—they're awful. I want the real thing. I was thinking it's an awful lot of work to wash swiss chard, wash them all, chop it up. Maybe I can't do that. Then, ah ha! Now Pat comes in the morning and can do that for me. She cuts up onions and puts them in jars so I have that ready. Cuts up carrots if I have any. Eggplant too. So then I can keep on cooking. She comes four mornings a week or more. She does all kinds of things that I can't do. She fixes my breakfast, chops up my vegetables, makes my bed, does my laundry, waters flowers, or whatever else needs to be done.

To Ruth H., Pat is part housekeeper, part health care aide, and part enabler. Most importantly, Pat enables her to maintain the "creative kitchen rituals" and good health that make Ruth H. who she is. Beyond eating fresh local produce, Ruth H. loves being outdoors; this is both mental and physical exercise, and practical. When I met Ruth H. in 2006, she walked to the nearby farmers market on summer days, and enjoyed daily walks around the block by herself. On icy winter days, she used her special "Yaktrak" shoes to grip the ice, and her beloved down coat to stay warm.

Three years later, at the age of ninety-six, Ruth H. confessed to friends that she feels increasingly wobbly, and prefers to walk outside with her cane and another person supporting her, particularly in the winter. Not wanting to give up her walking routine, she manages to get the exercise and the fresh air she desires one way or another, using a variety of creative strategies. She has advertised her interest in a walking partner in a variety of locations, including at the local university's volunteer center.

As a result, Ruth H. has found regular walking partners through the Adopt-a-Grandparent Program when school is in session. On the days Ruth H. has a student walking partner, she maximizes her opportunity to walk as far as possible, generally avoiding "sissy walks" of only a block. A companion can help her to zip up her coat (which is getting harder), and can listen as she reminisces about the neighborhood and how it has changed, and breathes deeply to feel the cold winter air in her lungs. On days when the weather is bad or a walking partner does not materialize, Ruth H. says she goes "stir crazy" and either does forty "laps" around the house or walks on her own, staying near the house. In an e-mail in January, Ruth H. gloated, "During the last two warm days I walked up and down in front of my house by myself! Hurrah!"

Mary and Bill and Their Do-Anything-Guy

The centerpiece of Mary and Bill's daily care, besides their neighborhood supper club (see Lesson 10 on redefining families), is Ray, who plays a role similar to Ruth H.'s helper Pat. Rather than hire a variety of service providers, or an aide who comes at the same time every day, Mary and Bill prefer their one flexible, on-call source for everything:

> BILL: We were talking to our pharmacist one day and said we needed help, and he said, "I have a young man who used to work for me, and he retired and is looking for something to do." And he introduced us to Ray. Ray is our right-hand man, now.

> MARY: He used to deliver drugs from the pharmacy. He would tell us jokes. Now he's available to us anytime we need him. We just call him. I had that one fall on Delaware Avenue and I drove myself up to a clinic. . . . I called Ray because they told me I shouldn't be driving back home so he came up and got me, and then he took me back up because I had left the car there. He's very available and accommodating. He'll come sit with you [at the doctor's office or hospital], two to three hours sometimes.

> BILL: Initially we wanted someone to take out our trash. See, I suffer from vertigo now. . . . I was going down one night and I had kind of a weak moment at the top of the stairs, and my foot caught on one of those stone steps and I pitched forward and went right on down, and the only thing that saved me was an empty trash barrel. . . . I

thought it was about time to have someone bring the garbage out. . . . So he comes around 4 o'clock Monday and
comes back around Tuesday morning and brings it back.

Gradually, as Mary and Bill gave up driving and tried to keep up with house maintenance, they enlisted Ray for more and more help, such as washing windows. He was also a pleasant companion and a fellow jokester for Bill. And Mary felt that as long as Ray was driving them to the grocery store, he might as well help with the shopping, especially heavy things. This way, Bill could continue to push the cart (for balance and to help with his vertigo) and joke around with others. With Ray's assistance, Bill and Mary can continue to live in their downtown row house, maintaining both home and autonomy. Ray also provides structure and companionship, particularly for Bill, who struggles with boredom.

Diva: Recruiting a Grocery Runner

I met Diva, a small, scrappy woman with short grey hair who carries a small dog in her handbag, because she was worried about her husband's poor health. Leon had fallen once or twice while climbing the stairs to their small apartment with grocery bags in his arms. She barely had the strength to help him up, which scared her. So she was looking for someone who would do a weekly grocery trip for them. The volunteer coordinator at Senior Services matched Diva, a retired professor, with me, who lived two blocks away from them.

Diva and I hit it off immediately. We visited for an hour or so every Wednesday and chatted about our research, the news, movies, our families, and our dogs. We laughed a lot. Diva, I learned, was one of the original founders of the women's studies program at her university. She had left an important legacy, one that I, being trained in the same academic discipline, appreciated more than most. She had a reputation on campus for being bossy and difficult. Now in her mid-eighties, she was taking control of her own household in new ways. She feared losing her beloved husband to diabetes. And later, I realized that she also feared losing her own memory and her mind.

At the end of our visits, Diva would print her grocery list, in large font, from her computer. The list was similar every week—sugar-free cookies for Leon, fresh fruit and vegetables, canned sardines, sliced meat from the butcher, gourmet dog food, bread, and milk. She listed her favorite brands, but in most cases noted that I should buy generic. Later that evening, while my husband shopped for us, I would fill another cart with food for Diva and Leon. When we arrived back at their apartment with bags of groceries, Leon and Diva were always thrilled to see us. They opened each bag like it was a present, delighting in the smell of the peaches and the softness of the bread. They were extremely gracious, thanking us many times. Leon would then get out his checkbook, and in a slow scrawl, wrote out a check to reimburse us for the cost of the groceries.

The necessity of shopping for groceries can cause countless problems for the oldest old aging alone. Logistics and transportation can be major barriers, as well as physical strength and stamina. Unlike Mary and Bill, Diva and Leon could no longer shop for themselves. They were lucky; they did not have to hire help or lean on a family member to meet their needs; a local service provider offered this volunteer-based program at no cost to them.

After a year of shopping for them, I learned that it wasn't just a fear of falling and a frugal ethic that led Diva to recruit a volunteer grocery shopper. She also gained in several other ways. She retained ultimate control over her husband's sugar intake, and they avoided tension at the supermarket. This was also an excuse to interact with someone else; someone she could trust and who understood who she was. When her memory started slipping, or she repeated things several times, she knew my husband and I would not judge her, and, most importantly, we would not threaten her autonomy. One year later, a variety of emergency circumstances aggravated her shaky sense of control.

Ruth L.: Creating a Medical Team She Can Trust

Ruth L., the Holocaust survivor who sings, stages walkers, and remains fiercely independent yet mostly homebound, leaves the house mostly to see her doctors. Over the years, Ruth L. has assembled her medical team (including a dentist, a heart doctor, and an eye doctor) because they all have at least one thing in common: they are all married to Holocaust survivors' daughters, or belong to families of survivors. Because of this, Ruth L. feels she can trust these doctors to protect her independence, understand her background, and prioritize her care. Most importantly, she says, "These doctors are human." This means Ruth L. can talk with them about her life without having to explain herself too much.

Ruth L. has much in common with war veterans who have access to specialized-care institutions. She had great respect for the doctors who "saved her life" and helped her to recuperate after the war. She also has unique medical and psychological needs; for example, years of starvation left Ruth L.'s stomach extremely weak and sensitive. Her hand-picked doctors understand her special needs, her simple and bland diet, and why, for example, she reacted violently to an MRI injection.

I witnessed the power of Ruth L.'s personalized provider network when I took her to appointments with her "leg doctor," Dr. Darling, at a major teaching hospital. Each time we visited, we were told that the doctor was in surgery and wasn't able to see Ruth L.. She was then asked if the nurse practitioner could help her. Each time Ruth L. said no. She asked again to see Dr. Darling, and explained that she was old and that this was her doctor, and that she would wait, sometimes for forty-five minutes or an hour. She would tell nurses and ultrasound operators about being a survivor. And then, the doctor would appear, saying he came straight from surgery to see her, and he would spend twenty minutes talking with her about her life and her leg pains.

Alice: Moving into Assisted Living

In 2009, I was surprised to learn that Alice, now ninety-two, was no longer living alone in her condo. Karen, the fifty-something step-daughter of Alice's brother, had offered to come and live with Alice for a year following a period of illness and hospitalization. Alice explained the circumstances that led up to this: her "legs gave out" when she was talking with a neighbor. "Just like that, I fell backwards and sustained a concussion." Alice sums this up as the "the attack" that left her with "new challenges" including balance, then breathing and heart problems, then sickness. Alice needed help recuperating, and welcomed Karen. Karen took care of cooking, and a good portion of the household shopping, and Alice thoroughly enjoyed Karen's companionship and assistance. Even with all these benefits, the diminished capacity for self-care, autonomy, and privacy led to worries about becoming dependent.

Despite her weakening strength and energy, Alice took steps to assert her autonomy and was optimistic about eventually caring for herself again. She insisted on going to the bank (with the help of a driver) and managing her own finances. She continued to use the local service agency for driving and maintenance services. She focused on improving her health, particularly her balance, eyesight, and strength. She tried various medical approaches (injections, surgeries) for improving her eyesight and asked her doctor to send her to a physical therapist to work on strengthening exercises for several months.

As Karen prepared to return home after six months of caretaking, Alice took stock:

> I do think that I'm going downhill physically. My eyes are weak and I'm a bit off balance, probably because of that. I use the walker to steady myself always. It is a godsend. But I think with my lack of eyesight, that doesn't help. So I'm going to the Association for the Blind for help with these things. They say they have things for magnification and for computers so that I can see what I'm doing. So I remain optimistic. At the same time, I need to look into my options. Karen leaves in January, and I need to figure out what to do. I do like my space and being on my own, but I'm just not sure . . .

In early 2010, Alice did "a lot of research" and decided to move into a continuing care retirement community (CCRC) managed by the same nonprofit entity she had served years ago. Having exhausted medical and nonmedical treatment options, Alice was becoming blind, and with this disability and her related balance issues, she could no longer envision caring for herself in her condo until the end of her life. She realized that if she was going to move, she needed to do it while she could adapt and see her way around. And so she made a very difficult decision and set about organizing the move, working the phones, and asking for favors. When I arrived with a dozen boxes, Alice showed me a floor plan of her new apartment, marked up with locations for her furniture. She and Karen had just a few days to pack, and Alice had a crew (both paid and volunteer) scheduled for the big night.

On moving night, Alice sat awkwardly on the seat of her walker in the middle of her empty, newly painted apartment, directing movers and helpful friends this way and that. Alice's driver friend stood nearby, reading from the floor plan that Alice had created. A week later, exhausted, but proud of all that she had accomplished, Alice admitted that she had a knack for organization and execution. It was what she had always done.

> I hate to ask anybody for help, as you know. When you've been independent all your life, it is difficult. . . . I felt like I was [a manager again] the other night when I had all those people to help with moving. In fact, the other day I had a group—the director [of assisted living] was here, and the recreational director, and the woman who drives for me. I sat there and when I got through I realized—it was just like running a community—it just came naturally! (laughing)

Alice likes her bright and airy new apartment, and appreciates being in a care environment where she is treated "as a human being, where staff look you in the eye and don't talk down to you." Her biggest concern now is losing her independence in the context of being legally blind.

> I love this apartment, but practically every thirty minutes someone is in here helping me with something, eye drops, or medicine, or making my bed. And even the tea—you helped me to set that up—I couldn't see it to find it. So with all this help you can get dependent. We'll see how it all goes.

Alice knows that many nursing facilities, in the context of limited staffing concerns, have historically made it difficult for residents to continue patterns of self-care, and in so doing limit residents and make them more dependent when it comes to physical capacity. For example, large-scale dissemination of incontinence pads for those in long-term care has led to increases in incontinence, as has increased use of wheelchairs. Alice wanted to avoid these types of learned dependencies.

So, while Alice followed the doctor's orders and allowed nurses to administer eye drops every hour, she also created her own schedule, skipping breakfast in the mornings, and getting to know people on her own terms. She unpacked her boxes a little every day, and borrowed "handy gadgets" like a magnifying reading machine and a "talking calculator" from the local association for the blind, whose staff affixed red stickers to her microwave, phone, and thermostat so that she could always see the buttons. Alice said she was "fascinated by the tricks" she was learning, like moving her head back and forth to see as much as she could, and feeling for the edge of the grass outside to know how to stay on the path. She had friends read her mail to her, and she planned to hire a helper, retain her driver, and hold on to her condo until the spring, as she still had "much to go through and throw out."

PERSONALIZED CARE "SYSTEMS"

In this chapter, the oldest old are managing their own care and mobilizing local resources. Whether asking a neighbor for help or outsourcing one's needs to a formal service provider to stay home and in control of their lives, these elders must negotiate a careful balancing act between autonomy and dependence. They draw on a mix of professional services and family and friends to meet their changing needs. Beyond managing their day-to-day living, many also plan for the future, making decisions and discussing preferences for end-of-life care with others. All of these activities make elders active agents in their own care, comfort, and well-being, even in death.

This chapter began by asking what it takes to get elders to take advantage of formal services. In this case, services do exist; New York State is one of three states with the most home- and community-based resources for seniors (along with Oregon and California).[7] (See appendix for local and national "Best Practices.") Then again, it is unclear if elders know about these options, or if these options are accessible where diverse elders reside. And, as mentioned earlier, the confusion associated with too many choices can deter elders from asking for formal help in the first place. In fact, research shows that elders prefer having fewer choices when it comes to their own care.[8] This became evident in 2005 with the launch of Medicare part D, when elders were asked to choose from countless prescription drug plans.

The scholarship on aging shows that most individuals do without formal care for as long as possible. This is true of the elders profiled in this chapter and may be, in part, because community- and home-based health care is not available to most. Most who are middle class or wealthier must pay out-of-pocket for long-term care.[9] Prohibitive costs may further delay formal care, with serious implications for informal caregivers. As people live longer, family and friends—mostly women—must provide care for longer periods of time. This group constitutes our first-line health care providers, devoting time and resources to elder care with little to no reimbursement for services.[10] In contrast, formal service providers may enter elders' lives only in times of acute need.

Alice's case reveals how formal service providers can lighten the load for elders (and their family and friends) who want to retain autonomy, but confront daily difficulties. Nevertheless, access can be an obstacle. Those living in urban locations, like Alice, Ruth L., and Diva, are surrounded by what can be a confusing array of service providers. When they become desperate, however, the help they need and choose is generally not far away. Alice hires a driver from a local service agency, and later moves to a care community not far from where she lives. Ruth L. is able to hire a certified nursing assistant who works at an area nursing home. Diva is able to utilize a nonprofit service provider to help with grocery shopping, without paying a cent. Those in rural locations tend to have limited social services at their disposal, and community members tend to pick up the slack. Margaret and Ruth H. have learned to ask for help where they live. They are particularly thankful when the county office for aging is able to assist with aspects of their needs, as Margaret's aide does.

Disability also contributes to mobilization of resources: 40 percent of men and 56 percent of women in the eighty-five-and-over age group report that they have problems with physical functioning or are unable to perform one of five activities of daily living. A longitudinal perspective allows us to see how Alice's physical needs and care system expand and shift over time. Likewise, for many of these elders, physical limitations increasingly constrain their ability to operate independently. For example, a number of the elders in this chapter have asked for help in the aftermath of falling. Acquired disabilities require adaptability when it comes to a daily routine. As Margaret described, able now only to "take care of the little things," she outsourced a portion of her care. (See Lesson 12 for more on how elders adapt to acquired disability and physical difficulties.)

While many of the other elders complain of decreased overall energy or physical weakness and increased bodily discomfort, their health situations have not worsened dramatically over the last three years; they continue to have episodic difficulties. Instead, they face other types of challenges. Many face financial and family health-related issues. For example, Olga's daughter needs support in her fight against cancer. Mary worries about caring for her husband and an ever-growing list of household responsibilities. At times, Ruth H. would appreciate an overnight caretaker, to feel more secure when it comes to personal health and safety.[11] Still others depend on assistance with food preparation and house cleaning, among other things.

Although many of these elders say they have "lost" aspects of their independence in their nineties, they all retain control over the majority of their care, planning for the future, weighing decisions, advocating for themselves, and even the most stalwart independents emphasize the benefits of embracing an amalgam of autonomy and dependency.

For these elders who are aging at home and who are mostly alone, self-care is a full-time job. And like all care providers, they desire and deserve a break from carework every once in a while. Outsourcing responsibilities is one way to take a break. But there may be other ways as well. One day, when Ruth L. was feeling exhausted from caring for herself (before her fall and subsequent hospitalization), she outlined a sensible idea. She said she wanted to "go on a retreat," or stay somewhere where she could be cared for, for a short time, to get her strength back. She was feeling "worn out" and also imprisoned in her home. Couldn't someone take her in? Generally, when those living alone like Ruth L. are hospitalized, they end up in a rehab facility to rest and recover. But Ruth L. was not injured, hospitalized, or particularly sick. In fact, she disliked such facilities because she associated them with death and suffering. She was looking for a place that emphasized living and compassionate care. I think Ruth L. was imagining a localized retreat center that would allow her to be closer to nature and meet her needs. She wanted her tea made and brought to her in the morning, and a change of scene. Eventually, Ruth L.'s son and daughter-in-law took her in for a week, and she raved about the treatment she received. But they were working full-time, dealing with their own health issues, and lived three hours away. They needed their own breaks, and it wasn't clear if she could count on them next time. Ruth L.'s comment is an important reminder that all care workers deserve breaks. If we want to support people aging at home, we owe those doing carework (including the oldest old, their family members, and their aides) opportunities for respite.

As in Lesson 2, we have seen here how place, or geographical location, matters when it comes to the range of resources elders can access for support and care. We have also noted how social location, or communities, networks, education, and previous work experience, as well as gender and economic resources, enable and constrain resource mobilization. It is no coincidence that this chapter highlights women asking for help and mobilizing resources. In fact, lack of formal power and gender socialization may uniquely prepare girls and women to be particularly proficient at these aspects of self-care. Life experiences have only enhanced these proficiencies, as all have cared for family members and managed personal households. Beyond this, each of these women has had (at least) a college education and careers or part-time jobs that involved business or management skills of some sort, whether they were managing students in a classroom setting like Johanna and Diva, or helping a husband run a business like Ruth L., or coordinating door-to-door sales for Avon like Margaret. This mixture of skills, knowledge, hands-on experience, and economic security have no doubt enabled them to mobilize resources throughout their lives and continue to do so in later life, even with health limitations. The next several chapters focus on a crucial aspect of self-care: fostering connections with peers, family, and social networks.

LESSON 6
Connect with Peers

Johanna and her Thursday Scrabble Group

At their monthly American Association of University Women (AAUW) Book Group meeting, eight female university graduates, all sixty-five and older, are eager to discuss *I Feel Bad About My Neck,* a bestselling book of humorous essays on aging by Nora Ephron. The group is meeting at a local diner attached to a motel. Elizabeth, today's facilitator, is wearing a lavender blouse and skirt and a colorful scarf tied around her neck.

I am Elizabeth's guest and she introduces me to the group. Most of the participants are former educators in their seventies. These women are all acquaintances; nobody knows last names, but they do share common histories. Elizabeth, age eighty-five, tells me that she fears the group is "dying out" because new members are hard to come by. On the other hand, she stays involved because "the group is fun, and only one woman has a cane."

Over lunch, I overhear and participate in conversations about family, libraries, and education. Elizabeth tells stories about being in the navy and working as a code-breaker for the WAVES during World War II. Another woman discusses how she had to take away her mother's car keys, and another talks about nursing homes. It is clear that this group is about books and also about supporting each other.

After the meal, Elizabeth begins the formal book discussion, reading selections from her favorite chapters aloud. The first is about the sense of rapture one can feel when lost in a book. Elizabeth adds that she needs at least one book a week to feel fulfilled. Then Elizabeth reads a section about how her generation, as well as the baby boomer generation, feels as if they have to "do something about everything," turning to creams, pills, and even crosswords if it will better themselves. The women nod in agreement.

When Elizabeth turns to the title essay, she announces, "I just discovered this thing on my neck—a waddle, like a turkey has. I'm putting lotion on it now." Another woman contributes, "Did you all notice that I wore a scarf today and tied it tight around my neck?" At this point, I noted to myself that more than half of the participants were either wearing turtlenecks or neck-obscuring scarves. The conversation about necks stopped there, after a series of loud noises emerged from one participant's hearing aid, and someone shouted, "Gerry, you're playing a concert over there—it is on!" Not long after that, Gerry left through the side door with her walker, followed by the others.

GROUP MEMBERSHIP

As we saw in the last few chapters, loneliness is a challenge that all individuals, young or old, must face, particularly if they live alone.

Social isolation can be exacerbated as individuals outlive their peers and confront health problems and disabilities that make it difficult to regularly attend regular book club meetings or church services. As more individuals age at home, staying connected becomes a pressing challenge in their lives.

This chapter highlights the importance of social integration as we age. Looking ahead to more individuals aging in place, it is easy to miss the significance of social networks. While Americans value independence and autonomy across their lives, they also value a sense of belonging, friendship, and being known. Decades of social science scholarship examine the positive effects of social ties across the life course, positing that social bonds can translate into social safety nets, buffers, and general benefits in terms of good health and well-being.[1] Debra Umberson et al. conclude their review of this literature by stating, "Humans are wired for social connection. Without social ties, distress emerges and health fails. In this sense, social connection seems to be a biological imperative." This link between social ties and health behavior is so widely accepted, it is now emphasized in efforts to promote population health, for example in the U.S. government's planning report, *Healthy People 2010*.

We know that healthy behaviors can be contagious, so if your friends eat balanced diets, you are likely to do so as well. At the same time, social networks can teach unhealthy behaviors, or reinforce stress. Elizabeth's book group, for example, offers a healthy sense of community and reinforces the value of reading, learning, and growing. Group members care for each other by offering a listening ear. At the same time, the group can reinforce commonly held ageist notions of aspiring toward youthfulness and good health, as evidenced in the group's frustration with Gerry's hearing aid and Elizabeth's emphasis on "fun" and able-bodiedness when she notes that "only one member uses a cane."

The next five lessons emphasize the act of connecting, caring for others, reaching across generations, and redefining family. This chapter focuses on establishing peer connections. For most, peer interactions occur in group-based recreational activities. Groups meet regularly in homes, churches and synagogues, community centers, fitness centers, and eating establishments. Many elders are drawn to a group context for individual reasons, such as a desire for physical exercise or mental stimulation. The collaborative context also becomes a platform for being together, a catalyst for friendship, and stimulates overall health and well-being.[2]

Like anyone, the oldest old tend to have a range of friends, from casual to intimate.[3] Social research on close friendships at any age reveal that they tend to be homogenous, based on shared religion, marital status, ethnicity, and gender, as well as attitudes and beliefs. However, most of the very old do not know others in their age group; and because of their age, they tend to have friends at least a decade younger. (See Lesson 10 for more on intergenerational relationships.) Across all ages, women have more friends than men.[4]

Gerontologists have argued that the value of friends may increase in old age, as the number of friends decreases. Psychologist Laura Carstensen's socioemotional selectivity theory posits that as adults age, they invest more energy in fewer relationships. They shed those relationships that are not particularly rewarding, and invest most heavily in spending time and talking with those whom they value most.[5] Further research shows that having just one confidant can buffer the effects of social losses. For the very old, friends and spouses tend to be confidants, more so than family members, due to common experiences and needs. Beyond this, friends can be life-long relationships, sometimes pre-dating spouses and offspring. In these ways, close friendships represent strong ties.

Interestingly, some sociologists have argued that acquaintances, or weak ties, may be just as crucial as strong ties.[6] As we will see in this chapter, weak ties represent raw potential for friendship. In social groups made up of weak ties that strengthen over time, such as Ann's early-morning water aerobics class, Johanna's Scrabble group, and Ruth H.'s discussion and research groups, identities are affirmed, sorrows and joys are shared, and members can be uninhibited and authentic. It is not surprising the number of "accidental friendships" that arise out of these group contexts. Particularly for the oldest old, being the "last survivors" in a group can create unexpected bonds. Beyond this, these groups can be the source of new, useful information and provide a sense of belonging and peer resistance against ageist tendencies in society. Perhaps most important, elder groups can be sites where peers help each other to cope with aging.[7]

Many ethnographies emphasize how caring communities can emerge from ordinary interactions. For example, Mitch Duneier's *Slim's Table* focuses on a group of working class African American men who are regulars at a cafeteria on the South Side of Chicago. Barbara Myerhoff's *Number Our Days* focuses on elderly Jewish immigrants who live together and frequent the same community center. And Frida Kerner Furman's *Facing the Mirror* focuses on the mostly middle- and upper-middle-class elder Jewish women regulars at a beauty shop in the Midwest. In all of these contexts, as individuals share stories and become familiar with each other over time, they begin to look out for one other, offering a collective antidote to boredom, discrimination, and loneliness. In the process, they maintain these intentional communities that meet a need for camaraderie and support.

On the surface, Elizabeth's book group may not seem like a caring community or a contemporary women's consciousness-raising group. There are few intimate connections here—participants know each other on a first-name basis, and they do not see each other outside of their monthly meetings. Despite these weak ties, coming together to joke about neck "waddles" and wearing turtlenecks can lessen individual anxieties about aging by exposing the similarities women share as they age. Beyond this, the ability to share information over a meal (and be listened to) regarding personal histories, nursing homes, and parental care may be enabling in terms of sharing fears and troubles, exchanging information, and venting. Finally, there is excellent potential for a friendship to emerge in the context of this group.

This chapter asks: how do elders, who are mostly aging at home, make and maintain connections with others and create empowering microworlds? I joined elders in their social worlds to understand how they came to belong to particular social groups, frequent favorite establishments, and connect with their peers. All reported that these social connections were beneficial in their lives, providing structure, support, and stimulation.

Ruth H.: Laughing and Learning with Friends

For the past several decades, Ruth H. and her friends have gotten together on New Years Eve. While some come and go, there is a core group of eight, mostly in their seventies and eighties, and Ruth H., now in her late nineties. According to Ruth H., the first time they did this they stayed up until midnight, but now they have supper at five and go home at nine. No matter how late they stay up, they always have fun.

> Nobody talks about how wonderful it can be to be in your nineties. I never imagined that old age was about laughing and having fun. But I was sitting with friends [at our annual New Years party] and I found myself doing that. Laughing! It is wonderful. You know, my father lived to eighty-eight, and he wrote a piece called, "The Joys of Living Longer than Expected" in a church monthly. Now I think I understand what he was getting at.

Ruth H. would be the first to point out that interpersonal connections are crucial to living a long, intellectually stimulating and socially supported life. She says "this village is the best place for a widow, because you are taken care of." That this rural village of three thousand is focused on education and social support is partly her doing. Years ago she helped to found a nursery school and a continuing education group for retirees. She's also been a long-time member in a number of clubs, including a women's research club and a religion discussion group. In these contexts, Ruth H. can continue to meet new people and "exercise her brain," two things she has valued throughout her life.

In Ruth H.'s Fortnightly Club, a women's organization that has been in existence since 1893, roughly thirty members research different aspects of a core theme and then report back to the group in a formal presentation of no longer than twenty minutes.[8] Looking back, Ruth H. particularly enjoyed writing a paper (in English) about Hans Christian Andersen, and reading about him in Danish. Since she turned ninety, Ruth H. attends Fortnightly meetings as an "honorary member," or a member who no longer writes and presents research papers, but who enjoys listening and learning as others present their research.

In addition, Ruth H. is still actively generating ideas in her discussion group on religion, an organization started by two of Ruth H.'s male acquaintances. Composed of six to eight retired individuals who sit around a table every Wednesday morning, they informally discuss a variety of topics. The group started for people interested in religion, but who did not necessarily attend church. As current events shift, their focus shifts. For Ruth H., this group has been an opportunity to interact with diverse community members she may not have known otherwise.

Fred: Bocce, Trivia, and Companionship

It is Monday night. After coffee and dessert at their large twelve-person dining room table, six individuals line up on the carpet. Two are in wheelchairs, the others are seated. First, one rolls the smaller ball, the jack. Then each takes a turn gently rolling a bocce ball on the carpet, past the hearth, trying to hit the jack. Fred, the retired postman from Lesson 2, is the only one who leaves his chair to assume a bowling stance when his turn comes. Several months ago, he suggested a bocce night at the residence council meeting. After Alice rolls, Fred yells, "Looks good Alice! Motor skills!" Then silence descends as Ken rolls his ball, and when it rolls out of the zone, he cries, "It's the floor—it is slanted!" Everyone laughs. When all of the balls have stopped rolling, a staff member takes out her yardstick and measures distances. "What do you think? Which one is closer?" Alice is declared the winner, she squeals with delight, and round two begins.

This is a typical evening at Green House number sixteen, where residents enjoy a full schedule of their favorite activities after dinner. Depending on the night, they may play trivia or word games, bingo, do arts and crafts, have a cocktail hour, or watch movies from Ken's personal collection. For Fred, these "programs" are among his favorite aspects of living in the Green House. While he enjoys his mornings reading the paper, walking the length of the house several times, and completing two crossword puzzles, by the afternoon he is ready for social time.

Fred was a mailman for forty years. To place me each time we see each other, he asks my address. Then he says—"Oh yes, right there by Trinity Church." His memory is perfect. For this reason, he has a reputation as "the trivia guy" in the house. Lately, kids from the local school have come to play team trivia with elders in the Green House, and this is a highlight in his day.

> They are interesting boys—one is Arab and another is African, and they try to trick me. They ask all sorts of questions about this Indian tribe or that aspect of war history, and then they are surprised when I know the answer! We have a good time when they visit.

On nice days, Fred and Alice take their word games out to the porch. They work separately, but they take breaks to observe the happenings outside—birds, people, cars. Alice says Fred showed her how to use the ruler to neatly circle words in her word search book. They are good friends who talk about their late spouses with great appreciation. Fred is the more introverted one. He has been widowed twenty-seven years, but he still remembers every detail of his wedding day, including the exact street address of the church.

Johanna's Scrabble Group

Johanna, the centenarian who purchased new furniture in the last chapter, and a former elementary school teacher, still derives great satisfaction from working with words. She says, "When I wake up I am eager to get to the puzzles in the morning paper. To see if my brain is working. This makes me happy." While Johanna does daily puzzles on her own, the highlight of the week is playing Scrabble with friends. Every Tuesday, four friends from the synagogue come to Johanna's house to play Scrabble for five hours. They set up the "Fiftieth Anniversary" board on a lazy Susan, put out some snacks, and focus on constructing a high-point word and winning the game. Beyond spelling words, these women are cementing friendship.

On the day I observed Johanna's Scrabble group in action, Johanna won the first round and declared, "Well, I'm done for the day!" "Promise?" Her friend asked. And then they played for four more hours, laughing, helping each other, looking up words, discussing them, and reminiscing.

Over the course of their hours together, the group discussed their volunteer work (all different), their husbands (past and present), and together admired a family heirloom from Johanna's mother. At the beginning, Johanna's friend Dorothy passed around an article she had cut out of the morning paper, about doctors not knowing much about geriatric care. They also exchanged reading materials, *The New Yorker* and *Mountains Beyond Mountains*. For Johanna and the others who mostly live alone, this weekly ritual is crucial for mental and social stimulation.

Ann's Water Aerobics Class

Like Johanna, Ann lives alone. While she enjoys her solitary life, Ann, who loves exercise, ventures out once a week to a group exercise class for a good workout and the opportunity to connect with others. The literature on aging is replete with studies on the positive effects of physical exercise on the well-being of older adults, and separately acknowledges the positive effects of social activities. Very few studies put these aspects together, exploring how exercise groups, for example, can have social as well as physical benefits.[9] For Ann, her weekly water aerobics ("hydroslimnastics") class is the only nonsolitary exercise she does all week. Although she can be introverted, she appreciates the social dynamic and having an event on her calendar that she can count on. Ann may not know the names of everyone in her class, but they look out for her and each other. They call Ann at home when she isn't in class; they also offer her rides. There is a sense of belonging and accountability here that is friendly and reassuring.

The fifteen or so women of the water aerobics class consider themselves a family. Many have been in this class for decades. A few are life-long friends, but most just know each other from the class. They cover the gamut of topics in the locker room, sharing vital information about health and family, inviting each other to local events, and working together to celebrate special occasions like birthdays. When I asked Ann why she continues with the class, she said,

> I do it for the exercise. [In the water] I move body parts I have never moved before. And I think it does me good. Plus, it is a friendly group. We went to the diner last week and had a grand time.

To get a sense of this group and the role it played in Ann's life, I joined the class for a few sessions. Because of my age, everyone assumed I was Ann's granddaughter. The forty-minute workout was a mix of dancing, kicking, running, and stretching in the water. I bobbed up and down in the water, surrounded by gray and white heads, several bathing caps, and one pink shower cap (Ann's). The instructor stood on the deck, demonstrating moves and shouting out instructions over the loud music. She also joked with the participants, calling them by name, adding to the feeling of group intimacy. Beyond this, I found that the resistance and privacy that the water provided was physically supportive; you cannot fall or make a mistake in this context. The workout made me feel strong and capable.

At eight o'clock one chilly February morning, Ann is at the coffee machine first, then some more trickle in—Rita and Kate and a few others. They greet Ann, then they all sit for a few minutes in the lobby of the fitness center and talk about the weather and the news. The class doesn't start until twenty minutes after eight. Ann listens and sips her coffee, chuckling to herself here and there, as the members of her class chat about the weather ("It is so cold and windy—it is just wrong!"), the news ("Did you hear about that plane that crashed?"), and my research ("Oh, you're the one writing about Ann!"). At that point, Kate starts to talk about how "remarkable" Ann is. "You know, Ann walks to class—takes the bus and then walks. She's more active than I am. I don't walk anywhere!" Then it is time to hit the locker room. I was amazed that these women (and sometimes a man or two) could motivate themselves to get into a pool when the weather outside was ten degrees. For them, it was about much more than getting into a pool. It was an energizing way to start the day, and a crucial opportunity for social interaction.

I witnessed this the next time I saw Ann. She was in the locker room chatting with several women. Later she explained that she was "dining out on going to the inauguration," (a way of saying that she was garnering personal attention due to her unique experience). The news was so exciting to people, including herself, that she loved to share the story with everyone. She asked me, "Have you ever known anyone to go to an inauguration? Me neither!" and then she launched into how she rode the DC subway for the first time.

Josie: Taking People In

I met Josie at a party at the local century-old Women's Club. The party was in honor of their two centenarian members. At first glance, she was nondescript and unassuming: a white-haired, pale-skinned elder, dressed simply, staring off into space. One of the first things she said to me was this: she was planning to move to a care facility because she missed being around people. This centenarian had a plan. Later, when I visited Josie at her home, it was clear that Josie loved her independence. But she was having difficulty caring for herself because she was increasingly blind.

Josie's stories revealed a complex personality: part spitfire, part lonely soul. Josie told me that she was extremely shy as a child, daddy's little girl. When her father died young, Josie took a job "doing figures" for a local railroad to help her mother make ends meet. She became close friends with her mostly male coworkers, and spent her evenings at a local women's club, playing cards late into the night. She learned how to be an independent woman, and to talk tough. On Sundays, she left church services and went straight back to work because she loved it so much. Josie has been single all of her life, but actively surrounded herself with people to avoid loneliness. Even at home, Josie had people around.

After her mother died and Josie retired, she felt a need to have others around. She reached out to acquaintances and relatives she hardly knew who needed support and invited them to live with her.

I had my mother living here and she died in '68. Wow—that's a long time now. Then I had my friend's mother, my friend Agnes, who stayed a couple of times, and my aunt. They were in the back room. I thought I was going to put up a sign in the front that said Home for the Friendless. But anyway, Agnes was a good friend. And for me, it was better than being here alone, you know? Even though they were sick. And I'm not a nurse, but I managed somehow. It meant a great deal to have someone here.

She met Agnes, a neighbor who was also retired and living alone, at the bus stop. Josie seems close to tears when she describes how she took Agnes in when she broke her leg and then later got sick with cancer.

Agnes and I were standoffish at first, but then we got friendly. When we were both retired we used to go on the bus together, and go out to the only other place out there. The mall. And then of course we would take the bus back home and transfer. She was a good friend. When she had cancer she moved in with me. I said I'm not much of a cook, and she said, 'I don't find anything wrong with your cooking.' But she was in hospice before you knew it and then gone.

After being released from assisted living at the age of one hundred because she was deemed able to care for herself, Josie is now alone in her large house. Surrounded by meaningful things that family and friends have left—including her mother's chair and her aunt's clock—without people, Josie says she has never felt more alone (especially in the evenings). She knows that if she starts crying, she will never stop, so she stops herself from starting. Every day she weighs whether she should move back to the assisted living facility, where, at the very least, she would be near people. Ironically, giving up isolation also means giving up a familiar space and things that remind her of when she felt loved and connected.

THE MANY BENEFITS OF LINKED LIVES

Robert Putnam's bestselling study, *Bowling Alone*, exposes a marked decline in social connectivity as the generation known for bowling leagues and clubs ages out. Today it is common for the oldest old to feel socially isolated, and this feeling can be compounded as more age in place and outlive their contemporaries. In an e-mail, Seymour broached this subject: "We feel pretty isolated at times; I think people tend to leave really old people alone." He seemed to be talking about a mild form of elder neglect, and he wasn't the only one.

An article in the *New York Times* highlights a group of elder Indian immigrant men in Northern California who regularly meet in a strip mall parking lot, on concrete planters, and sip chai tea. They are the lonely parents of immigrants not wanted in their children's households. They turn instead to each other for solace and ritual.[10] Likewise, many housebound participants from this study confided in me that they were surprised at people's lack of interest in them. They complained that nobody calls or visits, not even the religious leaders they had known for years. The exception was on the big birthdays (ninety, ninety-five, and one hundred), when communities might roll out the red carpet for a day. Other than that, family members were busy with their lives, or so it seemed. Several elder women described very difficult childhoods, marked by poverty and starvation. Despite this, they insisted that *now* is when they most need companionship. They feel cast aside by family, friends, and community members, and confused about why this might be.

In this chapter we saw how mostly homogenous peer networks can be socially, physically, and emotionally beneficial. (In other chapters, elders defy social rules and reach across cultural and age-based divides in valuable ways.) The social function of peer groups operates similarly across the age spectrum, allowing for a sense of belonging, recreation, collaboration, pleasure, and potential for developing deeper relationships. In some ways, elders collaborating in a group exercise class, a book discussion, or a particularly competitive Scrabble game may be able to achieve a sense of deep engagement, flow, or gratification that comes with collaboration.

Networks are also gendered. Countless studies show that women tend to be more skilled than men at making connections and building social ties. Due to the sheer number of old women in society, community center programming tends to be women-dominated, further reinforcing men's underparticipation. Fred exemplifies this, as one of four men in his twelve-person Green House. On the other hand, Fred (whose closest friend is a neighbor named Alice) and most of the male participants in this research actively create and maintain regular social ties. For example, Glenn has a Tuesday morning breakfast group, Hy builds community among retired professors, Joseph convenes the Jewish community at his senior housing complex on holidays, Bill "hangs out" with his helper Ray, and Eddie regularly fraternizes with his buddies at the gym.

Proximity makes establishing and maintaining peer networks infinitely easier. Intentional age-based communities and others housing contexts, such as Fred's living situation in a Green House, offer ample opportunity for making connections. Despite living alone, Ruth H. and Ann make it a priority to venture out to connect with others on at least a weekly basis, and Johanna's friends come to her. They may or may not know the names of the people they interact with on a regular basis, however this type of recognition may not be necessary. The regularity of meeting is enough to create opportunities for shared connections, offers for rides, and further invitations.

At the same time, group dynamics are complex. In-group and out-group dynamics can make group membership daunting. Disabilities can preclude interaction or increase a sense of isolation, even when people are around. Introverts feel similarly awkward in social contexts. For those who do not have access to or interest in social groups that double as zones for esteem, care, and affection, how can they reach out, while staying in?

In the next several chapters we will see how reaching out to family members, friends, having pets, tending plants, and even interacting with strangers can make a difference in quality of life. This half of the book takes up the theme of linked lives and social capital, emphasizing the multiple and overlapping ways in which social networks bring value and meaning to a life, as well as enhanced health. Specifically, these chapters attempt to answer the question: how does one continue to engage with social worlds in old age? In Lesson 8 ("Care for Others"), elders actively contribute to neighborhoods, communities, causes, and other people's lives in a variety of ways. In Lesson 9 ("Reach out to Family"), study participants care for family, and vice versa. Lesson 10 ("Get Intergenerational") reveals elders reconfiguring family in the absence of biological kin, by reaching out to friends and caretakers, across generations and social locations. In Lesson 11 ("Insist on Hugs"), elders literally reach out through touch and affection. Next, Glenn and others reveal how humor enables elders to connect, communicate, and play with age expectations in surprising ways.

LESSON 7

Resort to Tomfoolery

Glenn the joker

Glenn, the modest Dane who enjoys reading, sometimes resorts to good-natured pranks. He has lived alone since the death of his second wife, and says that physical intimacy with others makes him "wonder and worry whether I shaved that morning and gargled after brushing my teeth." For these reasons, he says, he generally avoids it. Then again, he dislikes it when others assume he is "too old" for something. To keep others guessing and defy stereotypes, he likes to play jokes. In an e-mail, he described his latest shenanigans:

> I found a way to get a little more respect from my young, married cleaning lady who had lightheartedly indicated that she thought I was "over the hill" for your research subject. I stopped at a local garage sale and for fifty cents acquired a skimpy, translucent ladies nightgown that I flung . . . crumpled and casually disordered . . . next to my pajamas on my unmade bed. She comes every Thursday afternoon for three hours. I normally make my own bed but deliberately refrained that day. She did not say anything when she first saw it but did stop in her tracks for a second look . . . did not comment or ask me any questions (I was nearby, of course, watching and enjoying myself) but, before she left, inquired if "one of your church ladies had moved in?" I took the Fifth Amendment and did not answer.

Glenn describes his personality as happy-go-lucky. He strikes an outsider as a wise-cracking Danish man with white hair and a contagious laugh. He regularly wears a shirt that says "RETIRED: Please Go Around." When he holds the door for women, he announces "Women and children first," and then says under his breath "although I feel more and more childish as I grow older . . ." For Glenn, self-deprecating humor and caretaking go hand-in-hand. Once in a while, Glenn sends me a joke e-mail to "brighten my day" or "lighten my academic burden for a moment." He'll close with, "Please laugh with me and not at me and forgive me for wasting your time." And then, "Looking forward to seeing you in June for an update on my sedentary, reclusive, hermit life."

Every time I call to schedule an interview, Glenn has insisted on taking me out to lunch. He drives us in his little Volkswagen Bug fifteen miles to his favorite lunch place, all the while assuring me that he isn't lost, and that the police cars we keep seeing are not following him. He drives over a bump and immediately apologizes for going too fast; "I clearly regret what I did there and I learned from it, don't worry. We will be there in no time." When I take a picture of him, he whips out his camera, saying, "I'm turning the tables on you now, look here. I will send this to my whole family."

Glenn acknowledges that humor can accomplish many goals. First, it can be a strategy to confront ageism, to "make a point," as in his prank on his house cleaner. Glenn says that one thing that really upsets him is to be patronized or stereotyped based on age. At the same time, Glenn claims that he hates conflict, so he uses humor to avoid discomfort, diffuse the situation, and to send a message at the same time. Whether it is a T-shirt that pokes fun at his slowness, or a rumpled bed for a house cleaner to see, such humor not only confronts stereotypes, but also may help him to accept changes in his life. Joking is also an opportunity for Glenn to utilize his creative mind, to problem-solve, to laugh at himself, to establish masculinity, and to care for others. Most important, humor is a way to make others happy, a guiding theme for Glenn.

THE IMPORTANCE OF HUMOR

Humor takes many forms, including, but not limited to, teasing, insults, joke-telling, pranks, and self-deprecation. The enlightened philosopher Immanuel Kant (1724–1804) placed laughter next to hope and sleep as the most beneficial means of renewing the soul. Over a century later, Freud discussed humor as a medication against pain, and a barometer of mental and emotional health, believing that only a healthy person can enjoy a joke. Freud saw humor as a psychic process that offered psychological and social benefits; humor was a way to share joy with others, while on a psychic level, it was a release of repressed energy (and unacceptable feelings) to serve happiness. Finally, he discussed humor as a survival tool, a tool one can use to cope with fear.

More recently, social psychologists and gerontologists have identified physiological, social, and emotional benefits of humor and laughter.[1] Geriatric texts promote the use of humor when caring for elders, for health reasons. Like social connections, laughter can ease pain or let us forget it for a time. Physiological systems influenced by laughter include the immune system.[2] Laughter brings oxygen into blood, activates and relaxes muscles, with the effect of relieving stress. On a social level, humor can help with feelings of solidarity and cohesion, and in relieving tensions and conflicts. Humor can offer an escape from the humdrum, and overcome boredom and fatigue, through reinforcing a type of mental tranquility. In general, scholars have found that interactional humor (both receiving and telling) can predict and maintain well-being; as Freud suggested, it can be a barometer of health. Then again, because humor is always social, the social networks that allow for humor may be just as important as the humor itself. Finally, when surveyed, elders themselves say that a sense of humor matters when it comes to life satisfaction and well-being as we age.[3]

Joking is often an activity associated with masculinity. For example, a recent German study found that men tend to increase their use of humor after age fifty.[4] This gendered association was reinforced over and over in my conversations with the oldest old. When I told each elder that this book would have a chapter on humor and joking, many of the women said that joking was not a part of their lives. I understood where they were coming from; none of them identified as joke-tellers, an activity they associated with men's leisure time. That said, many of the women used wit, or delighted in telling humorous stories, and laughed readily during interviews. A good portion of the men in my sample fit the stereotype; many had jokes to share and admitted to using humor to connect with others, to test their memories, to achieve continuity, to hide their hearing handicaps, and to feel as though they were contributing to a sense of goodwill.

Gender scholars have shown how language, speech types, and humor are important aspects of doing gender, or accomplishing masculinity or femininity. Early scholarship on men's joking highlighted humor as a gendered interactional practice to establish and reinforce power. On the other hand, some have argued that the simplistic model of the actively joking man and the receptively smiling woman has lost ground.[5] Today, girls' and women's humor is now exposed through better research methodology, and through understanding of humor as interactional. Still, humor can marginalize women; many jokes contain sexist content, and male teasing can be a form of sexual harassment.[6] The act of teasing, telling jokes, or in Glenn's case, pulling pranks, may still be associated with the performance of masculinity.[7] In this case, humor can be seen as a tool or an interactional technique used to constitute oneself as masculine or feminine, as well as a tool for deconstructing gender.[8] Humor can be used to reinforce masculinity (and heterosexuality, power, and status) and feminine ideals (solidarity, friendship, leveling). As we saw in Lesson 1, Eddie manages to use humor to accomplish masculinity among men and connections with women. He has a reputation for teasing and building rapport with men in the gym and the locker room. With women, Eddie's humor turns into flattery and more serious attempts to build connections.

As Eddie's comedic shift reveals, context matters to the use of humor in interactions. Depending on the situation and audience, humor could be used to build rapport, to rib, to slight, to mitigate conflict, to connect with others, to shore up power and status, or to reject or deconstruct power. Humor, as we will see, can be used to establish race, class, or gender-based superiority, or to point out vulnerability. For example, humor can be used to construct and deconstruct gender (e.g., to emphasize masculine prowess or make light of men's vulnerabilities). It can also be used to highlight, embrace, and resist age-related expectations and stereotypes, such as balding, incontinence, and bodily changes. Lore, the German immigrant whose style has always been direct and brash, gets away with discourteous honesty (viewed as humor) because of her age and background. And Glenn plays harmless pranks to interrupt ageism and mitigate conflict.

Recent research on old women in Sweden and Japan has shown how the old use humor as a tool to make life manageable.[9] This chapter extends that thesis, focusing on how Eddie, Bill, Ann, Alice, Lore, and Josie use humor to (1) connect past and present, (2) cement social bonds and make others happy, (3) express needs, emotions, anxieties, and identity, (4) enhance health and social participation, and, perhaps most importantly, (5) respond to aging and ageism. By focusing on the strategic use of humor among those eighty-five and over, we see how they negotiate social rules and their own vulnerabilities. At the same time, we see the humanness and resilience of spirit of the oldest old.

Eddie: Joking to Connect

A key element of Eddie's regular exercise routine, which he describes as mostly exercising his jaw, involves friendly verbal sparring with others. Here's a sampling of his shtick: When asked what he thought about being an elevator operator for years, his eyes light up and get wide, and he retorts, "It had its ups and downs." Someone approaches, saying he looks good, and Eddie replies, "Compared to whom?" Someone else says, "Yeah, you look fresh and clean there Eddie." He replies, "I try to shower once a week whether I need it or not!" Eddie then leans forward, and in a loud whispery voice reports, "A woman came into the locker room by accident; it was just as I was coming out of the shower. And she squealed! I just don't know if she squealed for joy or what!" For his finale, the mostly bald Eddie heads toward the locker room and calls ahead to his friend, "I'd like to borrow your hairbrush!" His friend replies, "I brought hairspray for you too!"

Connecting with all types of people is what Eddie does best, and humor smooths these early-morning interactions at the gym. Humor about aging bodies (balding and showering) seems to go over well among the crowd of retirees. A humorous and outgoing approach ensures that Eddie is "known" in this public space. His presence is anticipated and appreciated, and his lifelong reputation as an "Albany institution" is reinforced. Not only does humor allow him to cement social bonds, but it also helps him to connect past and present in his own life by fostering continuity, as discussed in Lesson 1.

In a similar way, Bill's humor helps him to be recognized and acknowledged in public places—at the bank, the grocery store, and in his neighborhood—among a diverse constituency. Like Eddie, Bill has been using humor throughout his life to smooth interactions. In late life, joke-collecting and delivery have added benefits when it comes to reducing boredom, enhancing health, connecting past and present, and enabling conversation despite hearing loss.

Bill: Joking for Health and Participation

Bill, a former neighborhood dentist with a hearty laugh (and husband to Mary), uses jokes to brighten people's day, and always has. He contends that a "pleasant outlook on life and lots of laughter are the best medicine." Continuing his work as a community healer, Bill takes this responsibility seriously, enhancing his own health and that of others through his light-hearted exchanges. He uses his computer (and e-mail) almost exclusively to access and share new jokes. (The only exception is to play computer solitaire, as discussed in Lesson 4.) He keeps a new printout of jokes and cartoons in his pocket to share with others when he leaves the house, stopping the carpenter and the grocery clerk, or people who approach him with a smile. He is so successful at engaging others that his wife Mary complains she has a hard time getting him out of the grocery store. When Mary approaches, he even jokes about her, referring to her as his "child bride."

For Bill, joking is crucial to his good health and well-being, giving him a clear purpose in his community. Feeling like he can contribute in a group is particularly important in the context of his hearing loss; telling jokes helps him to feel he is part of the conversation.

Beyond self-empowerment, belonging, and health, Bill can use humor to review his life and amplify the positive moments in his past. Those who know Bill well have heard the small collection of stories he tells about his past that always make people chuckle. He tells stories of when he was in charge of a medical aid station during World War II that received limited supplies of grain alcohol (200 proof) for sanitizing. He took the extra alcohol, diluted it with a lot of water, mixed in lemonade powder and rationed it out to members of the regiment. This concoction was useful; it made his men happy and also eager to sleep, he notes.

At ninety-four years of age, his daily happy hour practice involves "two drops" of scotch diluted with water, and this ritual not only reminds him of his army days, but also goes along with a joke he loves to repeat that makes light of aging and incontinence.

> A woman walks into a bar and she says she wants a scotch with two drops of water and he rolls his eyes and says "Jeez I've got a freak here," but he pours a glass of scotch and puts two drops of water in it. Then, she has another one, she said "I'll have a second one" and finally, she says "I'll have one more before I go home." The bartender says, "Ma'am do you mind if I ask you a question? What's with the two drops of water?" and she says "Well, young man, I'll tell you, when you get to be my age, you know how to hold your scotch but your water is another matter."

When Bill asks for "two drops," this is shorthand for who Bill was and is at ninety-four; a medic in the army who took care of his men, lives for happy hour, and wants to help others to laugh. If anyone worries about his alcohol consumption, Bill shares that his "heart man" tells him that it helps to thin out his blood. "He's my heart man, so I tell him he can't talk to me about my kidney or liver," Bill chortles.

Ann: Laughing at the Unexpected

Like Bill, Ann, the exercise enthusiast, also delights in sharing funny stories about herself. While Eddie and Bill typically share stories in groups, preceded or followed by jokes, Ann prefers to share humorous confessions one-on-one. Over the course of an hour-long conversation, she loves to say "I'll tell you a funny story . . ." and then chuckles throughout the delivery. All of her stories are different, but most involve an element of surprise, or something unexpected. In the process, they allow her to expose herself indirectly. Here Ann tells about her search for bus fare and a pay phone, and two surprise offers from men she did not know:

> ANN: You can't imagine how hard it is to find a pay phone. . . . So I know Stewarts [mini-mart] always had a pay phone. I went into Stewarts and I said to the man at the counter, "Where is the telephone?" and another man came over and handed me his cell phone and he said, "Use my phone." Can you imagine a man doing that? The day before, I got twenty-five cents from the black guy on the bus and then, today, a free telephone call from another man!
>
> MEIKA: That's wonderful.
>
> ANN: I remember reading in the paper that you could easily pick up germs that way [through sharing a cell phone] (laughter) . . . But isn't that funny? I mean I couldn't turn him down. He said, "Do you want to use the cell phone?" and I said "Thank you very much." All I could think of was he's probably some guy whose got AT&T stock. . . . But it struck me as so funny that two men offered me things two days in a row!

Ann leads a quiet, solitary, ritualized life. She is cautious and practical. To find herself without enough bus fare and in need of a phone two days in a row was certainly out of the ordinary, and probably a source of desperation and embarrassment. Then, to be offered assistance from two strange men, one black, without the ability to turn either down or pay them back, likely led to discomfort. Here, gender and race stereotypes seem to contribute to the element of surprise and discomfort. Ann's inexperience with cell phones and fear of germs may have added to her anxiety. In a Freudian fashion, Ann translates these experiences of discomfort and embarrassment into a humorous story, perhaps as a way of coping with the unfamiliar.

Similar to Elizabeth's disclosure about her "waddle," or Glenn's disclosures about his uncontrollable drooling (see Lesson 10), these elders' use of humor to smooth out "painful self-disclosure" is not uncommon, particularly among the socially reserved. Research shows that women elders across a variety of industrialized countries may convert painful life events to everyday matters that they can laugh about with others.[10]

Ann's stories are self-deprecating or proud, but never boastful. For a woman of her generation, pride is unacceptable. Then again, framed as a funny adventure story about exercise or absentmindedness, she can highlight lifelong accomplishments as well as make light of her foibles. Ann tells about the waitress who asked her if she was the one who swims in the lake on Decoration Day, which made her feel like she was famous. As we know from the last chapter, Ann also likes to tell about how she went to the Obama inauguration at the age of ninety-three and rode in a subway for the first time. I first learned about this adventure from a note and a picture that she mailed to my home one week before the Obama inauguration. In the picture, Ann was standing in her living room, in a gown. The enclosed note said, "Dear Meika, I am going to the inaugural ball. How do you like my gown?" Later, over the phone, Ann shared funny stories about her daughter searching for a gown that would hide the age spots on her chest, her insistence on wearing flats, and how people in DC generously offered her feet-warmers as she stood outside waiting to see the motorcade. Every layer of this story, from the picture on, conveyed an element of surprise, a (sometimes slight) detour from convention.

As much as she delights in relaying humorous stories, she also delights in collecting them. In order to reciprocate, I shared humorous stories of my own and realized that I too was doing gender through using humor to connect and divulge details of my own life. Ann was able to delight in the little details of my stories, and this made for a fun interview session together. She was still chuckling as the door closed behind me.

Alice: Humor to Lighten the Mood

Somewhat similar to Ann, Alice uses humor to lighten the mood in a conversation, to care for and connect with all types of people, and to avoid negativity. Like Bill, Alice has spent a lifetime reflecting and improving upon this strategic approach. She says whenever possible, she takes advantage of opportunities to make new connections and construct new friendships, using humor and body language. She says, "I try to understand people and support where they are. To treat them as I would like to be treated." She prefers not to be negative. Instead, she works at lightening the mood. Bring up health concerns, and she's quick to change the subject, saying "Let's talk about something cheerful." She even did this in the hospital. She said, "When I was in the hospital, I tried to make my doctor laugh, but he is quite stern." For Alice the optimist, complaining is unacceptable. Humor is one way to avoid or divert discomfort, and to create a positive connection.

As a librarian for most of her working life, Alice had the difficult job of keeping others quiet. Rather than reprimanding students for making noise, Alice would joke with them, warning that someday they would have a whole gaggle of kids that would never quiet down. She used humor to diffuse the situation, and she says that today people still talk about her joking approach to shushing students.

While her university librarian duties did not always require humor, her later work with children, doing puppetry, reading and leading songs did. These days, when my toddler-aged daughter visits Alice magically transforms into a marching-band leader, cupping her hands and holding them up to her mouth like an invisible trumpet and pretending to march around to a familiar tune. She uses humor and imagination to connect and empathize with all ages, and most importantly, to bring joy.

Lore: Telling It Like It Is . . .

In many ways, Glenn, Eddie, Bill, Ann, and Alice accomplish traditional forms of masculinity and femininity through their use of humor. While reinforcing gender, power, and inequality, humor can also provide opportunities to bend gender rules. Humor, in its complexity, provides openings for women like Ann to reveal self-pride and for men like Eddie to express care for others. In contrast to Ann's indirectness, Lore and Josie are uncensored and direct, using what is perceived by others as humorous insensitivity as a vehicle to express repressed anger, transgressing gender rules in the process. Interestingly, old age only enables these transgressions.

Lore has always told it like it is. Growing up Jewish in a German town in the 1920s, she was told many times that she was odd or crazy. She says that anyone she befriended in her teenage years did not want to be associated with a Jew. Thus, she developed a rebellious spirit that got her thrown out of boarding school. Later, in Holland, Lore used her "crazy" label to get away from the Gestapo, and married a man only to escape "evil" as Hitler invaded. As a result, she found herself "free" but stuck in an unhappy marriage. She laughs loudly with pride when she announces that she traveled for many years without her husband. She excelled in the arts, teaching ceramics in New York City. As a grandmother, she took on the responsibility of "culturing" her grandchildren, buying the cheap seats for the opera and then moving everyone to the front rows after the intermission (sometimes to the surprise of celebrities who arrived late to claim their seats). Asked about her childhood and adult life, she sums it up in one word: miserable.

Today, Lore continues to have difficulty with trust and says she finds little happiness in daily life. Her mobility is limited, her memory is waning, and she is in regular need of oxygen. To cope, Lore turns to hostility, biting humor (sometimes viewed as honesty) and art. At ninety-four, Lore lives with her granddaughter, who uses humor to connect with her "goofy side," calling her the Queen of Sheba, and your highness, and using funny sayings from movies, teasing and taunting to "keep things fun and keep both of us sane." Without humor, Lore can get hostile, sometimes lashing out at caretakers or visitors she doesn't know.[11] In this context, both caretaker and elder rely on a common language of humor (or what Freud would describe as veiled hostility) to let off steam and cope with stress.

When she is up to it, Lore still attends a figure art class at the local university, where she has a reputation for her "edge." Along with powerful, vivid, artistic renderings, Lore makes brutally honest and politically incorrect comments in class and gets away with it because of her age. Lore says she has a "round friend" in the class, a descriptor that embarrasses Lore's granddaughter, but one that Lore, who responds to shapes and colors, stands by. She also describes her doctor as the man with "slitty eyes." While our ability to self-censor may wane with age, Lore seems to embrace this opportunity to be uninhibited in her nineties.[12]

When I visited the house Lore and her granddaughter share one Sunday morning, Lore's friend from art class was visiting. She told me she appreciates their time together, saying "Here, I can say whatever I want. And she can too. She has no problem that I live with a man. We talk about the pros and cons of marriage, we talk about sex, and we have a lot of fun." Lore adds in, laughing, "We're not ashamed of anything, are we?" In this friendship, Lore's uninhibited persona is valued.

When I mentioned that Lore had a biting sense of humor, her friend told me the story of Lore's response to one nude figure model in art class.

> I remember one time we were in class and we sat down and the model got undressed. The African American guy. Lore announced to everyone that he must be cold because it was small! (laughing). Everybody heard too. But we all love our Lore, so it was fine."

Meanwhile, Lore continues to do what she has always done, delivering sometimes brutal truths that exploit racism, ageism, and other forms of oppression. In some of these moments, her hostility is not veiled, it is raw. Herself a member of a targeted ethnic group and a family that had little patience for her, Lore has likely stored up anger based on her own oppression, and may be projecting this onto others to cope. Then again, like Ann in this chapter, she may be uncritically reflecting generational and personal prejudice and ignorance. Lore's granddaughter believes that after a painful childhood and a difficult marriage, she is now freeing herself through uncensored art, humor, and occasional hostility. As Freud would say, humor is her medication against pain. Knowing what she has been through in her life, Lore's granddaughter uses playfulness and humor to connect with and care for Lore, invite compliance, and enhance her quality of life.

Josie: Being a Smart Ass

Much like Lore, Josie, the lonely centenarian who took friends and family into her home, spent years perfecting tough talk. For Josie, humor helped her to cope with shyness.

> I was afraid of my own shadow in those days [as a child]. I turned red as a beet when my mother was talking about my looking for a job as a

clerk somewhere. I was scared as anything, but I worked there at the railroad doing accounts for forty years. Now I get smart with people. See, people would tease me there, make fun of me, so I learned that type of talk.

Josie described herself as a young quiet business graduate who tended toward perfectionism. Her business professor praised her for bringing perfectly sharpened pencils to class. Then, when Josie's father passed away, she became the breadwinner of the family. Working for the local railroad, she was surrounded by teasing co-workers. Over time, the "good funny men" of the office teased her until she learned to protect herself. Eventually, humor enabled Josie to be accepted as one of the guys. Perhaps most important, besides mastering accounting, Josie gradually built her self-confidence and learned to connect through "getting smart with people." This work-place vernacular was ingrained in Josie for four decades as the rail-road workers became her extended family. Josie, who never married, lived for work.

These days, Josie vacillates from talking tough and loud, to being quiet and sad. In Lessons 9 and 10, we will learn of Josie's desperate loneliness in old age. Sometimes humor helps her to mask this sad-ness. I glimpsed this when I arrived at her home to do our first inter-view. When I shared the topic of the book with her, she immediately recoiled from my use of the term "oldest old," and then came on strong.

> OLD?! I don't like that word. No siree. I like the word YOUNG. After all, my friends are sixty and they are falling and getting sick. And here I am [at one hundred]. So old doesn't mean anything.

Sometimes Josie's scrappy style and tough talk get her into trouble, and then she feels terribly guilty.

> You know, when I was at [assisted living], I interrupted this guy who was giving a tour and using that word, old. "Sir," I said, "I wish you wouldn't use that *dirty* word here. We use the word YOUNG." And boy, he was upset. He is dead now, poor guy. I was being kind of a smart ass, you know?

Other times, as with Lore, Josie's direct, gutsy approach has won her friends and admirers, like at a recent ceremony honoring her involvement in a century-old women's club. There, she reminisced about being the first in the area to wear pants, and enjoying late-night card games with the girls.

HUMOR AS A TOOL

Is it any surprise that those who have lived long healthy lives have managed to make fun of themselves and others in the process? In this chapter, the oldest old use humor in various social interactions for multiple purposes. In some ways, the manner in which each of these individuals uses humor follows life-long gendered patterns. For the men, Glenn, Eddie, and Bill, joking and teasing have served them throughout their lives; they likely utilized these interactional tools in their public personas in sales (Glenn), dentistry (Bill), and elevator operation (Eddie), and they continue to do so now in public places (e.g., at the gym or the bank). This is also the case for Josie the railroad bookkeeper and Alice the librarian and child educator. Ann and Lore, on the other hand, may not have had to use humor to be successful in their careers (as social worker and ceramics teacher, respectively), and today they use humor mostly in private or one-on-one communication. Despite differences in context and styles, all seven appreciate humor for similar reasons. They use humor as a social lubricant, to express pleasure or playfulness, to connect with others, to entertain, and to poke fun at life or themselves.

Despite all of its pronounced social and interpersonal benefits, humor is not always constructive or enabling. Unfortunately, aging is itself a joke—as revealed in countless Hallmark cards and the infinite materials that jokers like Bill draw from. One negative outgrowth of age-based humor is that the subject of aging is rarely taken seriously. It can reinforce silences around difficult topics including death and dying, disability, disease, or depression. While humor can be used to reinforce stereotypes, it can also allow the humorist, in this case, the oldest old, to play with these silences in new ways, and in the process, to cope with their own troubles.[13]

While centuries of research emphasize the physiological and psychological benefits associated with humor, as a mechanism for managing the inevitable health stresses of *aging*, it has received limited attention in the literature.[14] As elders in this chapter reveal, humor can be a useful vehicle for interrupting uncomfortable silences about aging and exposing the complex realities of aging bodies, from balding to incontinence.[15] It can be a way to begin or divert conversations about frailty and vulnerability. In these ways, humor can be used to reinforce or reject age-based stereotypes; it can bring people together, or reinforce social division. Humor is one more tool that the oldest old turn to for fostering life-long continuity, happiness, and an ethic of play.

Beyond allowing for critical play, humor is social; so it can be used to smooth interactions and maintain social ties. In short, it can help individuals like Bill and Eddie to feel connected, and to continue to participate in social life. It can help Ann to express pride and embarrassment, and Alice to stay positive. Beyond health and social benefits, for all of these elders, humor is a way to confront and poke fun at age-based expectations and discomfort. Glenn uses pranks and visual humor to send messages about health, masculinity, and vitality. Ann, Eddie, Josie, and Bill use humor to cope with weaknesses and disability, or for deflecting attention away from aging. Bill's active joking helps him ignore hearing loss and interrupt the attendant isolation; Ann's funny stories and Glenn's disclosures allow them to share age-based embarrassments without losing face.

Humor can maintain and signal health; in fact, wittiness and joking can be a way to flaunt mental health (when others may not expect it), and also to test it. One elder says that her psychologist son tells her jokes to test her mental acuity. If she doesn't get the joke, he knows something is wrong. Likewise, when Bill cannot complete a joke or funny story he has told for years, his wife Mary becomes concerned. Finally, because humor can decrease pain and suffering, loved ones like Lore's granddaughter integrate teasing and jokes into everyday caretaking. Elders do this too—particularly when health and end of life conversations get too serious, many use humor to lighten their interactions or to change the subject.

As we have seen in this chapter, humor can be one method of caretaking—a way to bring joy to others in a community. In the next chapter, the oldest old care for others through a variety of methods including daily check-ins, telephone calls, e-mail and written correspondence, community involvement, and commitment to a cause.

Care for Others

Juana in front of her church

How does one actively contribute to society in old age? This is a question that many elders grapple with. Alice, the nonagenarian with an intricate personal care system, has always derived great satisfaction from helping people. Now, at age ninety-two, waning eyesight and limited mobility constrain the ways Alice can reach out to people, and this frustrates her. Even so, she perseveres:

> I feel very selfish now. As you know, I spent many years helping people, or at least I'd like to think so, and now I have to ask for help. That is hard. But I have figured out that I can listen. And sometimes people call me and what they need is to get things off their chest. So I listen.

While she is no longer able to visit and work in care environments (other than her own), Alice can still offer a listening ear. She hears about health concerns, family tensions, and financial worries, the matters that animate our lives across the life course. The telephone enables Alice to continue to do what she has always done; to listen, reassure, and offer support to those she jokingly calls "clients," or friends in need. Many of these "clients" have cared for Alice at some point or another; so this practice enables her to give back.

Just as Alice cares for friends and strangers by listening, Juana does this, in part, through sharing her poetry. This New York Yankees fan cares for her family and her Catholic community in numerous ways, acting as "mama" to many. After the terrorist attack on September 11, 2001, Juana focused her love and attention on the city that took her in as an immigrant from Puerto Rico decades before. After watching the terrorist acts on television, Juana sat down to write a poem. In four-stanzas she wrote in beautiful Spanish about "towers that trembled as if made of satin or paper," and the horror of an attack "like nobody has ever seen." She implored the gods to save America and to see that these grave acts of terrorism not go unpunished. Juana ended her poem with a request (translated from Spanish):

> *A prayer to the Lord,*
> *and a moment of silence*
> *for those who died are not forgotten,*
> *our brothers who had to go*
> *because of terrorism.*

After a social worker friend typed Juana's poem, titled "Terrorismo in Nueva York," followed by her name and her hometown in Puerto Rico, Juana packed hundreds of copies, and took a bus 140 miles from her hometown to New York City. On streets and in train stations, Juana passed out almost seven hundred copies of her poem. She says the people thanked her for sharing her poem. She thought this was something she could do to share her grief with others in a city that she once called home. She used her poetry to care for others and give back.

THE OLD AS CAREGIVERS

This chapter emphasizes the ways in which elders take care of others and, in the process, help others to feel good. When middle-aged and older adults were asked to define well-being for a psychological study,[1] these groups emphasized an "others orientation," or being a caring, compassionate person and having good relationships, as central to positive functioning. For many like Alice and Juana, being a caring and compassionate member of social groups (families, clubs, and congregations), has been central to living a meaningful life. Scholarship highlights how aligning oneself with a cause (or something larger than oneself), and practicing reciprocity can have a grounding effect, adding to a purposeful life and offering a reason for living. While social relationships are usually a barometer of happiness, studies show that caring for others is sometimes more beneficial than receiving help. We need the give and the take, the sense of feeling needed.[2] Particularly for old women, carework can be central to a sense of well-being, continuity, and meaning. Without the ability to care for others, Alice, Juana, and others may not see their lives as worth living.

While the oldest old may be limited in ways in which they can feel helpful, Alice and Juana have come up with creative and pragmatic strategies for contributing to the lives of others the best they can. Depending on health, mobility, and social location, elders utilize tools like telephones, computers, prayer, backyards, recipes, checkbooks, wills, and their voices to make a difference. Elders who live by this ethic of caring for others defy scholarship that tends to focus on old people as recipients of care, but not as caregivers contributing to others' lives. In reality, most of us are both givers and receivers throughout our lives.

When elders are providers of care, we assume this takes place in the context of familial or professional relationships. However, new studies reveal caretaking patterns based on friendship and a sense of moral duty. In a study of over a hundred naturally occurring care relationships in California communities, nonpaid, nonprofessional, and non-kin relationships lasted anywhere from one month to fifty-seven years and were established out of a sense of moral obligation. More than half the sample used kin terms to characterize their relationship. While heterogeneous in form and function, all involved socializing and help with at least two instrumental tasks. Forty-seven percent of the caregivers were aged sixty-five or older.[3]

This chapter emphasizes the wide variety of caretaking activities that nonagenarians take part in, including care for family, friends, strangers, and plants. Rarely do elders discuss the care they offer others in their daily lives, or the contributions they plan to make after death. Instead, like Alice and Juana, caretaking is something they have done throughout their lives or have learned to do in times of desperation, and now care rituals are just part of a quiet ethic of service that pervades what they do. A few nonagenarians talked about volunteer work as part of their daily routines, or made comments during interviews. In most cases, I stumbled upon stories and chance moments of observation when I got a glimpse of these caretakers at work. I heard Alice telling a "client" she'd call her back, I helped Ruth L. tend to her plants, I watched Shana connect with a neighbor, I heard Ruth H. lend support to a dying friend, and I observed Joseph at a community center dinner. It was only after following up on these observations that I began to understand how central providing for others can be in maintaining a meaningful life.

I begin with Glenn, a man who baked strawberry shortcake for our first interview session, apologizing all the while for his novice baking skills, and then showering me with proud stories of his children and grandchildren. Although he can be a prankster, Glenn's life also exemplifies an ethic of care for others, care that is emotional, physical, and relational. Like Alice, Juana, and others, tending to others has been a guiding theme in his life from childhood, through his time of service in World War II, through his marriage, and through his work and educational history. Because he still walks and drives in his mid-nineties, is e-mail-savvy, and is always up for travel, Glenn is able to tend to his five children and grandchildren in a variety of ways. In his humble, unassuming way, Glenn would be the last to admit he is a caretaker, insisting that he is "just an ordinary man" who delights in making others happy.

Glenn: Tending to Loved Ones

Glenn was raised by a single mother in Denmark. He has great respect for his mother, who was "straitlaced and a good mom," and later his mother-in-law, who was "the sweetest lady you'll ever meet." Glenn learned from these mother figures in his life that caretaking is both an obligation and an expression of love, and his own experiences have only reinforced his identity and role as a caretaker.

Today, Glenn tends to his five children, five grandchildren, and two great-grandchildren, none of whom live locally, staying up late into the night to make calls around the world. For all of his children, he listens and asks about the details of their lives, and travels to see them and learn more about them. He makes daily calls to his son with Parkinson's to try and cheer him up. He hosts family reunions in the summer as he always has, and, like any proud father and grandfather, he boasts about his children and grandchildren to friends. He longs to know and understand his grandchildren better, so he creates opportunities to facilitate this. Over lunch, Glenn told me how he just offered his grandson, who is a budding musician at age fifteen, $50 to play "Taps" and "America the Beautiful" on the trumpet on the deck of Glenn's summer home in the Catskills. With his son's help, he purchased a trumpet for $30 on eBay, and it is ready and waiting to be played this summer.

Glenn speaks fondly of his two wives, both of whom he took care of for many years. He says of his first wife of forty-three years, "Would you believe our fondness for each other increased in those three years she was sick? It was because I knew I would lose her." This case exemplifies how physical infirmities and sickness can shift the degree of closeness and interdependence in a relationship, sometimes in positive ways. Glenn says his wife's doctor complimented him on his care ethic after his second wife died. "I was stunned to learn that there are many husbands who do not care for their wives. I have never imagined any other way."

Glenn continues to care for his wives by nurturing their old networks. He visits family members and stays in touch using a variety of methods. Since Sylvia's death in 1985, he helped to memorialize his mother-in-law, contributing to a book and documentary film project on her life as a Norwegian homesteader. He keeps Sylvia's sorority sisters group going (established in 1942, now with only three members left) through round-robin correspondence, and he sends letters and cards on birthdays and holidays to their close friends. On one snowy February day, Glenn shared with me that he was busy putting the final touches on a letter to an old friend, originally Sylvia's best friend, Jean. In this letter, marking her ninetieth birthday, Glenn reflects on their common memories over the course of many years, first describing meeting his future wife Sylvia at St. Lawrence University (she was a transfer student from the University of Oslo and Glenn was asked by the Dean to translate her grades, which he embellished slightly), then meeting Sylvia's closest friend and her boyfriend Johnny (who, he says in the letter, was reputed to be a good kisser and a rare individual who owned a car) before enlisting in the service. He goes on to describe the long-standing family bonds he and Jean's family enjoyed over the course of many years. He concludes his letter with sentiment and an invitation:

> Jean, think back and shed a tear of happiness for the great times we have had . . . your family and mine. . . . and we are not done yet. You must come to Maplecrest this summer and we will have a ramp ready for yours and Roger's wheelchairs to buzz right up on the deck and into the living room.

Correspondence allows Glenn an opportunity to reflect upon and review his life's joys, and to reach out to faraway friends. He appreciates that he now has the time to write letters. Sometimes letter-writing is all he can do in times of crisis, as evidenced by his recent attempt to secure release for his lifelong friend who was moved by his children to a dementia facility. Sadly, those concerted attempts at communication, like many, seemed to fall on deaf ears.

Besides reaching out to family and old friends, Glenn works hard at cultivating new friendship. From our first interview, Glenn welcomed me as a friend. Soon, I was invited, along with acquaintances from his exercise classes and some neighbors, to lunch at his home.

Most of us were decades younger that Glenn, but that didn't matter. Glenn prepared his now-famous strawberry shortcake for dessert and delivered a short speech expressing his gratitude for friendship. This is just one example of Glenn's regular caretaking regimen that extends beyond his family and continues to give Glenn's life meaning. All of these acts of engagement with family and friends not only express Glenn's generous spirit, but also give him a sense of purpose and serve to temporarily relieve him of his loneliness.

Ruth H.: Appreciating the Dying

Like Glenn, Ruth H., described earlier as a female Mr. Rogers, delights in people and community. Ruth H. helped to found several local educational institutions, and in this way she has contributed to each community member's life, from childhood to old age. She and her husband raised four children and watched her parents live to be very old in this community. Today, Ruth H. still lives in the same house, and appreciates how many in the community look in on her. (One summer evening I knocked on her door, and she said with pride that I was the seventh visitor that day.) At the same time, Ruth H. cares for the community that cares for her. As she says, "When the shingle on the window across the street was hanging by a thread yesterday, I let them know. This is what we do in this small village; we look out for each other."

As I sat with Ruth H. on a cold winter day, the phone rang. It was immediately clear that this was a different type of call. Ruth H. quietly repeated into the phone statements like "Yes, you have done so much in your life that you can be happy about." And "You have had a very full life." She was talking with a friend who was dying of cancer. After she hung up, Ruth H. said she would prepare an "appreciation letter" to celebrate her good friend's life. This is something she likes to do. She explained that even if it does not reach her friend in time, at least the family will have it. This is one way Ruth H. believes she can continue to be of service to others. In her ninety-seven years, I imagine that Ruth H. has grown deft not only at formally appreciating countless individuals, but also in helping others to embrace the dying process.

Ruth H.'s phone and written communication reminded me that at any stage of life, it is helpful to communicate with peers who may be having similar experiences. As a first-time parent, I gained tremendously from talking with others who were also figuring out their new roles. Likewise, I know my students appreciate the support of others who are making their way into the work world, as they are. It makes sense then, that those experiencing "old age" could be a great support to others, when it comes to embracing life, and ending a life too. Ruth H. is someone who has formalized this role, providing comfort and clarity around life and death.

Margaret: Checking In on a Neighbor

Checking in with others is a common way to lend support in old age, especially in close quarters, such as age-segregated apartment complexes. Margaret has counseled others and knocked on doors throughout her life. She led a church group for many years and worked as an Avon salesperson, offering support and encouragement to women on a regular basis. Today she continues to counsel and knock on doors in her senior apartment complex.

This all happened when Margaret lost her good friend, Fran. Fran regularly checked in on Jackie, a woman who lives across the hall from Margaret. Margaret talked with me about how, after Fran's death, she decided to check in on a daily basis with Jackie, as Fran would have done. Here she describes how she came to be Jackie's confidant, supporter, and cheerleader:

> What told me to befriend Jackie? We were friends, but not friends if you know what I mean. I would meet Jackie when I went into Fran's apartment, but we were never on a one-to-one basis, so it was only after Fran's death that I took it upon myself to take Fran's place and to help Jackie through her trials. See, Fran was sort of looking after Jackie. Fran would go into her room and make sure Jackie was taking her medication and this and that. So I decided well, I'll go and at least there was somebody coming in and I'd make sure she was all right and what have you. I also . . . I have a great deal of faith in God. [Jackie] lost her sister in the meantime, and I have been going to her and I was able to help her through that with my religion and so forth. So she really appreciates me. I will say that much. She always says "Don't ever stop, Margaret."

Check-ins can operate like regular phone calls; they can shift a mood or remind someone that others care. Margaret kept a regular schedule; her visits to Jackie were predictable and anticipated. While they may have been unwelcome or intrusive at first, Jackie came to appreciate the effort, particularly at a time of grieving, and began to regain some independence. Margaret explains:

> So now she is going down and playing cards and this is making her better. I said, "Jackie, you don't know what that's doing for you—you're a completely different person since you're getting yourself down there and meeting people and playing cards." Before, she got so she was depending on the help too much instead of doing for herself. She just sat in that chair crocheting—a wonderful crocheter—and that kind of life. Now she's dressed, she looks lovely, she comes down and she's a different person.

Margaret offers social and faith-based care to neighbors like Jackie. Jackie, who is a former nurse, also shares her expertise with members of the community. This reciprocal relationship became clear one day when Margaret wasn't able to move her arms. Jackie came across the hall with her stethoscope. According to Margaret:

> I didn't know I was having [a heart attack]. My arms were heavy like lead. No pain in the chest whatsoever. And Jackie has a stethoscope so we always call her—she was a nurse—when we want our blood pressure taken or anything. So Jackie came and she said she thought I better go to the hospital. So we called the ambulance and so I did. I had a heart attack. I wouldn't have thought it. So that's why I feel so comfortable here, because we take care of each other.

The story of how Margaret and Jackie care for each other in their senior apartment complex epitomizes the ways social networks can play important roles when it comes to preventative health care, and the ways in which elders can be caregivers and contributing members of communities.

Olga: Great-Grandparenting

Besides caring for their peers, many who are aged eighty-five and beyond continue to provide for family members. At 6:20 every morning, Olga's caretaking routine begins, when she gets a call from her great-grandson. Then a sister calls, with stories of arthritis and a son with cancer. Eventually she speaks with her daughter who also has cancer. She says there is so much suffering everywhere, and if she can be of service she will. After a day "floating," serving meals and checking in on others at her senior apartment complex, Olga puts some money in envelopes for her family and puts aside something special for her daughter.

> My daughter has cancer and I am old, so we are giving each other these little things that we happen to have now. This (points to candy dish) was given to me by a customer, I [will give it to] my daughter. . . . I always kept that in my bedroom on a special shelf. Now I want to let her enjoy it for a few years. She likes blue glass, and I have piles of it.

At age ninety-seven, Olga is caring for her great-grandson most weekends, and supporting him emotionally as he begins his first job.

> I have a great-grandson, age twenty-one, that was born disabled with one hand. He spends every minute of his weekends here with me. Just something we just love—we just love each other. He has a real grandmother, she never takes care of him, and I said to his mom the other day, "He calls me every morning before he goes to work." I said, "He's mine as much as he is yours."

While contemporary scholarship on grandparenting is expanding, the work of great-grandparents is less acknowledged. As a great-grandparent, Olga takes on significant caretaking responsibilities that carry physical and emotional tolls as well as satisfactions. As with her children and grandchildren, Olga has taught her great-grandson the important things, like saying thank you, cleaning, and cooking. He also cares for her; his is the voice on the phone in the morning that helps her start her day.

Joseph: Caring for a Family, a Community, and a Cause

Like Juana, Joseph feels a strong sense of belonging with his religious and ethnic community. Joseph is a tall, bald, and blind man with a strong Latvian accent. He says his memory is all he has. This is a source of daily survival and satisfaction as well as great pain. For years, Joseph worked as a barber in his native Latvia. In 1942, he was sent to a concentration camp in Latvia simply for being Jewish. There, he was about to be killed (for picking up a discarded cigarette butt) when he begged for the opportunity to shave the commandant's beard. That opportunity eventually saved his life and helped him to locate his wife Myra in another camp.

Besides pain and pride, memory can also bring satisfaction. For example, Joseph remembers all dates, including anniversaries, birthdays, Jewish holidays, and doctors appointments. At a Passover Seder with fourteen of his family members, Joseph asked everyone to quiet down for a moment, because he wanted to "test his brain." He proceeded to name every single birthday and wedding anniversary around the table, without error. He said his family was shocked at how good his memory was, and he was quite proud. After telling this story, Joseph added, "I even sent a card on the birthday of my granddaughter's dog, which made her very happy!"[4]

Joseph and Myra live together in a small one-bedroom apartment. He is mostly blind and she has severe dementia. He says, "We are together; she is my eyes and I am her memory." Today, his life is about caring for family and community. This involves sharing memory, song, prayer, sharing food, and giving money to organizations. Joseph and his wife light candles every year to memorialize the six million killed in the Holocaust for Yom Hashoah at a local synagogue. Joseph's wife was among the first to record her memories for the Holocaust Museum in Washington, DC, and after many years, Joseph has agreed to share his story with others. When he shared his story with me, his memories were so clear and fresh, it was like he was living it all over again, with tears streaming down his face.

Jewish tradition and community bring Joseph solace and joy. He looks forward to holidays with his extended family, where he can "make the prayers" and be surrounded by the family he helped to create. Watching them grow and thrive is a thrill for Joseph. He says, "My great-grandchildren keep me going. Pretty soon they will be calling me Papa . . . and I can hold them. That's what you live for."

Jewish tradition extends beyond his family to his community. He leads the prayers at Jewish holidays at his apartment complex and at the community center. He and his wife also attend two meals a week at the local Jewish Community Center. While many friends who have sat at his table have passed away, this community center still feels like a place where they belong. Community meals are something to look forward to at the end of a day; and they feature two of Joseph's favorite things: music and food. This sense of joyful belonging was evident when I visited Joseph and his wife at community dinner; while a pianist played music from the thirties, Joseph introduced me to others at the table, and then sang and tapped his feet in between bites of food.

Finally, Joseph contributes financially to the causes he cares about. "There are so many Jewish organizations asking for money. I wish I were rich!" he says. But Joseph does what he can, despite his blindness. He asks his aide to read him the letters he receives and then to write out the checks and mail them to the appropriate organization. As we talk about important causes, Joseph takes a framed certificate from the wall and asks me to read it to him. It says that he invested in the new state of Israel in the 1950s by purchasing an Israeli bond. As I read, Joseph smiles and explains. He had only been in the United States for two years at that time, supporting his wife and two children on a barber's salary. Despite this hardship, he managed to purchase a bond for $25 to make a personal investment in the freedom of his people. Small financial contributions like this still carry tremendous emotional and symbolic weight for Joseph.

Shana: Being Neighborly

Shana's cause is just as personal and familiar as Joseph's, but increasingly local. Her most immediate project is reaching out to family and neighbors, providing a community hub and nourishing others with her garden. Particularly in the summer, neighbors, children and grandchildren swim in her pool, eat home-grown vegetables and the food she stocks in the fridge, and occupy her upstairs bedrooms.

Shana has lived in the same home for forty years and has watched neighbors come and go, grow up, and die. She is so connected to this land and residential community that she hopes never to leave her home and backyard. As she has aged, so has her neighborhood, and now the population surrounding her home comprises mostly retirees, and has been officially designated as a Neighborhood Naturally Occurring Retirement Community (NNORC). As a result, the neighborhood has received state grants to fund picnics and trips, and has distributed lists of resources for home maintenance and care.

Shana says she has always been active in her community, and she has a great neighborhood association. She likes to get to know her neighbors, especially in the summer, when everyone is outside and friendly. She tells me she is helping to plan a picnic for those in the neighborhood who are seniors. She also tells me about one neighbor who became a close friend over the years,

> He's in his eighties; he'd do anything for anyone. He was so kind. He's in a nursing home now, for over a year. With a feeding tube. It has been a while since I visited. . . . His poor wife and kids.

On the day I visited, a neighbor was swimming in Shana's pool, and he stopped to talk with her about the new young couple on the block. She said she loved the idea of having a new family on the block. Besides sharing her pool with neighbors, Shana spends a lot of time in her garden, harvesting flowers and vegetables that she shares with old and new neighbors alike. She says this past summer wasn't so great for the vegetables, but she had quite a few beans to share.

Ruth L.: Tending to Her "Children"

Ruth L. is an interesting contrast to others featured in this chapter. Like Shana, Ruth L. is growing old in a home she has occupied for half a century, filled with memories. Nevertheless, she is generally wary of people. She has watched the neighborhood change, and doesn't know who to trust. A former kindergarten teacher in Poland, Ruth L. spent a good portion of her adult years in the United States educating others about hate, speaking at synagogues and schools with children of all ages about surviving the Holocaust. She did it for the children, she says. But in recent years Ruth L. rarely leaves her home, except to visit her doctors (see Lesson 5 for more on Ruth L.'s doctor network).

Ruth L.'s lack of trust comes from many factors: she was raised Orthodox Jewish with a firm sense of right and wrong; she is a Holocaust survivor; she has been the target of anti-Semitic hatred in the United States; she has lived a life of giving that, in her mind, has not been reciprocated (more often than not she believes she has been exploited for her story of survival, a story that depletes her every time it is shared); and she has picked up on ageism, regularly repeating, "nobody cares about the old." Ruth L. spends her days feeling secure behind an elaborate system of locks and two-way mirrors, set up by her late husband. Given these psychological and social obstacles, Ruth L. may be more isolated than most, but she has also made connections of a different type.[5] She talks to her plants and her deceased relatives. At age ninety-seven, she believes this is the only reason she is still meant to be on this earth, to care for what was lost. Meanwhile, she has little need to leave her home. A son delivers groceries, a daughter-in-law does laundry, another son and a small group of friends call on the phone, and her most beloved companions are there with her—her books, her memories, and her plants.

On one of my early visits with Ruth L., she directed me into her dining room, and pointed to rows of potted plants, all different, arranged along the side with the large windows. She introduced me to each of them, sharing memories of when she received the plant, and from whom, or explaining how she created the plant from seed. Ruth L. emphasizes how, when caring for her plants, or "children," they come alive for her.

> These are my children. Forty-five years for most of these. Most were just tiny plants and look how they have grown. That's what I do—I talk to my plants. This one is from grapefruit and orange seeds. Just that and look, this beautiful plant. And this one I have a seedling if you replant it right away.

For Ruth L., human contact is mostly disappointing. Caring for plants, along with ritualistically remembering lost family members, keeps her engaged and feeling needed. Caring for her plants enables Ruth L. to do four things: review positive life memories (many associated with marriage), celebrate natural beauty and longevity, experience pride, and share this pride with special people. Perhaps most important, Ruth L. is able to experience companionship and some degree of healing with the help of her plants. They listen and respond to her, and she can protect them from dying. After she has been away for any length of time, she proudly talks about how she brought her "children" back to life. Partly because her home is filled with that which is most important to Ruth L., she has fought hard to stay at home (with her plants) until her death, making it known to her sons and doctors that she would not have it any other way.

INVISIBLE CIVIC ENGAGEMENT

Taken together, the oldest old in this chapter help us to see aging in both new and familiar ways. While we may expect the oldest old to be recipients of care with diminishing social networks and increased isolation, this chapter tells the opposite story. It exposes old men and women as providers, caring for others. This carework may occur in the context of expanding networks and a sense of social and civic belonging. By caring for others in creative and familiar ways, each individual in this chapter experiences social benefits, including a sense of belonging or feeling needed by another individual, a neighborhood, a friendship group, an organization, a community (real or remembered), or other life forms. When Joseph misses dinners at the community center, when Alice misses calls, when Margaret doesn't visit Jackie, or when Ruth L. doesn't tend to her plants, their absence is felt. In these ways, belonging and contributing is caring for others, and being cared for. Scholars have shown that reciprocity like this strengthens social bonds and well-being.

Continuity and reciprocity can also be motivating factors in carework. When they care for others, these elders are continuing to do what they did earlier in their lives: Ruth L. the kindergarten teacher tends to her "children"; Ruth H. honors the dying; Margaret uses her Christian faith to support a neighbor who suffers; Glenn extends a care ethic to many; Joseph participates in Jewish community and ritual; and Shana builds community around her home and her garden. In all of these cases, a sense of obligation and reciprocity keeps the oldest old engaged. Many are now caring for those who have cared for them.

These activities broaden the definition of carework to go beyond biological and marital bonds, to include community, friends, strangers, and even plants.[6] In all of these cases, elders expand their networks of giving and receiving. While they may lose friends and contemporaries to death, they continue to gain new connections and opportunities to grow, learn, and heal. Through the loss of a dear friend, Margaret gained another. Ruth L. creates new seedlings and brings her "children" back to life. Joseph welcomes new family members and new community members. Shana welcomes new neighbors to the block.

These elders' lives reveal the care-focused dimensions of civic engagement. While plenty of attention has been given to elder civic engagement in the form of participation in organizations and clubs, less is given to care for neighbors and friends, which is equally as important for health and quality of life. When Shana distributes vegetables in her neighborhood, Joseph supports causes, and Alice counsels by phone, each is engaged in what sociologists Pamela Herd and Madonna Harrington Meyer would call invisible civic engagement. This work, "predominantly performed by women, paradoxically limits, enhances, and even constitutes a vital form of civic activity." Perhaps the widely heralded social decline in civic engagement isn't really a decline at all, but a shift to less visible sectors of society.[7]

Ruth L.'s case reveals that elders' carework can take many forms. Her caring activities take place in a context of purposeful civic disengagement and partial isolation. Selectively social, Ruth L. engages with remembered worlds, plants, and a very tight circle of family and friends on her own turf. In these ways, this world-weary individual continues to create a life of continuity and meaning. This approach flies in the face of "successful aging" paradigms that emphasize social productivity, but epitomizes comfortable aging.

Psychiatrist Marc Agronin, in his book, *How We Age*, describes the unique challenges of healing-work with the last generation of Holocaust survivors. His experience has taught him that sometimes the perpetual sadness of an elder is not to be healed but shared. Further, survivors of great trauma can sometimes find healing when they give others what they need themselves.[8] These reminders are helpful in thinking about the daily lives of Ruth L. and Joseph, who both carry deep sadness—sadness that cannot be healed. However, both find comfort in ritualistic forms of caretaking and through giving.

While the carework literature may not fully address the oldest old as caretakers, it does address the joys and stresses of carework, usually in a family or marriage context. Carework can be a way to experience intimacy with others, as Glenn points out, or a way to stretch and grow. At the same time, caring for the living can be emotionally draining.

Outliving one's friends and loved ones can be painful and destabilizing; many nonagenarians feel that they are constantly grieving. Many of the oldest old worry about caring for loved ones after they die.[9]

Informal caregiving, especially when unanticipated, can be intrusive. Jackie took a while to warm up to Margaret's regular visits. And during my hour-long interview with Olga, we were interrupted by two unanticipated visitors: one who offered a ride and then continued to chat for a while, and another who delivered cookies. The visits were made with goodwill and generosity in mind, and didn't seem to bother Olga (who told me she couldn't eat the cookies because they contained chocolate), but I couldn't help but wonder how residents in this senior apartment complex managed to protect their privacy in such a social setting. Not answering the door or phone was one strategy elders used. And in her quiet residential neighborhood, Ruth L. protected her privacy by leaving a chair outside her front door and instructing postal carriers, friends, and delivery services to leave mail, packages, and foodstuffs there.

Caring acts help us to think about gender in nuanced ways. Gendered caregiving patterns are certainly evident here. Many of the old caring for others are old women. This is no surprise, as women outnumber men in this age group and are taught and expected to actively nurture others throughout their lives. But men like Glenn and Joseph have honed caregiving skills throughout their lives, as they performed service-oriented work (Glenn in sales and Joseph as a barber), raised families, and lost loved ones. While old women and men may go about carework differently[10] (with an emphasis on connection rather than task-completion, for example), there are more similarities than differences among diverse research participants. Why? In part, the skill set that we associate with feminine domesticity earlier in life is crucial for self-care for all in late life, especially in the context of widowhood.

The next chapter emphasizes the ways in which elders continue to provide for their families, while also depending on family for care. This unique give-and-take enables us to move beyond discussions of weak and strong ties within one's generation or peer group, to look closely at familial capital, and the forging of intergenerational bonds.

LESSON 9

Reach out to Family

Margaret in her favorite chair

For years, Margaret had lived next door to her children and had established a close relationship with her grandchildren.

I took care of my grandchildren through school while my daughter-in-law was a nurse, which I am so thankful for because it has given me the opportunity to become so close to them, you know? We reminisce on the things we did, we played hopscotch on the side together . . . it was just great that I had that experience with them. (laughing) And now to think they're in their thirties, and my grandsons are in their forties!

After her husband died and Margaret retired from Avon, Margaret's family wanted her to move in with them.

Did I tell you they were looking for a home with two rooms for me, and the real estate woman suggested this senior apartment complex? I would have had my meals and everything with them. Which would be fine, but I would be alone, whereas here I have people. So it is much better to be in a place like this where you are meeting with other people all the time and you make friends. And as nice as [my family] would try and make it for me there would be some lonely times. You know they have got to live their life too. So I am happy here, and they are only twenty minutes away.

In 2002, Margaret moved into a senior apartment complex, where she enjoys spending time with her peers, checking in on a neighbor, and arranging her space to keep things handy. A nursing aide helps her in the shower and with heavy cleaning. In many ways, the tables have turned and Margaret's children and grandchildren are now assisting her, at age ninety-seven, with daily living. Her granddaughters cook for her on holidays. Family members take her on excursions to the mall and out to lunch.

Margaret says while it was hard at first, to accept their care, she now makes the most of it. She asks her kids for hugs. She gets to know the nitty-gritty aspects of their lives, following up on the details. She works with her children to prepare for her death. Recently, she has established an enjoyable daily routine of phone calls with her son.

When the kids went to Florida this summer (first summer without her), they said I should call every morning at nine. So I did, and we got to gabbing and sometimes it would be thirty minutes. It really is a joyous note to start the day, and it cuts down on loneliness. They are far away but I can talk with them, so you start the day off strong. So it was hilarious, because I said to my son "I really like the conversations." And he said, "Why don't you keep calling?" I have to laugh, because I think he likes it. And he's not a phone person! And if he's not there I get to talk with my daughter-in-law, which is wonderful. So now we talk every morning.

In a number of ways, Margaret reaches out to her family, and they to her. Spending time connecting with family members, she asks for assistance and continues to offer a listening ear, a hearty chuckle, and help with planning for the future. Far from being passive receivers of care, elders like Margaret actively embrace familial care, and reciprocate with their own caretaking rituals.

MAKING FAMILY CAPITAL VISIBLE

Most children born today will have at least one (and likely more) living and healthy grandparent, and many grandparents can expect to see their grandchildren grow to reach adulthood.[1] An overwhelming majority of older adults have children (87 percent) and grandchildren (80 percent), and these family members are central to their lives. Half of older adults with children say they communicate with a son or daughter on a daily basis.[2] Those without children connect regularly with siblings or nieces and nephews.

As individuals live longer, the potential for care within multigenerational families grows.[3] Sixteen percent of contemporary households contain at least two adult generations or a grandparent and at least one other generation, a rate that has increased slightly since 1980.[4] This growth in multigenerational families accelerated during the Great Recession in the context of economic need and in the context of sociocultural shifts, such as a rising share of immigrants in the population and later average age of marriage.

Sociologists identify family as the primary socializing institution for individuals. Families shape us as social beings, meeting our basic human needs and exposing us to language, social norms, and values. Generally, when we think about family, we emphasize the role of parents in helping a child to develop. Yet we may neglect to consider the role that grandparents play. We may also forget to consider the role that children will later play when it comes to familial reciprocity, sharing resources with parents.[5] No matter the life stage, one can accrue diverse and varied social advantages from family, and these advantages constitute part of what is called social capital. When it comes to health, support, and well-being in old age, there may be nothing more important than family capital.

Family capital can be understood as the aggregate of family resources or investments and efforts that can be mobilized to advance class status and achievement, for example. Like social capital, family capital is multifaceted, encompassing material, social, linguistic, emotional, psychological, and cultural aspects. While many sociologists study family capital from the perspective of parenting children into adulthood, capital can accumulate for parents as well.[6] Beyond material resources, familial care, communication, interaction, cultural patterns, and social networks can translate into a lifeline for an elder or a child, or can be disabling, depending on the individual's experience of family. Children (particularly daughters), like mothers with their children, can be "intensive" in their approach, investing extraordinary amounts of time, energy, and labor in their parents' care.[7] Or, on the other end of the spectrum, progeny can be hands-off or distant (generally read as neglectful) when it comes to social and financial investment in their parents' care.

A vast gerontological literature demonstrates the "flows" of support from elders to younger family members, including financial support and care in the form of grandparenting. Grandparents provide broad and crucial safety nets for children all over the world, as Ted C. Fishman reports in *Shock of Gray*. In the United States, one out of every twenty children is cared for by one or both grandparents. A Urban Institute study estimates that grandparents provided $39.2 billion worth of unpaid services to their grandchildren. Americans over age fifty-five provided $100 billion in family care, taking into account care for spouses, older parents, children.[8]

The resources families can offer members may be shaped by a host of social and economic factors. Sociologist Teresa Toguchi Swartz reports, for example, that white families and higher socioeconomic status families tend to exchange more financial, material, and emotional support, whereas black, Latino, and lower socioeconomic status families, particularly the women in these families, are more likely to be involved in practical help and housing support. For example, black Americans and Latinos use nursing homes far less than white Americans; most will make whatever arrangements they need to avoid a care facility. This may be due to strong distrust of institutional care, or a sense of familial obligation.[9]

Juana exemplifies the flows of family capital. She cares for her children, and they in turn care for her. Living in a duplex with her daughter further enables this regular exchange. Higher rates of inter-generational co-residence among racial minorities like Juana have been linked to structural variables such as social class, health status, marriage patterns, or recent immigration. According to this view, family members reside together to pool incomes, share expenses, and offer other forms of instrumental support, such as child care, transportation, food preparation, and so forth that contribute to the well-being of one another and the whole group.[10] Importantly, not all elders have kin upon which they can rely. Single, childless elders constitute one out of five Americans sixty-five and older, and closer to one third of the baby boomer generation. In general, childless rates are on the rise in industrialized countries, and in these cases, the definition of "family" commonly includes extended kin and lifelong friends. Social scientists have found that many childless elders have built strong friendship networks over their lives and depend on small networks of siblings and friends in place of children.[11] In Lesson 5 ("Ask for Help, Mobilize Resources"), we saw how Alice, a single, childless elder, exemplifies this pattern. Josie and Pauline, also childless, depend on friends and siblings for support. Even some with biological ties prefer to depend on social families, or a combination of both friendship and familial bonds.

No matter how "family" is defined, this form of capital is gendered. Research shows that women like Margaret cultivate more kin-centered networks, as well as friendship networks.[12] Many of the participants in this study, including Margaret, benefit from family capital in the form of instrumental and emotional support from several generations. On the other hand, Margaret also associates well-being with autonomy and a wide variety of social connections. With health and financial resources, she chose a living situation a short distance away from family that allows her to emphasize peer friendship as well as familial closeness. To her mind, moving in with family would have made her more lonely and isolated than moving into a senior housing complex. Further, having her own apartment allows her to avoid dependency and emphasize autonomy. While this choice may seem odd, she sees it as the best of both worlds. The mix of autonomy and control combined with Margaret's close proximity to family enables her to expand her networks while being able to embrace and borrow on familial capital on a regular basis.

Like Margaret, many of the oldest old treasure their families. According to a Pew Research Report, the majority of elders say the most important benefit of aging is spending time with their families.[13]

Beyond this, the MacArthur Foundation found that elders who live with children benefit from their time with family; they are healthier, and they have sharper mental and social skills.[14] It is also possible to imagine scenarios where families may not be beneficial to health or well-being, in contexts of abuse or neglect, for example.

Because the research for this book focused on the oldest old aging in place, only Lore, who lives with her granddaughter, lived in a multigenerational household from the beginning of the research. Several others lived with siblings or spouses. Many, like Margaret, insisted on their independence, declining offers to live with family. Interestingly, by the time I sat down to write this book, two study participants (Ruby and Pauline), both black Americans, had moved in with their families for ease of care.

Over the course of three years of meeting with elders, I have met only a small handful of family members.[15] Most study participants live alone, and thus they tended to be alone when I visited with them. Nevertheless, evidence of family is always there. As elders like Margaret talk about their lives, many share pictures of siblings, children, and grandchildren. Indications of family care became increasingly obvious to me over the course of time, in the form of rides, phone calls, newly framed pictures, clean laundry, furniture that had been moved or purchased, and full pantries.

Informal caregivers such as family members provide an astounding 80 percent of care to elders living at home.[16] On the other hand, like most forms of carework, family care is easily rendered invisible or taken for granted in a society that assigns little value to it. Because these efforts occur in the midst of everyday lives (e.g., before and after the workday), they are difficult to measure and quantify, even for elders themselves, who often depend on this informal carework. Simply put, family care is a crucial aspect of successful aging in place. Some scholars have suggested that "aging autonomously" (or doing anything autonomously) is just not possible when most of us regularly rely on others.

Research shows that women play a central role in actively maintaining family relationships, doing the work of kinship and caregiving throughout their lives. In most of these cases, it was daughters and granddaughters who were taking on the bulk of this invisible labor.[17] This gendered carework was made visible at particular moments, like when Glenn gave me his daughter's phone number in Paris (as an emergency contact), or when Ann's daughter picked up her mother after an interview session at a cafe. Both Glenn and Ann have sons, but their daughters were somehow designated as the primary caretakers, even when they lived at a distance. (Interestingly, Japan has created a home care system that aims to relieve women from providing the bulk of the carework. There, a rotating crew of caregivers, subsidized by government assistance—each with their own functions, cares for housebound elders so that the burden never falls on one caregiver in particular.[18])

Since our conversations were focused on "living alone and making it work," I relied on elders to bring up the topic of how family members (and others) figured into their lives, and then I asked additional questions. In general, elders' stories about family care fit well with the patterns in the literature. Most were so invested in their own independence that they avoided asking family members for help or downplayed these moments. In some cases, they didn't feel they needed any assistance, and, in fact, some provided more care than they were receiving. In other cases, they were worried about being a burden to their "busy" children, especially their sons.[19] Despite such concerns, these elders were often not alone. I was able to see a relative or two in the background, washing clothing, calling care providers, and running errands.

In Margaret's case, independence and being with peers was important enough for her to insist on living apart from her family. Margaret says her health and financial situation (including her regular Social Security check) helped her to make this decision. On the other hand, retirement, a move, giving up her car, proximity to family, and then a heart attack pushed her to accept aspects of her family's care and prepare for "whenever God calls." At the same time, Margaret continued to care for her family in ways that she always had, and to delight in their company.

This chapter is based on three major ways elders talk about reaching out to family: spending time together, offering assistance, and asking for care. We would assume that for the oldest old, asking for care and feeling like they still have something to offer can be challenging. On the other hand, spending time with family can also be difficult, particularly in the context of family tensions, over-protectionism, or neglect.

PRIORITY ONE: SPENDING TIME TOGETHER

Most study participants spoke with me about family-centered, intergenerational social rituals that they looked forward to on a regular basis. For example, Ann spends many weekends with her daughter's family at a nearby lake retreat, and enjoys regular dinner dates with her son.

Mary and Bill host their daughter or their two grandchildren at least once a month. Joseph and his wife enjoy Friday night (Shabbat) dinners with their daughters. Alice's daughter-in-law takes her to the ballet every spring. Glenn hosts his family at their summer cottage every summer. And Olga receives a call every morning from her grandson.

Rarely did the oldest old wish for a live-in family member. Instead, regular social engagements with family provide opportunities for closeness; for children and parents alike, this is an opportunity to catch up and monitor family members' health and well-being. It is also an opportunity to maintain close bonds. While delighting in grandchildren is common, elders like Margaret acknowledge how nice it is to know and engage with their children almost as if they were peers.[20]

Despite these regular rituals, many elders are eager for more opportunities to spend time with extended family. "Watching them grow," Joseph explained, "is what you live for." On the other hand, he and others are convinced their children and grandchildren lead busy lives, and that asking for more is not an option. This doesn't keep tempers from flaring, especially when busy lives and distance prove frustrating. When I asked Florence about her children, she hastily replied, "My children all live far away. Some kids they are!" And then, after a moment, she added, "I'd prefer if they lived closer, you know?"

On the opposite extreme, Emma and Josie say they rarely see their family members. Emma adds that she doesn't even know her grandchildren, especially those who live far away.

> I don't know them grands. The other day, someone came in here—a boy, and I said "Who are you?" and turns out he is that one in the picture over there. But if I saw him on the street I wouldn't know who he was. I say, "I been here since 1990 and you just now come?" And he sat there and lied and said he'd be back with his kids every day. Humph. Haven't seen him since. No, they don't come around. And my kids, they got enough of me when they were coming up. (laughing)

Josie, a childless elder whom I described in a previous chapter as part spitfire, part lonely soul, describes a recent bout of desperation and loneliness, which led her to beg her nephews to visit with her.

> You'll notice I talk about friends a lot, not family. I only see my family once a year, Christmas Eve. And when they picked me up from the

hospital and took me to a nursing home. The other night I was so lonely, I called my nephews and asked if they would come over. . . . When they got here I said, 'I am sorry; I have nothing to offer you.' But they just sat and watched the Country Music Awards.

Josie's story is perhaps the most powerful example of reaching out to family, simply for companionship. She appreciated their company, but felt bad about not having beverages and snacks on hand. She also felt generally confused about her relatives, sharing that several years prior she was incensed when they "dumped [her] off" at an assisted living facility, without consulting with her. Others have described moments when spending time with family is not easy; getting caught in family friction, being told what to do without consultation, or feeling ignored by relatives. All of these examples point to ways in which family ties can be the opposite of enabling.

Familial neglect can go both ways, and the social repercussions can be traumatic. While I did not systematically collect perspectives from family members, two elders volunteered information about detaching themselves from family members they did not want to support. Elders break off contact with their families for a variety of reasons, from differences of opinion to debt. In this case, the two elders mentioned grandsons who were gay, and the limited support that came from the extended family for them. One participated with the rest of the family in cutting off contact with a gay grandson, and when he later committed suicide, the elder responded with a great deal of guilt and pain.

As with most of us, the vast majority of elders describe desiring a balance of family closeness and independent living. Like Margaret and others, this ideal is something they strive for on a regular basis. Technology such as the telephone and Internet can help to achieve this desired closeness at a distance.

PRIORITY TWO: OFFERING SUPPORT AND ASSISTANCE

The previous chapter focused on new caretaking relationships with friends and peers. At the same time, many elders continue to care for their family members—socially, financially, and emotionally. This continuation of caretaking can be a source of comfort and pride. A

Pew Research Report finds that 40 percent of all parents aged eighty-five and over say they have given money to their children in the past year, and 20 percent have assisted their children with childcare, errands, and/or housework. In this section, we get a taste of how the oldest old offer assistance and care in this way, particularly through communication, grandparenting, and running errands.

Glenn and Fred: Calls and E-mails

Over the course of their lives, women of the Greatest Generation were taught to embrace communications technologies. A few, like Margaret, worked as phone operators in major cities. The majority spent years in charge of family correspondence and continue to use this skill in old age, fostering and maintaining crucial friendships over the phone.[21] Two male widowers, Glenn and Fred, learned the art of family communication in old age.

Glenn reaches out by phone and e-mail to connect with his five children, scattered from Haiti to Seattle. He generally acts as the social hub for family conversations on an almost daily basis. On a typical night, Glenn is up late calling across time zones and sending humorous group e-mails. He says that when a family member is discouraged, "a friendly word is almost as good as flowers, and a lot cheaper." Glenn admits that he is in the daily business of "lifting spirits," particularly for a son who is seriously ill with Parkinson's disease. In general, though, he is intricately involved in all of his children's day-to-day lives and vice versa. For example, recently Glenn e-mailed his kids to let them know that a friend of a friend, a kindergarten teacher, would be coming to live with him during the week, and that she would be bringing her cat. (This was followed by a more formal memo detailing the arrangements, sent via snail mail.) This elicited countless amusing responses recalling mice in the house at Christmas and expressing hopes that the cat would be a good mouser. In the process, Glenn's daughter attached a picture of the blossoming tree outside her window (in Paris), and this, as well as other stories, were circulated to all.

Like Glenn, Fred also reaches out by phone, calling both of his daughters daily. One daughter he calls mid-morning, after doing his morning exercise routine. And he recently decided to add the other daughter to his call list after her husband died. He explained, "My other daughter—after her husband died, I thought maybe she needed a little cheering up. So I always check in." Unlike Glenn, Fred lives in a Green House, where nurses are on hand twenty-four hours a day. He makes these calls for his own peace of mind, to connect with family, and to assure them that he is okay.

Olga and Mary and Bill: Grandparenting, Hosting, and Offering Financial Help

Like Margaret, many of the oldest old find comfort in continuing to care for family members, especially their grandchildren. While a growing literature addresses the increasing caretaking roles that grandparents play, we tend to assume that nonagenarian grandparents no longer take on these responsibilities. Olga and Mary and Bill, who are still healthy and strong in old age, continue to do what they have always done.

In a previous chapter, Olga described how she keeps money envelopes for her family members, and has started giving meaningful things away to her daughter. This type of financial and material support is coupled with emotional and social support for her daughter, who has cancer. Every weekend, Olga spends time with her grandson in her small apartment. She teaches him to cook and clean, and they enjoy each others' company. Recently, when he turned twenty-one, she encouraged him to find a job, and they celebrated when he was successful.

Mary and Bill have offered similar forms of support for their grandkids ever since their daughter's divorce. When their daughter was going through her separation, she and her two small children moved in with them. Today, Mary and Bill still open their home to their grandchildren and daughter on many weekends and holidays. Mary prepares beds and meals, and delights in their company. So far, she finds it is mostly worth the exhaustion. After all, it is family.

Juana and Eddie: Cutting Hair, Preparing Food, and Running Errands

A friend of Juana's introduced her this way, "This is a woman who, at ninety-one years old, still makes food for her family!" It is true. Juana is still mothering her children much as she did back in Puerto Rico. She says her life is better now that her children are grown. But she still wakes up at 6:00 every morning to begin making food for her son's family. He picks it up a few hours later. Then, she might make rice and beans for her daughter, who lives downstairs. Or she might prepare flan to share with family and friends. Juana also cuts and dyes her children's hair (to cover the grey). She shows off her daughter Miriam's newly dyed dark hair. She says she uses the electric shaver on her son. When all of this is done, she makes time for her poetry. This is what she has always done, and she likes staying active and busy.

When I met Eddie, I realized that he played the role of personal shopper for several siblings and other surviving relatives. Eddie offers a service that many need in old age. In his hometown, the local senior services organization offers a grocery shopping program. Volunteers visit elder or disabled clients, pick up their grocery lists, and shop for them, just as I did for Diva in Lesson 5. This tremendously popular program is a huge help to elders who lack transportation, mobility, or the wherewithal to visit a grocery store. In previous chapters, Eddie discussed how he takes his sister grocery shopping and out to lunch, and drives her to and from her appointments. Sometimes he includes neighbors in his errands, especially when a new food store opens in the neighborhood:

> This new place—SaveALot—they open on the eleventh of February. I got to pick up some neighbors—they want to go. Some of them can't drive for one reason or another. So we'll go opening day to see what they got. Just to be inquisitive.

Eddie also shops for his uncle, a semi-retired elderly priest, and takes him out to dinner on a weekly basis. The day we talked, Eddie had just picked up underwear for his incontinent uncle, and was compelled to guess on the size. He joked, "Thank gosh socks are all one size!"

Healthy and mobile elders who are able to lend a hand generally do assist their families socially, financially, and emotionally. But what happens when an elder can no longer shop for herself, host others, afford care, or reach out in general?

PRIORITY THREE: ACCEPTING ASSISTANCE

Elders are not always comfortable asking for care from family members. Forty percent of the oldest old say they worry about being a burden to their children, and the poorer they are, the more they worry. As a result, elders tend not to ask, or ask for less help than they need to avoid being burdensome.[22] As one classic sociology study found, elders desire "intimacy at a distance."[23] Sixty percent of the oldest old surveyed in a Pew study said they receive help from adult children for errands or appointments, and 40 percent receive help with housework or bill paying. This work is primarily performed by family members. Of those children who perceived their parents in need of help, only one in ten had hired help. Instead, daughters and sons tend to take on these responsibilities themselves. In fact, daughters are twice as likely as sons to play the role of primary caretaker.[24]

In previous chapters we have heard from elders who depend on family members regularly. Many rely on children to handle their finances. Two say they depend on their granddaughters for regular check-ins and care; for Johanna, this is her closest-living relative, and Lore lives with her granddaughter. Alice, who is childless, called on her brother's daughter-in-law and a distant cousin for in-home care after she was hospitalized. While some of this family care comes on the heels of health concerns, other elders are proactive about asking for assistance and reaching out to family. In this section, we see how Shana, Pauline, and Ann have come to terms with personal assistance over time.

Ann: A Few Hours of Assistance

When I met Ann, she talked very generally about her daughter's help with clothes shopping, her son's assistance with grocery shopping, and how she enjoys spending time with all of her children. It was clear that they worked together as a care team (sometimes in concert with grandchildren) to meet her needs. For example, all of her children recently collaborated to take Ann to Obama's presidential inauguration.

Over the years, Ann's children's regular caretaking roles have become increasingly specific. They seem to have divvied up the core responsibilities: daily check-ins, companionship, shopping, and transportation. Ann's out-of-town son calls every night at 7:30 p.m. Her in-town son has dinner with her twice a week. Ann's daughter drives her to and from her water aerobics class once a week. Ann sees all of these moments of contact as bonuses in her day. She describes her morning ride this way:

> My daughter picks me up at 7:45 a.m., and she has a thermos of coffee there for me in the car. Now that's service! And then she goes for groceries and picks me up when the class is over. Isn't that wonderful?

Getting a ride with her daughter, instead of taking the bus, is made all the more attractive with the promise of coffee and groceries. Meanwhile, Ann continues to walk daily, prepare meals for herself, and volunteer at the Lutheran home once a week. Her experiences highlight the delicate balance of offering and receiving assistance, and how that balance can shift with age and health concerns, without threatening a sense of autonomy.

Shana: Help with Home and Transport

When I first met Shana, she was planting and weeding and caring for her home without a lot of help. Several years later, Shana tells me that she has difficulty bending over in her garden, carrying heavy things (like garbage cans), and needs help with some transportation. Together, Shana's extended family meets these needs. In exchange for her hospitality, her nieces from out-of-state help out around the house and the garden. For day-to-day care of her home and transport to the doctor, she relies on her children, who live nearby.

> My son will come today and take out the garbage since it is Monday. I hear from him regularly. I just got a black-eyed Susan from his place and brought it over here. . . . He calls on Sundays, and my daughter calls every night. I still drive, but my daughter-in-law will take me to the blood test today. And my granddaughter used to take me around too. Just yesterday she was a small thing! My niece, she cleaned out the cellar this past weekend and found an old picture and my God, everyone is dead in that picture. Last year they came from Colorado and made three raised beds in my garden. And now I can pull the weeds out of them!

Pauline: A Sister's Care

In Lesson 2 we met Pauline, the Southern-born pie-maker who creates her own safe haven in a crime-ridden neighborhood. Only a year after Pauline and I met, she moved back South to live with her sister. Pauline and her sister have always helped each other out. As young adults, the two sisters left South Carolina for New York. Her sister enlisted in the air force. Pauline held down various jobs in hospitals, shirt factories, and military arsenals, saving money to purchase a home and visit her sister in her various military deployments. When I first met Pauline, she was in her mid-eighties, taking an exercise class and planning to stay in her small home as long as she could, despite the rising crime of inner city neighborhood. She was upbeat, though worried about her health. When she ended up in the hospital a few months later, it was her sister who insisted that she move back to South Carolina, where she could live with family. She explained over the phone,

> I told [my sister] "Sometimes I don't feel like making breakfast." And she said "If you don't feel like making it, you don't eat it, so you're gonna need some help." So, after fifty-four years, I'm going home to South Carolina. This was a lot sooner than I had hoped, but I feel good about it.

WHEN FAMILY CANNOT ASSIST, OR WHEN CARE GOES TOO FAR

Almost everywhere, family is associated with a sense of reciprocity and obligation. In countries like India and Japan, loving family service (or "seva" in India) is built into the culture; familial elder care is (until recently) the unquestioned duty of the son and his wife.[25] This familial ethic is also particularly salient in Latino-American households. However, in the United States in general, an ethic of individualism and choice shapes how we do everything, including how we approach aging. The aging in place movement is one example.

Despite our cultural ambivalence around family dependency, nobody can do it alone. Margaret, Joseph, Ann, Shana, Fred, and Eddie are fortunate that they live near some of their relatives, and they see them frequently. They regularly contribute to and draw upon family capital, epitomizing multidirectional flows of familial support. While the vast majority of the oldest old have siblings or children, these relatives rarely live close-by or have much extra time to devote to care. Some distant relatives care from afar, making time for daily phone calls and helpful visits. These simple overtures can be a lifeline for the oldest old. When an elder's health or well-being becomes imperiled, not having a local safety net can have far-reaching consequences. Pauline's hospital would only release her if she had a caretaker. Rather than move into a care facility, she chose to move back to South Carolina to receive family care. Josie, who does not have children of her own, is expected to move into assisted living.

Since the passage of the Family Medical Leave Act (FMLA) in 1993, family members have the flexibility to take up to twelve weeks of unpaid, job-protected leave to devote themselves to caring for certain defined family members. When family cannot assist, what options does an individual have? One can purchase long-term care insurance or pay out-of-pocket for home health care. For those with limited financial resources, many senior-oriented nonprofits offer free visiting companion services, daily phone call services, and hot meal and grocery shopping programs. Additionally, state and federal monies are starting to be put aside for home health care for those who cannot afford it.

Not all elders have kin to care for them. They may be estranged from family, too far away, or childless. Some elders who do not have family to lean on are fearful of outsourcing their own care. They do not trust others to know what is right for them. They fear becoming dependent too early, on the heels of a major health event or an acquired disability. Alice has told me about close friends who lost their independence very quickly in the context of increased care and learned helplessness. These friends many times become the "clients" she counsels over the phone. In some of these cases, well-meaning doctors and family members have stepped in to take charge of a changing situation, making decisions about health care, housing, finances, food provision, and other things. As their rituals of daily life were "taken care of," her friends have lost control and independence. As a result, some lose the ability to walk or control their bladders, as they learn to become dependent on wheelchairs and diapers. The experience of Alice's friends highlights how care contexts can force dependency, a reminder that elders' personal desires must be central to any care program.

Beyond family care and professional care, there are still other options. Most older adults say they have people they can rely on, other than family.[26] These friends provide support and companionship, and sometimes play the role of a social family in their lives. In the next chapter, Glenn, Mary and Bill, Alice, and others create intergenerational bonds with friends, neighbors, caretakers, and housekeepers who can act as a stand-in for family in their daily lives. They create new flows of support, and new forms of family capital through fostering these close friendships. By redefining family, these elders can avoid being a burden to their kin (if they have biological kin), and create new, crucial friendships in their last years of life.

Get Intergenerational; Redefine Family

Rose at church

Many elders create bonds that can substitute for kin, and then turn to these individuals for support and companionship. They may do this when family members live far away, to create family where none exist, or simply to supplement familial bonds. These bonds can be equally or even more valuable than ones with family. This chapter is about how elders create strong intergenerational relationships that they come to depend on, and in the process, how they end up redefining family. Rose exemplifies this trend, through her family-like relationship with her newly "adopted" friend, Eve.

The creation of a social family is nothing new for Rose, an African American nonagenarian who adopted three children as a married adult. Rose remembers how she and her husband doted on these kids. Then one tragic day, as mentioned in an earlier chapter, a social worker knocked on Rose's door, and removed the one white child (then three years old) from Rose's care to place her in a white adoptive household. This was one of the most traumatic moments in Rose's life. As she described earlier, this was an ugly reminder of the "color line" in America. Through persistence, Rose was able to stay in touch with her baby girl over the years, and even attended her wedding.

Over eight decades later, Rose went through the adoption process again. This time she didn't need an agency. She adopted a close friend who was "like a daughter," Eve, someone who could check in on her regularly. Rose and Eve met at church. She describes her church as her second family, where everyone shares their troubles and feels loved, and she plays a mother role. In this familial context, it felt natural for Rose and Eve to form more committed caring relationships.

> I take them all as children—they call me Mother. I'm the oldest in the church, although another lady is creeping up on me. So Eve is just like a daughter—we adopted each other—at this late stage of life! She's seventy and I'm ninety. She lost her husband around the same time. So Eve calls me every evening before bed. Every night. And if I need anything, if Peggy [my daughter] can't get something for me or can't get to it, she'll do it. She will take me to see a dress shop [clothing store], for example. Eve has more time for me now.

Even for Rose, who has adult adopted children living nearby, having a companion and community to whom she can turn is important. Like many African Americans, Rose has always created and maintained familial connections with non-kin, and continues to do so in old age.[1]

CLOSE FRIENDSHIPS, RECONFIGURED FAMILIES

Contrary to expectations, social networks do not disappear as one ages. In fact, later-life transitions, such as retirement and bereavement, may prompt greater connectedness.[2] In Lesson 6 ("Connect with Peers"), we saw how one's degree of social integration in classes, clubs, and neighborhoods influences the characteristics of elders' social safety nets. Likewise, strong social ties are often crucial to quality of life, visibility, and countering loneliness, particularly among the oldest old, who tend to invest more energy in fewer relationships. These ties are integral to social support, especially since elders tend to turn to informal systems of support (kin, friends, neighbors) before asking for formal support.

Social scientists make a distinction between strong and weak ties, both of which are central to social capital. Weak ties are associated with low intensity and emotional distance, and strong ties with frequency, loyalty, and trust.[3] In previous chapters, we have seen how weak ties associated with group membership and caretaking responsibilities can be beneficial in feeling a sense of belonging in social networks. Strong ties and kin-like relationships, particularly important in the context of increased isolation and loss, offer frequent contact and material and emotional support. Today, Americans have fewer strong ties than ever, with most listing spouses and an average of two friends. Twenty-five percent of Americans claim they have no close confidants at all.[4] Sociologists also point out that our most intimate ties may not always be available to help, as in the case of elders who live far away from their children. As elders move away from or lose friends and family members, they may create new close relationships with younger individuals to fill the void and to help with daily needs. These ties can be vital in old age and even in death.

Changing demographics means that extended kin networks will become increasingly important as people live longer, move more often, live farther apart, and enjoy fewer family ties (fewer siblings due to decreased fertility rates). These networks already exist. In a Canadian study of elders, longtime residents in communities were asked: "Are there any people who are not related to you who you think about as almost family?" Forty percent said they have at least one fictive family member, within one hundred miles. Most described these people as "just like family" (invoking descriptions like sister or daughter), explaining that they act as confidants and lend material and emotional assistance.[5]

Gender, race, socioeconomic status, and age all contribute to innovation when it comes to friendship and family. Rose is not alone as an African American elder of limited means who relies on an extended kin network as well as the church for social support. Broadening support networks beyond biological bonds has been crucial for many blacks to survive in America.[6] As we will see, Julia and Alice, in contrast, grew up with housekeepers and friends cycling through their white middle-class homes. In the absence of a spouse, these lifelong sources of support now fit with a sense of family and shared home. For the childless, ethnic background can have important implications for whether family plays a role in one's care. Medical anthropologists have found that the families of childless blacks place more emphasis on a collateral form of organization that capitalizes upon the sibling bond as a link to nieces and nephews. In contrast, white families emphasize vertical ties between generations, which potentially can exclude the childless.[7] These fictive kin relationships may also follow the substitution principle, or the notion that individuals who have no kin tend to convert close friends into quasi-kin.[8] Research on aging ethnic minorities and gays and lesbians has pushed family scholars to acknowledge "friendship families."[9] Scholars of aging must now consider this reality for elders like Rose and future generations of elders without "real" family ties.

These close relationships and friendships are particularly significant for elders, many of whom struggle with social isolation. For example, Rose has outlived spouses, most friends, and many family members. She has no siblings living nearby, and has spent more than a decade living alone. Over time, however, Rose has actively rebuilt and expanded her social networks. A testament to her resilience, she has cultivated new friendships in late life, working at reciprocity in order to maintain strong ties in intergenerational, kin-like relationships. In turn, this work has paid dividends in the form of common rituals and financial, emotional, and social support.

How do these kin-like relationships emerge? Elders like Rose use ethnic, religious, and community ties to connect with younger peers. In the stories that follow, Julia, Alice, Ruth H., Mary and Bill, Christine, Glenn, and Joseph reveal how they foster and maintain intergenerational connections in their everyday lives, and all are different. For Julia and Alice, it is about reaching beyond socioeconomic and ethnic differences to foster strong ties with household employees; for Ruth H., it is about setting friendship goals in a close-knit community; for Mary and Bill, it involves being active participants in an intergenerational, multi-ethnic neighborhood that regularly breaks bread together; for Christine, it is sharing memories and emphasizing ethnic and immigration-based ties; for Glenn, it is about opening his home to a stranger; and for Joseph, it is befriending and trusting a fellow immigrant and formal caregiver. In all of these cases, strong ties and family-like relationships result from elders' efforts at cross-generational friendship.

Julia and her Homeless Friend

At Julia's funeral, family members and friends were eager to meet Mo, a homeless woman who was probably Julia's closest friend in the years before her death. We met Julia in Lesson 3 ("Live in Moderation"), warming up canned soup for dinner. Julia grew up white and middle class in a small town, with a hardworking father, a sister, and a nanny; her mother had died in childbirth. Her sister was her best friend, and when she died young, Julia says she took it hard. Socializing and physical closeness with others was important throughout her life to ease loneliness and to stay healthy. She told me:

> [Socializing] keeps my brain from getting scrambled. . . . It is important to get with people. I do the library book group and the bible study at church and read and watch TV. I sometimes go to dinner or lunch, although I shouldn't drive at night. Mo comes every night except Sundays. . . . She is good for me, really.

Julia paid Mo, a homeless woman who was sleeping in various garages in her residential neighborhood, to vacuum her home, rake leaves, and set up holiday decorations. Julia knew that Mo had schizophrenia, but still delighted in her company. Julia explained, "Most nights Mo would bring a frozen meal she recovered from the grocery store dumpster, and I would eat a can of soup." This regular dinner date was something Julia looked forward to.

Alice and Her Housekeeper

Not unlike Julia, Alice became close friends with her housekeeper, after years of spending time together. While they had very different backgrounds, they found themselves in similar situations: both on their own, living away from family. Even after the work relationship ended, a friendship continued, with each doing favors for the other:

The housekeeper I used to have—she does all kinds of things for me, and her family has pretty much gone. I'm not a member of her family, but we know each other and that's a very good relationship. She can no longer do the work, but she calls me almost every day, tells me what she's been doing. She doesn't have the same interests as I have, but we have a bond. She will take me grocery shopping, or anywhere I want to go. . . . She picks up things very fast but this is a woman who is British—she only went as far as eighth grade in school. She was so good to me, I bought a few shares of stock for her and myself and said, we'll go to the shareholders meeting. I was interested in what was happening with the business. What she cared the most about was the food. So that's a difference, and yet we have a bond. I did finally find that I could not figure out her checkbook. I tried to help her with finances. Sometimes I went to the bank because I don't want her to be taken advantage of. I know what can happen. I'm very fond of her, and she of me, you know?

Today, Alice considers her former housekeeper one of her closest friends, despite their differences. They speak on the phone regularly, and support each other socially and emotionally. Like a parent or sibling, Alice aims to protect her friend from financial exploitation, as well as to support her financially.

Ruth H.: New Friends Every Year

When I met Ruth H., she told me that she had a rule: make one new friend a year. She wanted me to know that I was one of several new friends she had made in 2006. Four years later, Ruth H. still delights in new friendships. A first-year student at the local university has volunteered to walk with her every Monday, and Ruth H. says, "It is such a pleasure to see college through her eyes." The vast majority of Ruth H.'s friends are many generations younger than she, and Ruth H. is quick to point out how the energy and enthusiasm of the young can be contagious. When December rolls around, Ruth H. has piles of holiday cards on display in her home. She makes a list of all of the cards she gets, and feels proud of the number of friends she has. She says living in a small, close-knit community makes a difference when it comes to social connections.

Ruth H. is a pro at creating and maintaining loose and strong ties, and this range of connections can translate into respect and a sense of belonging. For many years, she worked to improve the services in this small rural community. Today, Ruth H. loves when she is greeted in a public place. She is already planning her 100th birthday party, which will involve setting up a tent in the yard, with food, and inviting the community to come and enjoy themselves.

Amidst her vast web of social connections, Ruth H. tells me that there are ten or so individuals whom she could call to ask for a favor. This small handful is her local social family. A group of them coordinate among themselves to respond to emergencies, provide transportation and help around the house, and offer emotional support. A few are part of her morning phone tree. Sometimes they seem to understand Ruth H.'s needs better than her own children, who live across the country and visit three times a year.

In sum, Ruth H. has lived in the same community for more than half a century, and draws from a web of lifelong social connections in this place, while supplementing losses with new friendships.

Mary and Bill: An Intergenerational Neighborhood as Family

Mary and Bill are active participants in a close-knit intergenerational neighborhood, partaking in community dinners, sharing local resources, and planning "field trips." According to an article about this group in a neighborhood newspaper, "It was a health crisis and a do-it-together attitude that led to the formation of their multigenerational supper club, with members ranging from thirty-something to their nineties."

> On this Center Square block, people already helped shovel each others' walks, accepted delivery of packages and collected mail during vacations. So, when a neighbor who had lived on the block since the 1940s was going to have surgery, it was fitting that a group of five neighbors banded together to take a turn—once a month—cooking for her and her husband. But according to Kathy Linhardt, who moved to Albany from Iowa in 2003 and organized the effort in 2006, the "dinner brigade" has led to so much more.
> "Not only do our neighbors look forward to a home-cooked meal and visitors every Monday evening, but we often get together for potluck meals, holiday and birthday celebrations, and the occasional

dinner out," said Linhardt. "We know we have something exceptional on Lancaster Street, and we do our utmost to keep connected by sharing interests, getting involved in projects and organizations together, and, basically, just finding any excuse to have fun together. We all care about our urban neighborhood, but, most of all, we truly care about each other. We're family now."[10]

The supper club continues; every Monday night, neighbors get together on Upper Lancaster Street. The first Monday of each month is a potluck, with themes that represent the cultural and ethnic diversity of the neighborhood (with Irish, Polish, Italian, and Jewish-themed meals). Every other Monday, a different neighbor takes a turn bringing a meal over to Bill and Mary's home, where they provide the wine. In the cold wintry months, these small and large meal rituals keep everyone from feeling housebound or lonely, also enabling neighbors to keep up with each other's lives. Mary says, "It would be a dull existence without them. I like when we all get together, and it's a different slant on things to hear [them] talking—[they have] been out there and talking to others and I like to listen to the chatter." The neighbors, in turn, enjoy hearing Mary and Bill's stories about the people who lived in their houses before them, and how the neighborhood has changed.

MARY: At [the community dinners] it's everybody all together, and you get a lot of opinions and laughs, too, and it really is interesting. When they come here it's a one-to-one basis and it's really nice. We really look forward to both.

BILL: This is truly unique. It's like living in a fraternity. It's just great to live on a street and to think we have this many friends.

MARY: If [the neighbors] have leftover soups, they bring it over.

BILL: Not if they have left over scotch. (laughing)

MARY: I mean it's great. Yesterday I was talking with Kathy about going to this meeting, and she offered some leftover meatloaf, and I took her up on it. But you know, it really is about companionship. You're never really alone.

I spoke with Mary and Bill about the communities they belong to and how they matter. They said that their church community is still important to them, but the membership has changed dramatically, and they get to church less often. The neighborhood group, they say, is the community they could not live without. Like church, a loose yet formal structure allows for regular interactions, sharing food, and a chance to ask for favors. Recently, Mary and Bill have programmed several neighbors' phone numbers into the "speed dial" function of their phone in case of emergency.

While sociologists have shown that social capital tends to decrease with age, neighborhood socializing, religious attendance, and volunteering increase with age, and elders in general demonstrate a high level of flexibility and adaptability in the maintenance of ties over time. In many ways, Mary and Bill exemplify this. As a member of Mary and Bill's neighborhood, I have also experienced the community's support and love. Before my daughter was born, the neighborhood put together a surprise shower. The next year, we all planned a joint birthday party for the baby, who was turning one, and Mary, who was turning ninety. Mary says having the baby in the mix just brings everyone even closer together. Mary says, "Watching [the baby] grow and progress, it takes you back to when your children were that age. And it keeps you young! It really does."

For most of us on the block, family members live far away. The block is our social family and a huge reason this place feels like home. On special events, this is particularly evident. On Mary and Bill's sixtieth wedding anniversary, the neighborhood planned a surprise party for them, and invited family and friends. At the gathering, it was not clear who was related to the couple and who was not, and it didn't matter. All were family.

Christine: My Family in America

Sometimes it takes a major event, like a move, a birthday celebration, a hospitalization, or a death, to expose social networks. In the days before her death, Christine had a steady stream of visitors, none of whom were official family members. (Christine's surviving cousins, nieces, and nephews were scattered in New York City, England, and Ireland. They wrote letters, called, and visited once in a while.) It was a local family made up of friends and careworkers in the Albany area upon whom Christine depended on a regular basis. When I visited Christine in early February, she said she was expecting several friends that day. Although she was extremely hoarse and in terrible pain, she answered her phone and invited all to come. She sat coughing in her wheelchair, with mittens on her hands and a blanket on her lap. Three drinks with straws were arranged on a TV table in front of her. She told me that Linda, the nurse at the Green House, was keeping her strong, "fighting against [her] death." She said she was well cared for by the staff, and her closest friend Ileana visited her daily. When she died of respiratory failure two days later, Ileana was the first to be notified, and she handled all of the details of the memorial service. The guest book contained many comments from Christine's social family—aides and friends. Perhaps most telling, in the obituary, surviving friends and family members were listed together.

After hearing about Christine's death, I contacted Ileana, and we met in person for the first time. After knowing how tied Christine was to her ethnic heritage, I was surprised to find that her best friend was Puerto Rican, a well-educated professional in her sixties. Ileana described the "divine intervention" that brought her and Christine together ten years earlier, and how after that first drive to Sunday Mass, they became close friends. Christine was like a grandmother to Ileana's children, wanting to see pictures of new babies and asking after everyone. As Christine struggled to care for herself in her late eighties, Ileana would stop at her apartment after work and help with showering, and put her in bed.

> I always told Christine, "If you die first, I will make sure we are buried right next to each other." So her niece and nephew took some of her ashes and the funeral director gave me a small container. So I tell my daughters, "when I am buried, you bury her with me. She will be with me forever."

Christine's experience as a first-generation immigrant motivated her to reach out to others and to create strong friendship bonds. She moved to America in 1954 to be a domestic for a family in Long Island. After many years working in New York City as a bookkeeper, she moved to the Albany area to retire and be near friends. She never married or had children; instead, she was welcomed in by various friends and their families. She lived independently into her eighties in an apartment, where she kept things neat and tidy. One night she fell, and it was hours until a friend found her. After a hospital stay and a rehabilitation period, her social worker advised her to live in a nursing facility because she had no family to care for her and she was mostly wheelchair-bound.

Christine and I first met in the nursing home. I told her I was writing a book about ninety-year-olds, and she welcomed the opportunity to take part in interviews, review her life's details, and to hear about the book project. I was drawn to her warmth, her quiet optimism, and her Irish brogue. She described how she "made memories" (or took visual pictures in her mind) every time she visited Ireland. She spoke of her strong sense of smell, and how the nursing home smelled like chemicals, but she remembered "walking around the country roads in Ireland smelling the wild woodbine . . . it looked like a rose with little tubes coming out of the sides, and it grew wild everywhere." After our visit, she asked me to come again.

Over several years, as she was moved to the Green House and dealt with a variety of illnesses, I visited her in the hospital, introduced her to a friend, and took my daughter to meet her (at her request) in the Green House. I also talked with her by phone. She wanted to know about the book and how my work was going. One day, sitting with her in her room, I described the concept of a "social family" that I would be discussing in the book. She knew right away what I was talking about, and chimed in.

I've always had a new family [in America] and they are always younger than me. Ileana, Amy, John, and you . . . Ileana is my very good friend. She was in [my home town] at the hairdressers, and I was asking for someone to drive me to Mass and she offered. So then she became my good friend. And when she wasn't home, her father and stepmother would check in on me and make sure I had what I needed. Milk and bread. I miss them now that they are dead. . . . Ileana visits me most every day now. And Amy, she was the manager at the apartment complex, and she'd come with Irish tea and we would have a cup of tea and talk. I used to go every Easter and her mother would make dinner. Now we talk on the phone, and I love to hear about the kids. And John. When I was across the way [in the nursing home], I felt I was entering a dark cold dreary place. I felt so terrible then. I cried so much. John perked me up. He was training to be a doctor, and he came back again and again! (starts crying) He brought his girlfriend and his family, and they wanted to hear Irish stories. It was such a lift. He is doing exams now, but he will come and see me soon. And you also visit me regularly, which is nice.

As a first-generation immigrant who was curious about people and far away from family, Christine assiduously cultivated strong ties throughout her life. She worked hard to make chance acquaintances into close friendships, with the help of shared culture, Irish tea, and stories. And illness and disability did not stop her from actively cultivating friendships into her nineties. I watched as she asked people to visit her, and when they came, she gently requested that they come back. Like Rose, she actively "adopted" others, sometimes using ethnicity or immigrant status to cement social bonds.

At age ninety-two, Christine became a local celebrity at the Green House, quoted on the local television news, print news, and in *Parade*, a nationally distributed Sunday news magazine. The Green House was still a new concept in the United States, and the news media were drawn to this new alternative to nursing home care. Christine was chosen by Green House administrators as their resident spokesperson, someone who could speak to the power of elder-centered care and community, and the transition from a nursing home environment. Christine was proud of her ability to contribute, and welcomed another opportunity to share her story. She was also thrilled to meet and speak with the news anchor she watched every night. She recounted, "He was Oriental, but his name was O'Brien!" Ileana collected copies of the articles and sent them along to family abroad. Later, as discussed in Lesson 4 ("Take Time for Self"), Christine dictated a letter to the family (on my tape recorder) that acknowledged special friends like John and Ileana for "getting her out of [her] moods" and visiting regularly, and for the aides and staff who take good care of her. She reassured her family, "You see, I am very happy here." Each time I visited, Christine told me stories about aides like Teresa, who cooked wonderful meals for her (Teresa described Christine as her "angel"), and aides like Ashley and Jane who took especially good care of her, always keeping her warm and comfortable.

Glenn: Free Accommodations in Exchange for Companionship

Glenn has always shared his home with others. He built it in the 1950s for his large family—five children in all, and then his in-laws. Five years after his second wife's death, Glenn longed to share his home with someone once again.

Initially, Glenn talked about helping another in need. He had too much space and wanted to share it with someone who needed a home. Glenn worked with his church to locate an Iraqi refugee to occupy his basement space. Then he searched for a student, knowing that over the summer his children would return to stay in the house. Nothing fell into place. In 2010, Glenn told me he was still looking, and this time he emphasized companionship. I immediately thought of my friend Marion, a single mother and kindergarten teacher who needed a place to stay when school was in session. Glenn seemed quite interested in meeting her.

Glenn greeted us at his front door on a warm March day, and led us on a tour of his home, walking through the basement, complete with a sunny bedroom, bath, space for guests, and a television room. This was all space he did not use, and offered to his guest. Then, over tea and cookies, Glenn shared pictures of his five children and stories of his life and two wives ("not simultaneous, mind you!"). He asked the teacher about her life. They had much in common: love for Scandinavia and travel, dedication to family, and appreciation for privacy. They laughed about memory loss and the thirty-year difference in their ages. Glenn shared that he has a problem with drooling, "I have to apologize, I have this mouth and I just can't control it coming out!" Then, Glenn got serious and said,

> I know you probably think, "This Glenn is ninety-two, he'll die at any moment." So please know that I will tell my children that you have the downstairs for a full year, despite anything that might happen to me.

They agreed that the move-in would happen in September. On the drive home, Marion said to me, "This man is brilliant, and he's too good to be true. Now I can finally pay some of those bills." The move-in was eagerly anticipated by all. And so it began, after Glenn made his intentions clear in a characteristically humorous e-mail correspondence to his future companion (excerpted here):

Hi, Marion-allow me to chide you gently on my alleged "generosity" in inviting you to live in my house. This is not generosity at all but a "barter transaction." I fully expect to benefit in equal measure from your presence in my home. How so? Let me explain what is in the back of my head and how I arrived at my decision to invite human company to share my home.

. . . Now I have lived for five years, alone, after the death of my second wife. . . . I began to find myself "thinking out loud" and even laughing at my own, remembered jokes from time to time and it set me thinking that, hey, I might become a recluse if I did not challenge and counteract that tendency. I diagnosed myself. . . . yes, I practiced psychiatry without a license . . . and concluded that I really needed more human contact and a more structured life-style. I talked with my Church minister but his suggestion of more church involvement did not appeal to me. I am close to becoming a lapsed Unitarian!

More human contact and more structured lifestyle. . . . this is where you come in, Marion. With you and Kini [her cat] in the house, I will just have to stop trotting around playing my ukulele after midnight . . .

Let me stress again that no work obligations, none, zero, absolutely none, are expected or contemplated. I am keeping my cleaning lady—for the whole house, poor soul—and with your own set of house keys you can come and go as you see fit.

This must be one of the most strange e-mails you have received in years. I think I will copy Meika for her file on me. Do you mind?

It is late. I send you all good wishes.

Glenn

Glenn knew what he needed—structure and human contact. Glenn was also clear that he did *not* need a live-in caretaker, and he is not alone in this desire. For many, hiring a caretaker represents not only a loss of independence and money, but also a great interpersonal risk. In Lesson 5 ("Ask for Help, Mobilize Resources"), we saw how elders take great care in hiring aides and helpers. Home health care aides, house cleaners, and their elder employers generally differ in background, age, socioeconomic status, gender, and ethnicity. Such differences can be perceived as risky, and these perceptions may overlap with generational stereotypes and racism, as well as common fears of exploitation and concerns about safety. Furthermore, gay elders report serious concerns about having to go back in the closet in the context of care.[11] Sometimes trust and friendship develop out of these care relationships (as with Christine, Julia, and Alice), but sometimes not.

Joseph: Embracing an Aide Who Takes Good Care

Many elders living on their own rely on housekeepers or aides who share and care for their space, either full- or part-time. In interviews with me, most of the oldest old with hired help tried to emphasize the employee/employer relationship when they talked about these individuals. They rarely used names, instead referring to them as "my girl who comes once a week," "my housekeeper," or "my aide"; On the other hand, in a context of shared time and space, friendship can and does emerge, and these friendships can bridge generational as well as socioeconomic, gender, and ethic differences. For individuals like Alice, Julia, and Christine, frequency of visit, timing in the life course, level of dependency, and period of service blurred professional and personal boundaries over time. In Christine's case, seeing and spending time with the same nursing assistants day after day created a sense of familiarity and comfort; she missed some of them terribly when they were gone. Alice and Julia also became close with the women they employed in their homes, despite having little in common.

In Joseph's case, while he makes the professional relationship clear (sharing that his aide's pay comes out of his pocket), commonalities in experience, disability-based dependencies, and barriers to communication with his wife (who has severe dementia) have contributed to strong ties between him and his aide. Being blind, Joseph relies on his aide for much more than cooking, cleaning, and driving. A typical day's work (in a three-hour shift) includes these duties as well as reading his mail aloud, writing checks from his checkbook, and distributing medications into his weekly pill box. Once she was even there to pick him up when he fell. In other words, she knows a whole lot about Joseph's daily life, social circle, and finances, and, in turn, Joseph knows much about hers.

JOSEPH: She takes care of us very good. Same woman still over five years, she cooks for us, she cleans the house, she does the laundry, she does our medication, takes us to the doctors. Her name is Kim, and she's very good. My daughter found her. When she cannot come, she sends her daughter. . . . She's going to be a nurse so she goes to school, but once in a while she comes here.

MEIKA: Is she like a family member to you because you see her so often?

JOSEPH: Oh yes, oh yes. It is good to have somebody. And she's a child of ten, and I am a child of ten as well. But her family situation is not good. Not good at all.

When you ask Joseph about his daily life, Kim is part of the answer. He is the primary caretaker in the marriage, but in the context of his disabilities, this aide has been entrusted with a wide range of responsibilities. Meanwhile, Joseph and his wife have come to know Kim and some of her family members very well, and she theirs. Joseph and Kim have found many things in common. They share immigrant status (both are from developing countries in different regions), unique family size, and experiences of profound loss and tragedy. Joseph is careful not to share the extent of Kim's tragic story. He changes the subject to protect her privacy, another sign of his respect for Kim. This admiration goes both ways. Upon meeting Kim's sister, I was told repeatedly how wonderful and unique Joseph and his wife are, enjoying every meal together and observing rituals as a loving couple. She saw them as role models for marriage.

INTERGENERATIONAL CONNECTIONS AND COMMUNITIES

Intergenerational connections often arise out of daily interactions. Today, those interactions are most likely to occur in communities. In nineteenth-century America, these connections occurred in households. Multigenerational families worked and lived on the family farm together. By 1900, one half of adults aged sixty-five and older lived in a multigenerational household. Then, in the period after World War II, the prevalence of the extended family household declined. In 1940, about a quarter of the population lived in such a household, and by 1980, just over 10 percent did. Today, extended families sharing a household remains relatively uncommon (although slightly higher than rates in the 1980s). A range of shifts likely contributed to this decline, among them the rapid growth of the nuclear-family-centered suburbs; and the sharp rise in the health, economic well-being, and autonomy of adults aged sixty-five and older resulting from the enactment of social programs such as Social Security and Medicare and improvements in medical care.[12]

With these changes came what amounted to a new intergenerational social contract within most families—namely, that older adults and their children, who had the health and resources to live independently, should do so. The concept of the multigenerational family home has largely been replaced by the middle-class nuclear family household. By 1990, fewer than one in five seniors lived in a multigenerational family household; and this rate has increased slightly in recent years.[13] Amongst the oldest old, 21 percent lived in multigenerational families in 2008; 19 percent lived with a child. [14]

Several participants in this research have moved recently to be near their adult children or grandchildren. When I met them, however, only two (6 percent) lived with family members: Eddie lived with his sister and Lore with her granddaughter.[15] In addition, Juana lives in a duplex with her daughter, but they maintain separate households.[16] Many live far from their adult children.

As the stories in this chapter indicate, many elders create proximal bonds within their immediate communities that can substitute for kin and, in the process, redefine family. Many of these connections are relatively recent, representing friendships made in the last years of life. These connections translate into a structure for their days, companionship, and a sense that someone "is there," helping to foster health, perspective, and pleasure. One elder described how seeing children in her synagogue "chirping away" reminds her of regeneration and the cycles of life and death. Others, like Ruth H., talked about the joys of befriending young people. In these lives we see how something as simple as proximity to a different generation can help one to create and sustain a meaningful life. We have long known that diversity in our schools can enable growth and perspective. These examples show that exposure to diversity is important in all aspects of our lives and across the life course.

In an age-stratified world, on the other hand, we have overwhelmingly created segregated spaces in which to live, which can make reaching beyond generational lines difficult. Over the course of this research, I visited numerous retirement villages and senior housing complexes in the United States. Not one of them had a playground or a nursery school on site, as I had observed in European countries. Age-based segregation is only heightened by the fact that many gated elder communities do not pay school taxes, and thus actively negate connections across generations.[17] In addition, the neighborhood naturally occurring retirement community (NORC) where Shana lives, which receives state funding to build community among those aged sixty-five and over, does not involve the numerous families and students in the neighborhood. Efforts to create intergenerational communities are few and far between. These examples raise important questions about how ageist notions work to reinforce age segregation, and vice versa. We know from the civil rights era that separation of different groups can reinforce prejudice. Efforts to build age-based diversity and community in housing, public spaces, and classrooms would go a long way toward interrupting ageism from both ends.

Sometimes resistance to fostering intergenerational relationships happens on the part of youth, as described by Alice:

> What bothers me about aging is with young people particularly. When I meet them, they immediately pull the curtains down. Unless they had a particular relationship with their grandparents or something like that. But usually they pull the curtains down. . . . I usually say to them, "Give me a chance and then if you don't like me, that's fine." They are perhaps afraid or disinterested. . . . If I go to the university and someone introduces me to a kid, they are polite—they feel they have to be in that situation. But there's no contact as a person. They don't think of me as a person. I don't know how you get through it. That's what bothers me. I understand if you don't like my personality, but for goodness' sake, give me a chance! (laughs)[18]

Resistance doesn't always come from the young, as Hy, a retired history professor, describes.

> There have been some efforts to build a housing unit on campus for students and seniors. A learn-from-each-other sort of thing. [An emeritus professor friend of mine] recoiled in horror at the very thought: "I spent thirty-five years with students. Now live with them? Enough already."

As Alice and Hy reveal, age-based segregation has costs and bene-fits. That elders like Alice are perceived as less than human is trou-bling, and a clear outgrowth of ageism. On the campus where I work, I regularly hear students complain that they never see children or elders on their campus; they too feel distant from family, including grandparents and siblings. In visits to care facilities, some elders seem hungry for children to visit. Yet not all elders need or want intergen-erational contact, as Hy points out. Well-intentioned and familiar ef-forts to "brighten" the mood of elders by bringing children into care facilities can miss the opportunity for connection, and in the process reinforce ageism and "othering."

There are some hopeful signs of age-based integration in process. Beyond the stories of the elders in this chapter reaching beyond gen-erational differences, the co-housing movement has been successful at demanding and building several intergenerational housing com-munities across the country. Schools and community centers are pairing children and elder volunteers for tutoring and help with school work, in programs such as Americorps RSVP. I was delighted to find a nursery school for my daughter where local elders serve as teachers' aides. Many universities have "adopt-a-grandparent" extra-curricular programs. And more and more university communities are creating shared spaces for elders and students to collaborate on cam-pus. For example, the first time I taught a course on aging, a student in his eighties audited the class, and he became a crucial contributor to class discussions, bringing many lessons to life. Every semester I partner students with local elders, and they are always surprised to find many common interests and similarities across the generations. When successful, intergenerational connections can be healthy and enabling, and can push us to change popular conceptions about age.

At the same time, we must not forget how age-based segregation can be socially beneficial. Partly due to the value placed on youth, we learn to devalue the old. As a result, many elders abhor the idea of living in a retirement community or a care facility surrounded by "old people," with varying levels of ability and health and dependency. Many are personally invested in maintaining a distinction between the healthy old (like them), and those whom they perceive to be overly dependent or sickly. Despite this resistance, living among peers can help the old to appreciate differences across age and come to terms with aging processes and internalized ageism. It can also be a useful way to develop social capital and connect with those most like themselves, in terms of age and class status. For Hy and his partner, living in a retirement community near the university enables them to find like-minded individuals to converse with over meals. Similarly, in the Green House, Fred and Christine have been able to participate in new caring communities with others who hail from the same geographical area.

The last two chapters have focused on instrumental forms of support across generations and real and imagined families. The next chapter explores the importance of affective ties, a sometimes overlooked facet of social capital. Specifically, this chapter focuses on the crucial role of human affect and touch in relationships with family, friends, pets, and even strangers.

LESSON 11
Insist on Hugs

Lore and her favorite companion, Moses

E very time I see Alice, she greets me with "How about a hug?" Alice does not have children and has outlived most of her family members. Thus, she insists on certain forms of physical affection with friends, loved ones, and pets. In particular she believes in the importance of hugging.

> Hugs are good for people, especially old people . . . because time goes by. I remember as a thirty-something visiting old people who would hold onto my hand, and I just wanted to get away. But now I understand it. It is a need—almost involuntary.

Alice can trace her family back thirteen generations in the United States. (Alice is quick to mention she is not a member of the Daughters of the American Revolution because of their racism.) The family line comes from Britain and tends to be reserved, she says. Over the years, she has learned that warmth is a better approach. When Alice was younger, she worked with elders. Through this experience, she explained, she came to identify a universal need for physical closeness as we age.

As we talked about this need for physical closeness, Alice and I hatched a plan. We would get a table at the upcoming senior fair in the mall, with a sign, "FREE HUGS." Instead of the traditional freebies (e.g., pens and magnets) we would offer hugs to anyone interested as a test of Alice's theory. On the day of the event, Alice was unable to join us, but my daughter (then age one) and I stood at the table for over an hour, and then returned home exhausted, and reported back to Alice. Despite all of the giveaways at the fair, our table had the longest line, and the happiest customers. It seems that Alice's theory was true—people will line up for hugs, even if they are coming from strangers.

Alice also understands the importance of physical closeness with pets, particularly for those leading mostly sedentary and solitary lives. Just after I met Alice in 2006, she described how her pet cat Bart had become more rebellious with age, and while he sometimes bit her and others, she could not bring herself to say goodbye to him.

> He is my longest pet companion: thirteen years. Sometimes he will sit on my lap for hours, getting stroked and petted, before I have to push him off.

In 2009, after nursing an infected wound for over a year, Alice finally said goodbye to Bart. It was a bittersweet goodbye to a long-time companion. "I'll just have to insist on more hugs," she said.

By 2010, as Alice grew increasingly sight-disabled, she still insisted on hugs, and relied more than ever on touch to navigate her world. She showed me how, on elevators, she would feel the numbers on the wall to figure out what floor she was on. And in order to open her front door, she had to first feel the lock with her fingers, before slipping the key in. Alice never anticipated this, but in old age, her sense of touch was now a crucial factor in protecting her autonomy.

THE IMPORTANCE OF TOUCH

This chapter emphasizes touch and affection. While scholars are increasingly focused on aging and sexual intimacy, little has been done to consider other forms of intimacy, sensual pleasure, and tactile gratification. In fact, if it is human touch in infancy that makes us human and social creatures, then it makes sense that human touch and sensory stimulation would contribute to a sense of vitality and connection throughout one's life.[1]

In an ageist society, our view of elders as unattractive or sickly makes it all the more difficult for those elders who are not partnered to receive hugs, touch, or even eye contact, as Alice points out. One discussion I witnessed at the Green House reminded me of how integral human touch can be as we age, as well as the discomfort and embarrassment we tend to associate with aging and intimacy. On this particular visit, I overheard the certified nursing assistants talking about Joe, a severely disabled elder who lived for his bath night. Joe had a reputation for moaning loudly while he was being washed, and shouting the nurse's name over and over in excitement. The nurses joked about who would be in charge of bathing Joe that week. One joked that she was ruined for life and will never have sex again after Joe's moaning her name. The nurses performed what sociologist Julia Twigg calls bodywork for hygiene reasons, while Joe exalted in its therapeutic, symbolic, and perhaps even erotic functions.[2] As awkward as it was, all involved acknowledged that the bath experience was central to Joe's health and quality of life. Joking was a strategy for coping with the awkwardness in a twelve-person home where everyone knew when Joe was taking a bath.

In his book, *Shock of Gray*, Ted C. Fishman profiles one man, Mr. Shimono, who is a professional bather in Japan. Many elderly request, as their last wish, a Japanese-style bath. When they feel they might not get one, they despair; bathing in Japan has a spiritual dimension, particularly for those who are dying. When they do get one, family members send letters thanking Mr. Shimono for his service and describing how very important the baths were to the dying relatives. This mix of spiritual cleansing with human touch can bring a final sense of peace.[3]

In a similar way, Frida Kerner Furman's *Facing the Mirror*, an ethnography of elder Jewish women who frequent a hair salon, exposes how the daily rituals that took place there can be therapeutic and intimate. Affection and touching are commonplace. Women customers hug and touch, and staff massage scalps and hands during hair washing and manicures. This form of carework that relates to touching the body, creates a zone of physical enjoyment and well-being for the women in the salon. The women of the salon talk about being starved for affection, and appreciate the emotional reciprocity that takes place in this setting. In this context, we see how crucial physical touch and closeness can be, especially in old age.

Due to ageism, blunted sensory perception, and a general decrease in intimate connections as we age, a small amount of research published in nursing and gerontology journals emphasizes the importance of sensitive bodywork in caregiving. Studies reveal how certain forms of closeness and touch—such as directed eye gaze, affirmative head nodding, smiling, forward leaning, and affective touch on the arm and shoulder—can be crucial for connecting with elders, particularly those with dementia. These studies also show that instrumental touch, such as guiding someone by the shoulder, or expressive touch on the leg can help too.

The human need for touch and affection is not always easy to study, or to discuss, and this may contribute to the gaps in the literature about the importance of sensory gratification in old age. Those elders whom I asked directly about the importance of touch usually responded by saying, "Oh, I get that from my family," and quickly changed the subject or made a joke. Shana said she didn't remember the intimacy in her marriage and then explained, "That was the Depression era so we were both Depression kids. Everything was practical." Others, like Lillian and Ruth H. spoke candidly about their interest in partnered intimacy.

From my previous research on Viagra, I know that all too often touch and affection get confused with sexuality, making it a difficult subject to broach, particularly among a generation encouraged to see intimacy as a private matter. Beyond this, I encountered doctors and pharmacists "disgusted" by old people having sex, evidence of broad-based ageism that led to many silences. Thus, I was most successful at eliciting conversation about intimacy or touch when I could follow up on a comment made about holding a grandchild, petting a cat, or communicating with a partner.

The only national study to include sexual and nonsexual intimacy in their measures is the 2005–2006 National Social Life, Health, and Aging Project (NSHAP). This was a national survey of 3,005 men and women between the ages of fifty-seven and eight-five years, focused on intimate social relationships, including marriage, family, social ties, and sexuality. The study did pay some attention to nonsexual intimacies with grandchildren, pets, and others, but no survey can measure the diverse qualitative ways in which the oldest old experience and make sense of pleasure within and outside of traditional sexuality and intimacy.

In this chapter we learn why touch and affection are central to maintaining meaningful lives, as well as how the oldest old go about getting the sensory stimulation they need. Only a small percentage of those eighty-five and older are involved in intimate relationships like Seymour. Most have been widowed or single for many years, and are currently living solitary lives. In that context, some elders learn to maximize opportunities for touch and affection. Lore, like Alice, turns to her pet cat and her granddaughter for sensory gratification and affection. Florence and Juana frequent spaces where they are treated with affection and care. Margaret and Seymour insist on affection in the form of hugs and physical touch from family members. For Joseph, the simple sensory act of holding a great-grandchild in his arms, or being surrounded by the sounds of family, is crucial to knowing and experiencing his world as fully as possible. And for Emma, nothing is better than soaking in a bath or snuggling with her dolls.

Lore's Affectionate Side

When I asked Lore, the German-born artist with biting humor, what gives her pleasure, she was adamant in her response. After a short laugh, she declared, "Nothing." This was her official story. When I asked if I could take a picture of her, she insisted on having her cat Moses on her lap. She held the cat like a baby, almost purring

"Oh my Moses, my friend Moses . . ." Moments like these told a different story.

During interviews, Lore constantly chided Moses or talked to him. The cat provided a convenient distraction and a way out of any question. Instead of an answer, I would hear "Oh Moses, you're always going somewhere . . ." Or "It is a girl cat and I thought I had a boy!" (laughing) Or "You know, her name is Moses—it is a good Jewish name." Moses keeps Lore challenged, trying to understand the cat's comings and goings, and her fickle nature. Beyond this, Moses provides Lore with an opportunity to give and receive affection. Lore smiles broadly when Moses lies on her back and waits for her to stroke her belly. "Oh, my Moses. Look at that white furry belly!" For Lore's part, she makes it known that she loves her cat but can do without the others. Then, when her granddaughter returns from a short trip, it is clear that Lore missed her deeply. They snuggle together in bed, and Lore asks countless questions about the trip. The family is together again and all is okay.

Florence's VIP Lunches with Love

I almost didn't recognize Florence in the diner. She was dressed up, wearing large shiny earrings, a blouse, and slacks. She gave me a hug and shifted over so I could sit next to her in the booth. A year before, Florence, whom we met in Lesson 2, had introduced me to her mostly sedentary life in her recliner, resting her back and watching old movies. In subsequent phone calls, Florence would say "I'm still just sitting here, watching television for something to do. My girl still comes every day, ten to two." The one weekly ritual Florence talked about during that first interview was her Friday lunch where she got treated like a VIP. I invited myself along one Friday, to see Florence in her element.

Sitting across from me was Adrienne, Florence's "girl," who looked to be in her fifties. She started as Florence's housekeeper many years ago and added hours as Florence needed help with cooking and cleaning. Now she visits Florence six days a week. She and Florence explained why this weekly ritual at the diner meant so much to them:

Usually we drive up and park at the end of the [handicapped access] ramp, and they get the table all set up for us. They treat us like VIPs.

Today the girls aren't here, but they all know us. The waitress usually gives me a kiss. You know, we have been coming here for years. . . . It used to be Saturdays with the girls, when my husband was alive. He didn't go out to eat, so I'd go out with my girlfriends.

This eatery played a significant role in Florence's personal history, and as a "regular" for decades, she was known and appreciated. The personalized service, the warm greetings, the companionship, and connections to her past all meant a lot to Florence. The VIP treatment was worth getting out of her chair, and trading an hour of "resting the back" for another kind of comfort and personalized care.

Adrienne and Florence didn't linger long after lunch. Florence said she "ached all over," and her painkillers did not always ease the pain. As she walked down the ramp back to Adrienne's car, holding onto my arm, she told me she prefers "to hang onto people instead of using a walker or a cane. This is just nicer." And with that she was in the car, on her way back to her recliner and old movies.

As with anyone, I saw another side of Florence when I met her outside of her home. What stood out in particular was her affectionate side: hugs, kisses, and holding onto people were key themes. It was clear that beyond lunch and personal continuity, this excursion offered the promise of human contact and physical closeness with others.

Juana's Kisses

Juana, the Yankees fan and poet, is the eldest member of her Catholic church. She is treated with great respect, called Mama, Abuela, and Ma by most members of the church (much like Rose in the previous chapter), regardless of their ethnic backgrounds. Calling her Mother is the highest compliment the community could pay to Juana, who has worked very hard at motherhood as a single mother of seven, and values family above all else. She is also regarded as a mother by the leaders of the church, who hug her when they see her, and warmly receive her offerings, including homemade flan and cakes. In general, Juana's Catholic community treats her with great affection.

This affection is reciprocated by Juana, even in the most formal of contexts. When I met Juana after her Sunday Mass, she was hugging friends. She jokingly told one friend that an interviewer is here to help her find a boyfriend on the Internet. Later, she shared with me that, during Mass, when one of her favorite deacons passed with the communion cup, she kissed his hand. She giggles about this, and then explains that she calls this Dominican deacon St. Martin de Porres, the only saint she knows of with dark skin. She says the leaders of the church are wonderful men. They treat her like their own mother, so she reciprocates with affection and respect.

Margaret's Insistence on Hugs

Margaret, the retired Avon saleswoman who regularly checks in on her neighbor Jackie, says that she is not a "touchy person." But like Alice, Margaret sometimes insists on hugs from others. Being single for so many years, she misses the affection she received in marriage. So she turns to her family to satisfy her need for affection.

> I often say I miss my husband's hugs, so I ask my kids Ron and Barbara for hugs all the time. I'm not a touchy person with friends, but with my kids . . . they come right up and kiss you, but once in a while I have to say "I need a hug."

Beyond hugs, Margaret feels her family's affection when they call her on the telephone, take her on shopping excursions, cook with her recipes, and share their lives with her. After hearing stories about how her educator children and grandchildren educators are changing their students' lives, and how her son is always looking out for her best interests, I began to understand how Margaret reciprocated these affections. She finds joy in the moment, and expresses unconditional love and support for her family.

Seymour's Communication through Touch

Seymour, the technogenarian we met in Lesson 1, is painfully alone in his head. At his ninetieth birthday party, he could not have felt more so. He saw everyone socializing and having a good time, but he could not hear anything, and this made him feel frustrated and cut off. Since he became deaf as a teenager, his challenge has been to connect with others without sound. Much as the telephone is a lifeline to elders like Alice, Seymour relies on e-mail to stay connected. Some social scientists have found that computer ownership and Internet access can increase elders' total social network, frequency of communication, and quality of relationships, as well as helping to reinstate distant or past friendships.[4]

Beyond relying on his computer and other technological tools, interpersonal touch is central to Seymour's ability to communicate and feel connected.

> SEYMOUR: I wouldn't be here if it weren't for her, but don't tell her. [He points to his second wife Bernice, of thirty-six years.] . . .
>
> MEIKA: How is physical touch important to you?
>
> SEYMOUR: Touch is very desirous to me, if for no other reason than it brings the other person closer to me than if it was a conversation, which for all intents and purposes is very difficult because of my severe hearing impairment. This, of course, may not be true for others in my age group who don't have this handicap. I'm not nearly as interested in animals, nature, and other things that seem to be very important to other seniors.

As one of the minority in his age group with a surviving spouse, Seymour is able to experience human intimacy in ways that elude their peers. Despite his age and disability, his desire for affectionate intimacy in the context of a second marriage is not unique. Studies show that women in second marriages after age fifty said they value companionship, cuddling, and affection over sexual intercourse and passion.[5]

Joseph's Great-Grandbabies

Joseph has been married to his wife Myra for almost sixty-five years. When I visited Joseph in March, he was looking forward to the table of sixteen family members who would surround him and his wife on the upcoming Passover holiday. Unlike Seymour, Joseph can hear the sounds of family—he just cannot see them. Being able to taste the food (so similar to his mother's) and hold his great-grandchildren is what he lives for.

> It is my family that keeps me going. Pretty soon my great-great-grand-children, twins, are going to be one year old. Pretty soon they are going to walk around and say Papa. That's what we live for. . . . I cannot see

them so well—if they are close-up I can see them. But I can touch them and hold them.

Several months later, Joseph reported that he had held both babies. When I asked how that felt, he replied, "They were heavier than you would imagine, and one had more hair than the other. It was wonderful." He would always remember how it felt to hold and touch his great-grandchildren.

Emma's Sensory Delights

After our first interview session was over, Emma wanted to show me around her one-bedroom apartment. She wanted me to see that she had everything she needed there in that small space. It was clear the numerous pictures of grandchildren on the wall made her feel loved. The tour emphasized many of the sensory delights in her life, from bathing rituals and fabrics, to inanimate companions she could squeeze, to the written word. It was clear that each of these things brought her a great deal of pleasure and also tactile gratification.

We started in the bathroom, where she pointed out the two-tiered maroon and pink satiny shower curtain that she ordered from a catalog and loves. As a former "seamster," Emma knew her fabrics. She wanted me to see this to underscore how important the ritual of soaking in a bathtub was to her, especially for sore joints. (See her discussion of the pleasures of bathing in Lesson 5, "Take Time for Self.")

The next stop of the apartment tour was Emma's favorite stuffed animals and dolls situated in corners, doorways, in her bedroom, and on tabletops. Their location made it evident that they were major players in the scene. She snuggled and giggled with her Tickle Me Elmo doll, lifted three-foot-tall Aunt Jemima's bonnet to reveal the hair she braided, and then introduced me to a stuffed reindeer that sang "Jingle Bells." She squeezed it and laughed, saying "I gotta let you listen to this."

Amid the stuffed animals, several different Bibles were displayed on Emma's living room table. Emma said she loves reading passages in the Bible, and has memories of gingerly turning the pages of the family Bible as a child. She explained, "When I was a kid I had to get on a chair to get the big book, and it was a prized possession in that house. Mama said, 'Don't go ripping that!'" Emma rarely makes it to church these days, but she can sit and read Bible passages and feel companionship of another kind.

LITERALLY REACHING OUT

In the lives of Alice, Florence, Seymour, Margaret, Lore, Joseph, and Emma, we see how the oldest old literally reach out to give and receive physical affection with loved ones or bask in the affections of others. This need intensifies in the context of disability and social isolation, when many learn to communicate in new ways through touch. Thus, Alice, Seymour, Lore, and Joseph's blunted senses force them learn to depend on touch for survival and affection. Emma and Florence, who engage in limited social interaction, turn to new and familiar sources of warmth and companionship. And Margaret, after the loss of her husband, insists on hugs from her children.

Scholars of social capital, while emphasizing the benefits of social connectivity, tend to miss aspects of touch and affection that come out of a wide variety of associations, from weak to strong ties, family to non-kin, to pets and inanimate objects. In this chapter, elders explore the overlapping physical and emotional benefits of all forms of connectedness. Family holidays, lunch dates, living companions, second marriages, stuffed animals, and pet adoptions can create opportunities for interpersonal intimacies. The oldest old reveal that companionship and affection can be crucial to quality of life. Insisting on hugs, baths, touch, and other forms of sensory learning and tenderness can contribute to health and well-being. The need to connect with the living world—including pets, plants, children—in the last decades of life is real.[6] When elders like Emma are unable to do this, the next best thing can be a stuffed companion, or a comforting Bible verse.

For many of these elders, like Alice, Seymour, Joseph, Margaret, and Florence, the story of learning and communicating through touch comes in the context of life changes—acquired disability, loss of a spouse, or increased social isolation. The next chapter takes this theme one step further, focusing on how the oldest old shift their routines and perspectives to accommodate their changing lives and bodies.

LESSON 12

Be Adaptable

Eddie at the gym

E ddie likes his routines. In Lesson 1 ("Continue to Do What You Did"), we learned that on Tuesdays and Fridays you can always find him in the gym between 6:30 and 7:30 a.m. He chats with his buddy at the front desk from 6:00 to 6:30, works out from 6:30 to 7:30, and then "holds court" in the locker room until 8:00 a.m. On his way out, he greets all of his old friends waiting for the morning hydroslimnastics class, and anyone else standing around drinking coffee. This well-choreographed morning routine is part of a predictable pattern that structures his life, and the lives of those around him. Family members as well as morning regulars at the gym anticipate Eddie's regular routine and their role in it.

What may not be obvious is how Eddie's morning routine is a work in progress, always adapting to new changes and challenges in his life. Everything from his unique exercise techniques, to skipping meals, to reading and doing puzzles, is a recent adaptation in response to shifting personal, family, and health needs.

When I meet Eddie in the empty gym in the winter of 2010, he is walking counterclockwise and flailing his arms in a variety of ways, while greeting the morning exercise crowd as they walk through on their way to the fitness machines. He tells me he was up at 3:30 that morning, watching the news over a big breakfast. He said he used to have a cup of coffee and a cigarette when he was working. Now he breakfasts on cereal and fruit, coffee, and a Danish. I ask him to tell me about his workout and his morning routine.

> EDDIE: Well, I mostly exercise my jaw. But I think I told
> you I have circulation problems—I'm always cold. I
> told my doctor, and he said you don't have to go on all
> these things [exercise machines], just go around the
> gym and move your arms and legs as often as you can.
> So I do. And I feel a lot better after a workout. Before a
> workout, I have to push myself. I feel logy, and all that.
>
> MEIKA: And what do you do after this workout?
>
> EDDIE: Well, What's today, Friday? I'm going to get my
> sister. She gets her hair done on Friday. VERY important.
> I bring her over there, then I go home, . . . So she'll call
> me when she's done and I'll go pick her up and we'll go
> for groceries. We usually go to [two different] shopping
> centers. Then we go out to eat. We go to something like
> Applebee's. . . . On the days we go out shopping—rather
> than eat three times a day, we eat twice. We eat a full meal
> at 3:00. That's one of my secrets for losing weight. Two
> meals instead of three. You don't do that every day, just
> twice a week. Are you a good eater?
>
> MEIKA: Oh yeah.

EDDIE: Do you drink wine? I drink wine every night. That's a secret. My father said if you don't feel good, got a cold, have two glasses of wine. Not only that, but he said once a week eat food that is spicy—or hot peppers. Cleans you out. Get all those germs out. So I eat hot peppers or something.

MEIKA: What do you do after the meal?

EDDIE: We get home about 4:30, we don't do much. We watch TV, catch the news, and I'm trying to catch up on my reading. I got a stack of books to read. I'm way behind in reading. I have a bad eye so I get tired—but I got this *Reader's Digest* book of the month club. I've been reading all that stuff. It is wonderful. There are four stories in each book. I like it because these are things I didn't do when I was young. *I changed*, you know. I didn't like school. Now I get older and I do puzzles, I start reading. I changed my whole thing.

MEIKA: Why change at this stage of life?

EDDIE: I just wanted to get more interesting. More knowledgeable. 'Cuz I quit school early [to support the family], all these things. And I have the time. You know, you get older, and you get smarter . . . I believe that!

EVERYDAY ROUTINES AND ADAPTABILITY

Many of the chapters in this book suggest the importance of a routine to structure one's life, to provide familiarity and meaning. Many elders agree that a routine is central to self-efficacy and care, but as bodies and circumstances shift, routines must shift too. So, how do elders manage and meet the changing needs in their daily lives?

While Lesson 1 emphasized continuity, this chapter focuses on the ingenuity that elders exhibit as they strive for continuity while adapting to change. Tracking elders over the course of several years made it possible to realize that the story of our lives, no matter what age, is a narrative of continuity and change. In old age, versatility is particularly important to manage bodily changes and prevent health problems. Eddie adapted his morning routine to alleviate circulation problems, watch his weight, avoid smoking, and to pursue new hobbies in his free time. Despite these tweaks and transitions, Eddie is still the same guy, continuing to do what he has always loved to do, including socializing, helping others, eating, and drinking wine.

There are a variety of ways to measure adaptability. Sociologists are interested in the overall well-being of elders like Eddie, including physiological health, physical capacities, and psychosocial health (healthy habits, attitudes, and relationships). The fact that Eddie has recently changed his routine signals his adaptability on a number of levels. Eddie practices preventative medicine not only through cutting out smoking and moving his arms, but also by "exercising his jaw," and following a familiar daily routine; these adjustments can translate into improved health, social capital, and general well-being.

Physicians and nurses are taught that physiological health and physical capacity are first and foremost in assessing a person's ability to live on their own. The umbrella term "functional health" generally refers to the ability to engage in everyday activities such as bathing, dressing, and walking. According to the Centers for Disease Control, many older adults report physical limitations with respect to walking, reaching, stooping, and pushing.[1] Activities of daily living (ADLs), are frequently used to assess how well the elderly, mentally ill, and those with chronic illness can manage their self-care. For example, hospitals will discharge patients only after assessing their functional autonomy in terms of dressing, bathing or showering, and using the toilet. The ability to perform other ADLs, like driving (daytime and nighttime), eating, getting in or out of bed, walking across the room, and walking a block, can be central to self-care and aging in place. We know from the 2009 National Social Life Health and Aging Project (NSLHAP) study that driving, walking, and dressing (in that order) are the most common difficulties for individuals as they age.[2] About 30 percent of the population aged seventy-five to eighty-five report having difficulties in these areas.[3] Additionally, although women live longer, they tend to report more problems with physical functioning than men of the same age.

In contrast to ADLs, competence in the *instrumental* activities of daily living (IADLs) is not necessary for fundamental functioning, but does enable an individual to live independently. These expanded competencies include cooking and preparing meals, shopping, housekeeping, taking care of financial matters, using the telephone, taking medications, and carrying out minor repair work at home. For someone like Alice, who became legally blind in just a few years, most of these tasks are now nearly impossible to accomplish on her own. However, the inability to perform these activities does not mean that elders can no longer be independent. These tasks can be delegated to others or minimized. Some nonagenarians like Glenn are able to care for themselves without much help, revealing that aging does not always have to be associated with significant physical challenges, and that an exclusive focus on physical competency to determine "functional independence" might ignore other relevant considerations. For Glenn, loneliness is the most pressing challenge. Such psychosocial challenges (lack of social networks, anxiety related to safety, or low confidence) are difficult to measure, but are crucial to well-being.

It is not just doctors who measure functional capacity for independence in late life. Elders themselves seem to have internalized this paradigm as well, integrating regular capacity-testing into their everyday lives to assess their own health and well-being. In previous chapters we saw how Johanna uses puzzles and games daily to measure her brain health and others like Ann test their stamina and strength through exercise. Likewise, we will see in this chapter how Joseph intermittently "tests" his memory.

Measuring functional capacities is one method for assessing an individual's ability to age in place. But what do elders say are the major barriers in their lives as they age? How do they adapt to them? Over the course of three years, I asked about daily routines each time I talked with them, and together we paid attention to how they shifted over time. These daily routines can be a barometer for health and creative adaptability.

When coping with stress and loss, resilience has been the central paradigm in health psychology, but recently, researchers have begun to focus on the benefits of severe stress and grieving. They have found that confronting adversity can reveal hidden abilities. Severe stress can actually enable an individual to rise above the adversity. In this way, relationships can be strengthened, one's sense of self can shift, and individuals can become happier.[4]

Surviving two world wars and the Great Depression, the oldest old have all experienced adversity throughout their lives. In his research on the greatest generation, Elder has found that exposure to early adversity with the help of social support generally translated into growing up stronger and mentally healthier. Social psychologists have corroborated this theory, emphasizing that those who experience early challenges in their twenties or earlier may be stronger and happier later in life than those who do not.[5]

This chapter catches up with members of the Greatest Generation, detailing how elders creatively approach adversity in the last stage of their lives, in the context of health and physical difficulties and personal loss. Adaptability can mean a variety of things, from cutting back and slowing down (while holding on to what is most important), to making things easier and utilizing technology to assist with new challenges. It also often entails learning how to accept assistance.

Seymour: Deaf but Vitally Engaged in Active Living

In his sixteenth year of writing for the *Reporter,* and in his ninety-third year of life, Seymour declared in an uncharacteristically personal column that his response to his disability has enabled him to live longer and healthier.

> . . . I feel that if I were not profoundly hearing impaired, I would probably have joined the majority of men in my age group and become a sports junkie and/or a couch potato. And very likely I would no longer be around to type these lines. . . . So wrong or right, I have come to the conclusion that perhaps the "bad" handicap that I encountered early in my adult life has become a good handicap, in as much as I still feel great as I conclude this column. The moral is, of course, if you only have lemons, make lemonade. (Seymour, excerpted from his column in *Century Village East Reporter,* Jan. 2010 edition)

I called to schedule a first interview several years before he wrote this column. Seymour (communicating through his wife) was quite specific about the time of day I would visit him. When I arrived, he suggested that I sit at the kitchen table facing the window. With the help of his cochlear implant, he explained that he had the best opportunity to read my lips if I had the morning light on me. When he learned that I had published a book, he said, "After you leave, I will Google your name." These first moments of interaction with Seymour conveyed a man who was not going to let his disability get in the way of his social participation.

In Lesson 1, we learned about Seymour as a technogenarian. Today, along with writing, Seymour's structures his time around exercise and physical functioning. In all of our conversations, Seymour stressed this the most:

Our ability to function physically is extremely important. So every other morning Bernice and I lift weights—she does three pounds, I do five and we do fifty reps. Then the other morning we swim. The pool here [in New York] is a twenty-four meter pool. I swim eight laps. At first I could only do maybe two, but Bernice does ten, and I worked my way up.

For Seymour, physical exercise is a way to keep moving, emphasizing physical functioning and feeling alive. It also enables togetherness with his wife as well as a competitive spirit that reinforces feelings of health and masculinity.

You know, since I've been eighteen years old I've had this deficiency, and it has dictated my lifestyle since. I don't do movies, and TV and music (I have quite a collection but do not listen). Maybe in a perverted way I'm living longer because I don't do those typical things. I'm swimming while others are at the movies. I don't know.

Two years after our first interview, Seymour proudly reported by e-mail from Florida that he was, as ever, keeping up with his exercise routine, his driving, computer stuff, and "anything that involves math, taxes, or assembly (such as small furniture, etc.)." He theorized that the warm weather contributed to everyone living longer there. And he wondered if I knew of any research that showed whether physical exertion at his age would deplete already limited energy or enhance health. In addition, he confessed that he had "increased difficulty walking," and as such had concerns about their "migration patterns" as snowbirds who moved to Florida every fall. Finally, he shared that his e-mail contact list had decreased dramatically as friends passed away; these days, he mostly e-mailed with family.

We may opt to stay down here [in Florida] permanently. It is and always has been a very tough decision for Snowbirds. It gets very hot and lonely here in the summer, and remember, small talk is not my forte! . . . We do keep in touch with our children via e-mail, phone and Skype. We also now find that we feel pretty isolated at times; I think people tend to leave really old people alone.

Keep in touch, Sy.

P.S. We truthfully, and maybe wrongly, do not yet think of ourselves as old people.

For Seymour, who has lived for almost seventy-five years with a severe hearing handicap, difficulties are part of everyday life. His life story is about adaptability. For years he chose to cope with disability by emphasizing his strengths. As a nonagenarian, Seymour continues to adapt as his physical strength and stamina weaken. He still emphasizes ability over disability, and perhaps in a parallel way, youthfulness over old age. At the same time, Seymour, like most, says he never knows about tomorrow, and that changes the way he approaches everything, including travel and shopping. In a recent e-mail, Seymour added that he no longer buys green bananas, because he has no idea if he'll still be around tomorrow.

Shana: Weak Legs, Still Gardening

Like Seymour, Shana is also cutting back and slowing down. Shana, who always insists "they can take me out of here with my boots on," still gardens. While she no longer can get down on her hands and knees and feel the soil between her fingers, she gets great pleasure from managing and monitoring her garden, even from the windows of her home on wet and snowy days.

When I knocked on Shana's door in 2008, she greeted me with, "I was just deboning a chicken, come in!" In the midst of a tour of her kitchen and garden, she described her morning routine:

I have breakfast—toast, OJ, black coffee. I make my bed. Shower. Dress. I do my reading, the *Times Union* [local newspaper], till 10:00. At 10:00 I do weeding. Then I rest. Then lunch. I used to go exercise, but I have been taking it easy. Sometimes I swim [in the pool in the yard].

At age ninety-one, Shana was doing what she had always done. She prepared and ate similar foods, kept up with the news, and cared for her home. She kept her eye on the time. And her favorite activity was gardening. She explained that she came from a "family of farmers," with a history going back to what is now Lithuania. Shana had also made some changes to her routine. "Taking it easy" was more of a priority.

One year later, I asked Shana about the morning routine. Had it changed? Shana was less sure that she had a routine now. Breakfast, reading, and crossword puzzles were still part of the morning ritual, but the schedule was no longer so structured time-wise, and the activities list was shorter.

> I don't know that I have a routine. . . . I usually get up and read and then putter around the house and then shower and get ready for lunch. Last year I was swimming, but then I couldn't get up out of the water, so I have to wait for others to swim with me. . . . I love to weed, and I can't do that anymore—not on my hands and knees. My legs won't give me that push. Like I feel them right now—the feet are tingly. My doc says don't cross your legs but it is natural! (She laughs, realizing her legs are crossed as she is saying this.)

No longer comfortable swimming by herself or weeding on her hands and knees, Shana knew her morning routine had to change: she asked family members for help with weeding, for example. At the same time, despite concerns about strength and balance, Shana still took care of most things on her own, and she centered her day around her greatest pleasure, the garden.

> SHANA: I'll go out and look at the garden. Not every day. It has been so rainy and muddy. But today I need to go see if my transplants took. I saw this bush of black-eyed Susans there at my son's and so I brought it back. It would be great in the far corner there. I need to see if it took . . .
>
> MEIKA: Can you still weed and care for the plants?
>
> SHANA: Oh yes, my nieces put in three raised beds, and when the weeds get big I can pull them. I just lean over and pull them.

As when we met, Shana was in the process of adapting what she always did to what she could manage, such as experiencing her garden mostly from a standing position, to compensate for decreased bodily strength and increased leg pain. At age ninety-three, Shana's daily self-care routine includes many familiar elements, just with a slightly different pace and approach.

Ruth L.: Recovering from a Fall, Accepting Assistance

Ruth L. is the Holocaust survivor who sings, cares for plants as children, and reads to escape (with the help of her "apparatus"). Despite all of her careful efforts to stay at home and care for herself, Ruth L. had to agree to the one thing she never wanted—to live, for one month during 2010, in a nursing facility after falling and breaking a bone. While she lost much of her autonomy, she gained a home health care aide whom she loves, and with this, a certain peace of mind.

Fiercely independent and home-centered, Ruth L., at age ninety-five, spent her days in 2008 circulating through the downstairs rooms of her home, taking care of her plants, keeping up with the mail and reading, cleaning, and preparing small meals, and always lighting her candles Friday at sundown for Shabbat. To get going in the mornings, Ruth L. had developed a specific routine.

> I wake up at six and I listen to the radio for a while. . . . I also have a tape player and it has Mozart, Bach, and others. It is so lovely. Then I get up at seven and wash myself—standing—with a sponge. I used to think old people have a smell, and it is not right. So I am very thorough. It is very warm in there, but I get dizzy when I do this. I will not tell my sons, but it is true. I wear warm clothing like this (she points to her fleece sweater). Then I put the kettle on. I must have tea. I take my daily laxative—I have a weak stomach from the war, we all do, from not eating. And I take my extra strength Tylenol. I use this so that I will not move my wrist. I did not want the surgery, so I use these instead (Velcro wrist support that she pulls on and off). Two tea bags. Very hot and very strong tea. And I eat my wheat cereal. I slice a banana or raisin. And then I go back to bed. If I still have strength, I sit for twenty minutes and read. I am reading a very good book now. Then I go to bed and rest. I will get up in a few hours and eat something around eleven. Then back to bed—like this for the rest of the day, and it is very lonely. It is very lonely but we said in the concentration camps people do not know what it is like to live so closely with

people. We will move to places where there are very few people. So I do not need people. I just need this house. And if I were to go, which will not happen, I would take my books and my reading machine. I would not live without my reading machine. But I will not go.

Ruth L. always said she was "looking for someone to help her around the house." Countless possibilities who were sent her way never worked out for very long. Ruth L. wanted things just so, wasn't sure who she could trust, and found carework to be expensive. And she wasn't in the market for a nurse; she was looking for a companion (someone who could challenge her mentally), who could also be her driver and house cleaner. Nobody really fit the bill, but Ruth L. persevered, leaning on friends and family here and there.

In 2009, Ruth L. could no longer take care of everything. In December, she fell in her kitchen and broke her femur.[6] After a hospital stay and four weeks in a rehab facility, Ruth L. was back at home as she wished. She no longer had the energy, strength, or balance to care for herself as she had before. Ruth L. also believed that she experienced psychological trauma at the nursing facility. She described this to me several times over the phone:

I tell you Meika, I couldn't take it again. That place, the horrors I saw. Women and men who were working husbands, mothers, all of a sudden . . . in that state. I didn't believe it existed. (Did it bring back memories of life in the camp?) Well the camp was something else. But worse than the camp, mentally I thought my mind will bust. I got scared. I almost went out of my mind. I was in despair—and now I am so skinny. I don't feel like eating. I cannot stand too long on my feet. I cannot prepare meals for myself. I tell you, I changed physically and mentally in the past few months. And this weather doesn't help.

Today, Ruth L.'s routine is different, but only by degree. She spends the majority of her days in bed, listening to classical music and news. Whereas before she might steady herself by using walls and counters for leverage, now her walker is always with her. She appreciates phone calls; they help her to feel alive, she says. When she can gather the strength, she can still bathe herself, make her tea, eat something light (mostly cream soups and protein drinks), and read for ten-minute segments before lying down again. Reading makes the time pass and allows her to get involved in something other than her daily aches and pains. She leaves a chair by the front door (in the enclosed porch) for packages and deliveries, and she relies on her sons (one who lives nearby) and a few select friends who assist her with cleaning, shopping, laundry, and some meals.

Unlike many who fall and break a bone late in life and end up spending their last years, months, or days in a nursing facility, Ruth L. fought to recuperate and to be allowed to return home.

> The doctors all say to me, "You are too independent for your own good. Let people do something for you." But you know I don't care. Even after the Holocaust I did not do therapy. Never. We just helped each other. Now I help myself. And I told myself I must get better. I must get out of this place. Now I am home. It is lonely here but I will not go back there.

Ruth L. won her fight, but she was unprepared for how challenging it would be to resume caring for herself without assistance. She spent more time in bed and, as a result, became more open than ever to hiring a helper. Immediately after her release, Ruth L. had a nurse checking in on her. Several months later, she took the nurse's advice and hired someone to help out and clean. "She does it just the way I want and she comes highly recommended, so she is good," Ruth L. told me over the phone.

A few months later, Ruth L. is back sitting on her porch, watching the neighborhood. She motions for me to pull up a chair, and reflects on the past several months:

> The doctors put me back together like Humpy Dumpty. That's all they could do, and the rest I have to live with. I'm glad for my mind, it is the reason I can stay at home. But sometimes it is a curse. To be old is a terrible struggle. I have so much pain, and I cannot take painkillers because of my stomach. I can only read for ten minutes at a time, and it is amazing that I don't burn down the house when I turn on the tea. . . . But this woman, Elizabeth [the nursing assistant], has brought me back to life. She helps me in the shower and combs my hair. She does everything. And she has agreed to stay with me until the end of my life. I cannot tell you how much this means to me.

Ruth L. has come to terms with dependence on another human being, but not just any human being. Elizabeth, a Puerto Rican home health care aide, calls most evenings from her job at a nursing facility. Ruth L. describes Elizabeth as smart, with a big family, and a willingness to learn. Ruth L. says she has taught Elizabeth about planting, and about many other things. Together, they have created a type of symbiosis, where they care for each other in important ways. Ruth L. hopes that, with Elizabeth, she has won the fight to age, and die, at home.

Ruth H.: Tingly Fingers, Less Typing

In previous chapters, Ruth H., the small-town community-builder who describes herself as the CEO of her large home, admitted to feeling wobbly at times and having less energy at age ninety-seven. To help her care for herself and her large home, she enlists a gang of helpers, from the students and community members who walk with her, to the household helper who chops vegetables, to the group of close friends who call every morning, to a local techie who helps with her computer.

To accomplish daily tasks, Ruth H. says the computer is the one machine she could not live without. Despite having owned a computer for several decades, Ruth H. only recently took advantage of the benefits of e-mail and computer check-writing:

> I didn't discover e-mail until sometime after [my husband] died. It's too bad, the Internet was around, but we didn't know about it. E-mail keeps me connected with life, even if I'm housed, I am connected with the world, my children, and friends. I even write my checks on the computer. Nobody else in the village does this, I don't think. They may not know about it. I think it is wonderful. It helps me because sometimes I don't know if two and two is four or twenty-two! So this way I can see what I'm working with.

Ruth H. spends a few hours a day in her study on the computer. As she explained to me in 2008, she uses the machine for e-mail correspondence, typing and storing her memoirs, engaging in translation work (as a favor to academic friends), and monitoring her finances. Not only does using the computer provide Ruth H. with a steady hand (as opposed to a shaky hand holding a pen) and a clear budget, but it also reinforces her reputation as a technogenarian in her community, a reputation of which she was proud. In 2009, with increasing numbness in her hand and a new Google-based Gmail account, Ruth H. became frustrated with e-mail, but still used this method to communicate.

> These fingers are numb so that I hit all the wrong keys. Takes me for-ever to write a message and then Google . . . just threw them away somewhere. I sent two rather long messages this morning, one to Denmark and one across the street. It said sending but then I checked the list of things sent and it didn't list them. It is so frustrating.

Ruth H. isn't the only one with circulation-based issues; many elders report tingly, numb, or shaky hands. Because we use our hands for everything from writing to preparing foods, this seemingly small chal-lenge of decreased dexterity can have important consequences. Visibly shaky hands can also carry psychological baggage: a regular reminder of one's aging body.[7] While some elders have adjusted to these difficulties and accept decreased control as another sign of aging, others turn to medication or wrist supports for increased control and dexterity.

Despite having problems with typing, Ruth H. enjoys how e-mails can keep her engaged in the lives of her loved ones.

> My younger brother had a bad reaction to a drug, and his girlfriend sent me e-mail messages back and forth so I could keep up with how he was doing. Telephone isn't quite the same because you have to catch the person at home.

In 2010, I e-mailed Ruth H. to ask how the typing was going. She replied:

> My parents gave me a typewriter for high school graduation and sent me to business school to learn typing for a few weeks after that. I think on the typewriter—and now on the computer. And now with my hands weak, I could not possibly write by hand. It is hard enough to sign checks. I am doing well for an old lady, and still thankful to be able to live alone! Love, Ruth H.

Much like Seymour, for Ruth H., adulthood has always been about thinking and doing business on a computer, and she doesn't plan to give this up. While she limits her typing due to numb, tingly fingers, the computer is still her lifeline to family and friends.

Mary: More Time, Less Energy for Cleaning

In previous chapters we learned that Mary, of the husband and wife team Mary and Bill, continues to be resourceful, employing skills she learned from growing up without a mother in a poor immigrant community. She also continues to regularly host her grandchildren and has adopted her neighbors as a sort of extended family. When I tell Mary and her husband Bill that I would like to know more about their daily lives as nonagenarians, Mary immediately replies:

> Well, we get up, eat our breakfast very slowly, read the paper, do odds and ends and then go to bed again. That's our daily life. (laughing)

Mary's joking response is telling. The pacing of their lives has slowed in some ways, and as a result, the amount they can accomplish in any given day has diminished. This has important implications for Mary, who says she has a "big backlog" in keeping her home clean and presentable.

According to Bill, "Mary is a very good housekeeper. As soon as there is a little dirt she gets out the vacuum." But Mary says her approach to cleaning has changed at this stage of her life. She is okay with doing "an adequate job," most of the time, although she quickly points out that she's not beyond scrubbing the floors like she used to. Several factors reinforce her recent shift in cleaning standards: a loss of "zip and stamina" as well as strength, a big-picture perspective, delegation of some cleaning responsibilities to Bill, and new lightweight, time-saving cleaning technologies.

> MARY: I know I've adapted to not cleaning every corner. I find myself doing my cleaning a lot faster than I used to do. It used to take me a day to do a full room and it doesn't today.
>
> MEIKA: Why not?
>
> MARY: Well, I'm not able to spend that time, for one thing, I get tired too fast. And I got thinking that I didn't fuss too much when I was working because I only had Saturdays to do both floors. Now, these days

they have these Swiffers [sic] and I use those new things now, instead of using a mop and pail. Of course, once in a while I do get that out because I don't think those Swiffer things really get the dirt up, but if you're doing something . . . like today I knew you were coming and I could see a lot of spots on the kitchen floor. Some dribbles and drabbles. And I just got that out and used it there and in the bathroom. So, it's acceptable. But if I really wanted to, I could get down on my hands and knees. I used to do that.

MEIKA: Do you clean the first floor [where Bill spends time]?

MARY: Well, not really, but if it has to be done he has to do it. Or his bedroom. He has so much junk I just refuse to. That's his responsibility. . . . After all, he's a big boy. And it gives him something to do, which is important.

BILL: Yes, I have to do that on my own.

MARY: You poor little thing. (everyone laughing)

BILL: I've got to get one of those dusters. I think I have to adjust to that rather than get the vacuum out once a month.

MARY: At this point I think you need more than a duster. (laughing)

By adapting her cleanliness standards to fit her available energy, Mary avoids a stressful backlog of work and keeps her easily bored husband occupied. Meanwhile, she frees up time for more pressing or fulfilling tasks like giving things away, sewing a chair cushion, or stripping a coffee table.

Rose: Relaxing and Receiving Prayers for a Change

In previous chapters, Rose organized her small studio apartment into a comfortable "nest," celebrated a new presidency, adopted a friend, and visited hospitals, lifting the spirits of patients with song. When I called to check on her in spring of 2010, I was surprised to hear her daughter pick up the phone. She was cleaning out Rose's apartment. She told me that Rose had moved three hours away to live with her son.

Rose grew up on a farm in South Carolina; her stepfather was a struggling farmer and her mother was a "missionary," making peace with everyone and always taking food to neighbors. As an adult, Rose lived in the city where she trained to be a nurse. She was called "Smiley" by the veteran patients she served. Later, she and her husband purchased a house in the country and raised their four adopted children.

After her husband passed away, and she could no longer maintain her country home on her own, Rose moved to a senior subsidized apartment complex in the city. She settled into her new life, creating her cozy "nest" and playing the role of "mother" and "missionary" in her church. She was still caring for people as much as she could. When I met Rose, her weekly routine involved choir practice, church services, and visits to people in need. Visiting her church one Sunday, I saw her sing in the choir, smiling broadly.

Six months later, Rose fell during the night and was hospitalized. From then on, her attendance at Sunday services was intermittent, at best. In August, she explained on the phone that her job now was to relax:

> ROSE: I had a fall, so I missed my Sunday service, which I
>   don't like to do. Would you believe I was sleeping? I was
>   in my bed and then I was running and I ran into my
>   dresser! I don't understand it at all. I spent Sunday in
>   the ER and got the stitches and now I'm just being
>   relaxed, without dressing or anything. Just being
>   relaxed.
>
> MEIKA: If you needed anything, who would you call?
>
> ROSE: Well, that's where the pastor and my daughter come
>   in. And Eve. They all make visits regularly. They've been
>   visiting me—usually I'm out visiting our brothers and
>   sisters who are in need. But now they are visiting me.

Over the next six months, at the age of ninety-four, Rose was hospitalized at least three times, for extended periods. She no longer visited others. Instead, she was the one being visited, sung to, and prayed for. And she seemed to accept that. Meanwhile, it was getting harder to reach her by phone. When I did, Rose would explain that she had been sick, or in the hospital, and how things had changed for her in terms of energy, mobility, and care. "I don't get out like I used to, you see. I sleep a lot. And two times a week someone comes to help me. But I'm still doing things, and I appreciate your interest in me."

At some point, self-care got to be too much. Months before her ninety-fifty birthday, Rose moved to rural New York to live with her son James, who was out of work on disability leave and able to devote his days to caring for his mother. She was almost three hours away from her apartment complex and church community, but she was in a place that reminded her of her old country home. Her spirits were high; she spoke of her memories bringing up a family in the country, and getting treated like a "queen" by her extended family. "They love me so much, all I can do is love them back," she said. Her caretaking days were not over.

Over the phone, Rose emphasized the blessings, using an "every day is a new day" approach to life to stay positive about the move. In order to embrace her family's loving care, she had to give up what was uniquely hers: her nest, independence, proximity to her adopted friend, Eve, and regular time with the Christian community members who called her Mother. I was reminded of one of the first things she said to me, "I hope never to leave this place." Then again, she did not seem upset with the move. She had adapted to her new situation, and her health had stabilized. Her son promised to drive her to church once in a while. Meanwhile, she enjoyed the countryside and her family's care.

Joseph: Blind, Relying on Memory

As we know from previous chapters, Joseph and his wife rely on their remaining senses—her eyes and his memory—to take care of one another. When asked how he feels, Joseph says his body is not so good. He has now been blind for five years. He has recurring dreams about the Holocaust. But he is also thankful for his detailed memory. He can remember the nitty-gritty details of daily life—dates, times, and locations—and this means he can continue to care for himself and his wife, by handling logistics

> It is very hard. I have my wife here, but she is not well. And I cannot help her so well. She has dementia. She forgets everything. I try to help her remember. That's what I'm here for. . . . I cannot see, but I know where everything is. I have memorized it. My memory is perfect, thank God. I remember all dates.

Because it is one of his clear strengths, Joseph loves most opportunities to "test" or show off his memory, asking questions (that I know the answer to) and then answering them correctly, beaming with pride. When I ask Joseph about his regular routine, Joseph can recite a complex calendar of doctor's appointments and meal programs, including timing and related bus schedules, from memory:

Downstairs in room 108, two times a week we are at the breakfasts. Last Thursday we went to the Italian-American Club for dinner; it was very good. Usually we have dinner at the Jewish Community Center on Mondays and Wednesdays. And Sundays we go out with our daughters.

The ways in which Joseph has had to rely on his memory and adapt his routines to mitigate his blindness are particularly evident when it comes to grocery shopping. Weekly shopping trips give him something to do and something to be proud of. He has memorized where most things are in the store, but he still has to ask for help once in a while.

JOSEPH: Would you believe I go shopping?

MEIKA: Who takes you shopping?

JOSEPH: We got buses come every Thursday and take us to Price Chopper for the whole building. I get most of [the groceries]. Maybe just a couple of pieces I don't know, so I ask somebody. Last time I ask for help, "Where is the gefilte fish?" I tell them the gefilte fish I want has a red top. I remember this. So he brings me over there. But otherwise I know where everything is. And once he shows me I remember where it is. . . . I get five bags, maybe twelve bags of groceries. I don't carry, I use that cart, and it goes on the bus.

Joseph is not afraid to ask for help and mobilize local resources. While he appears to be extremely autonomous, Joseph depends on a range of people and resources to meet his needs, including community organizations, drivers, an aide, and family members. This web of resources, as for all of the elders in this book, undergirds Joseph's ability to age in place. But he does not stand by as his needs are met by others. By focusing on the things he *can* accomplish, Joseph is able to maximize his capacity for care and self-efficacy, and in the process, stay challenged.

EMPHASIZE ABILITY, IN THE CONTEXT OF DISABILITY

You could say that the oldest old have no choice but to adapt to their changing bodies and capacities. This may be true for some, particularly those who experience severe illness or disability. For most, difficulties come and go, which makes it tempting to live in denial and proceed as usual. The elders in this chapter recognize challenges and adjust by scaling back and honing in on what is most important, usually emphasizing comfort and manageability. All continue to do what they did, but in new ways. As they tell me about their challenges, most are not content to stay on that topic, turning the conversation to what they can and do achieve in their daily lives. Adaptability for elders is about coming to terms with aging, functional disability, and illness while also emphasizing capability. This requires a sense of resilience as well as access to resources and support.

In contrast to a model of "successful aging," popularized by pop-MDs such as Dr. Oz, elders like Ruth L., Seymour, Joseph, and Rose underscore how crucial comfort and overall well-being are to successfully aging on one's own. There is no one way to ensure comfort; diverse elders ensure that their needs are being met in a variety of ways, from cutting back, to hiring help, to emphasizing rest and relaxation or warm climates and moderate exercise.

Human resilience is complex and multilayered. Some might walk into Ruth L.'s home and see an emaciated bedbound woman who spends all day listening to the radio. But knowing Ruth L.'s background reveals a woman who continues to advocate for herself and teach others; a woman who capitalizes on ten minutes of strength to read or water plants; a woman who cannot take painkillers because of her weak stomach from the concentration camp, but does her best to manage intense pain through a daily routine of morning tea and music. That said, Ruth L. herself vacillates between bemoaning her loss of control to feeling in control. She will say she is eager for her life (and pain) to be over, and then comfort herself with the song lyrics, "Whatever will be, will be," voicing a lifelong technique of self-consolation. Long-term observation and attending to a broad definition of well-being beyond physical capacity captures the complex ways in which elders negotiate the final years of life, adapt to challenges, and continue to advocate for themselves while home alone.

When confronted with physical or psychosocial difficulties, most scale back in some way, perhaps to avoid asking for help.[8] Not all see their lives as diminished, however. In fact, we know from the disability literature that life's difficulties can have the effect of lowering expectations, magnifying the positive (including pleasures and accomplishments), and focusing one's attention on the moment. The oldest old all are growing and learning in the context of new challenges and vulnerabilities, routines, and environments. In this way, "bad" becomes "good" for Seymour, Rose counts her blessings, and Ruth L. sings a song of acceptance.

These creative and strategic elders also have numerous structural and embodied resources that enable them to stay at home. They have economic safety nets, as well as work and educational backgrounds that help them to problem-solve. They have support staff, medical professionals, family members, or friends assisting and advocating for them. They are able to access groceries, technologies, medications, and transportation when needed (or go without, if assistance is hard to come by). Their diminished physical strength, stamina, and overall health influences their ability to access some resources, but not all. They show us that when it comes to self-care, physical capacity is not everything.

And yet their bodies will have to fail eventually, and the oldest old must, at some point, come to terms with their own mortality. The next chapter discusses the ultimate form of adaptability, or how some elders accept and prepare for death.

LESSON 13

Accept and Prepare for Death

Olga in her kitchen

Olga, the former waitress introduced in Lesson 1, was a picture of good health and strength in her nineties, much like her mother, whom she described as a "tough old bird who lived to 101." Olga walked to the store once a week, even in the snow. She said it was this active lifestyle, coupled with healthful eating, her informal education from others (she only completed sixth grade, but had a lifelong curiosity), and her various efforts at "helping out," that kept her going. At ninety-seven, she still served hot meals for the County Department for Aging, volunteered at the Bargain Basement Thrift Store, and hemmed pants for three dollars. For years she talked about retiring from her volunteer work, but she never did. Olga also took care of her great-grandson, Casey. They had a special friendship—and his calls every morning helped her start the day. In many ways, her life at ninety-seven was not so different from her childhood years growing up on the farm—taking care of siblings and taking on jobs both indoors and outdoors.

Then, as the temperature started to cool in early September 2010, three things happened. Olga announced to those around her that the time had come to retire, saying "I am ready to retire. I think I will die soon." Around the same time, Olga's doctor ordered a bone marrow biopsy, not an easy or comfortable procedure. Afterward, Olga told her daughter and her doctor, "That was a bitch!" and laughed. She was diagnosed with acute leukemia, and was given six to twelve weeks to live. This was also the time that her great-grandson Casey started dating a serious girlfriend. This was hard for Olga, according to her daughter, but she was also very proud of him. "Olga had to let him go and accept that he was now a grown boy." Three weeks after officially "retiring," Olga said goodbye to extended family members from her bed in the local hospital extended care unit. Five hours later she was gone.

The obituary in the local paper described Olga as "the lovely little lady often seen walking around the Village for the past 15 years who was everyone's friend." It recounted her twenty-seven years of waitressing at a local diner, as well as her various volunteer jobs. It mentioned how she moved to her subsidized apartment community in 1995, where she considered all of her friends there to be her second family. Finally, it called for others to honor Olga's memory by doing "a random act of kindness."

ACTIVE AGING, ACTIVE DYING

British demographer and social scientist Peter Laslett described the last stage of life as the "fourth age," a period characterized by dependency, frailty, and decreased quality of life. According to Laslett, the fourth age can develop gradually or happen suddenly, generally following a period of post-retirement fulfillment. In an ageist society we sometimes refuse to acknowledge this period of decline.[1] For some, the dying process is long and drawn out; for others it is brief or nonexistent. The last three weeks of Olga's life were characterized by sickness and hospitalization. And yet, even at her most frail, Olga was vitally engaged in letting go.

Social scientists who study the end of life have found that we exercise some control over the circumstances of our death. For example, health care proxies, wills, and funeral arrangements convey our last wishes. Studies of obituaries reveal that many individuals delay their deaths until after celebrations or major holidays. These so-called "death dips" occur in every culture. In Asia, significantly more deaths occur on dates that are considered "lucky." American cultural anthropologist Barbara Myerhoff captured an extreme version of a ritualized death on tape, when an elder in a Jewish community center delivered a goodbye speech, and then passed away.[2] In all of these instances death is socially constructed.

The cause of Olga's death was cancer, but emphasizing this single physiological fact misses the overlapping social and relational forces that shaped her dying process. Nobody knows how factors like hospitalization, a diagnosis, an end to work and caretaking, and time of year might have shaped Olga's readiness to let go. Yet we can measure Olga participation in many of the circumstances surrounding her death. At ninety-seven, and the oldest member of her local apartment community, Olga chose not to avoid the reality that her death was always coming. She nonchalantly prepared others for her death, eventually declaring her own retirement and letting her great-grandson go. As we learned in previous chapters Olga had been busy putting money aside in envelopes marked for family members, and she had given her daughter some of her most valuable possessions. A year before her death, she eagerly participated in a life history project in my Sociology of the Life Course class. Olga worked with a student to create and narrate a digital story that looked back on her rich life of service and friendship. Olga was so proud of this three-minute film, entitled, "The Best People You'll Meet" (her own quote about the strangers she met while working at the diner) that her daughter chose to play it at her memorial service.

Taking into account Olga's financial preparation, life review, giving things away, and efforts in preparing others for her departure, her passing epitomizes the social construction of death. At the very end, she moved out of the single apartment complex away from her social family, and into a hospital setting. There, her family and friends were summoned to say goodbye. She died at the end of September, as the leaves were turning; winter was not far off. (Olga and I had wondered together, months earlier, how she would make it through another winter of walking in that same pair of old black shoes.)

As we have seen throughout this book, preparations for death can take many forms: from advance directives, to buying a cemetery plot, to living in the present (and perhaps avoiding making plans in the future). Health researchers Amanda Clarke and Lorna Warren remind us that an "active aging" paradigm, or an emphasis on aging and agency must be broad enough to acknowledge how individuals prepare for death. "Living for now" (for example, Seymour insisting on purchasing only ripe bananas) and "taking one day at a time"—and by extension, the accomplishment of everyday activities rather than the future-oriented goals of earlier years—are common strategies for dealing with the unpredictability of later life. Taking steps like entering residential care or cutting ties may be actively chosen and empowering, even though they are steps toward disengagement and dependency.[3] Thus, Alice's proactive move to an assisted living environment was an acceptance of dependency in the face of increasing disability. Similarly, Ruth L. ended many lifelong friendships in an attempt to tighten her circle of friends and loved ones in her ninety-seventh year. Margaret chose hymns for her memorial service to help her family in funeral preparations. And Olga, taking a step toward death, actively "retired" from work.

IMAGINING A GOOD DEATH

Most of the oldest old, like many others, define a "good death" as one that is quick, painless, and occurs during sleep. Most say this seems to be a peaceful and protective way to go; not waking up shields an individual from seeing pain on the faces of loved ones. This popular death script fits well with our cultural values: quickness, efficiency, and avoidance of dying. However, the dying process, like birthing, is rarely a quick, peaceful, or painless thing.

Many of the participants in this study acknowledged that they couldn't control the physiological aspects of dying, but many did imagine they could control the circumstances surrounding their death.[4] Many expressed a wish to die at home. For example, Shana repeated, "They can drag me out of here with my [gardening] boots on." Johanna spoke of how hard she worked to ensure that her husband did not die in a hospital, and emphasized that she too would like to die at home. Ruth L. cut ties with several longtime friends in order to focus her energies on her core group of supporters, who would help honor her last wishes to die at home and avoid another nursing home visit. And Lore made it known that she would commit suicide if she were sent away to a nursing facility. I knew that these four wanted to die at home from our very first interview, and they repeated this desire many times. By making their desires known to friends and family, each prepared others for their death and enlisted their help in achieving a comfortable death.

Scholars have shown that the delicate balance between autonomy and dependency continues through the end of life. Edwin Shneidman, a psychologist instrumental to the academic study of suicide and death (thanatology), takes us through his thoughts and preparations for death in his final book, *A Commonsense Book of Death: Reflections at Ninety of a Lifelong Thanatologist*. In the book, he writes "The decedent has a proactive role in his own demise."[5] He argues against the four official categories of death—natural, homicide, suicide, and accident—that treat the dead person as an object, neglecting intention. Instead he proposes these categories: intentional, unintentional, and subintentional. Shneidman spent a lifetime trying to prevent suicide, but he also protected one's right to end his or her life. He wrote, "As with a runner, no one should have the right to take your race away from you—you get to decide where the finish line is. The autonomy to run your own race is the ultimate freedom." The individualism glorified in this passage about a lone runner underscores an often neglected though key component of a "good death": a support system. It wasn't that Shneidman didn't have one. We know from his therapist's epilogue to the book that he hired her, as well as a secretary and health aides, to work with and care for him in his home. And yet, in his ten "Criteria for a Good Death," being surrounded by empathetic listeners, care workers, and a personal support staff does not figure into the list.[6]

HOW MORTALITY SHAPES LIVING

Whether they want to talk about it or not, the oldest old are acutely aware of death. In a culture where "old" is synonymous with disease and death, they are expected to treat death as imminent. Their great longevity in their communities accentuates their age, and death has become normalized around them. They regularly see the individuals who have shaped their lives (including those who are much younger than they are) in obituary notices. Alice and others fear picking up the phone because they cannot stand to hear more bad news. All of this contributes to their own preparations for and acceptance of death; most cannot help but think they are next.

Their own sense of mortality animates their lives. Some imagine their own demise, wondering where the death will take place, who will discover them, and how long it might take to discover their body. For example, in her fictional portrait of octogenarian Leo Gursky in *The History of Love,* Nicole Krauss describes Leo imagining others finding him half-slumped on the toilet, with his pants at his feet, or in a pool of blood at a remote warehouse where he has been summoned. Even more common is for an elder to imagine his own death after a major emergency, like a fall, or a call to emergency services, or after finding himself in a hospital. For example, when Johanna, at age 101, found herself with a nosebleed that would not stop, she called both a friend and 9-1-1. She said, "I was certain the end was near." After several days in the hospital, she returned home, surprised once again at her body's resilience, and maybe even a little frustrated. This wasn't the first time she was fooled.

A similar thing happened to Edwin Shneidman, the noted psychologist and thanatologist who argues that death can be subintentional. According to the final epilogue to his book, written by his therapist, and corroborated in a *Los Angeles Times* feature (narrated by him) titled "Waiting for the End, Alone and Afraid," there were times when Shneidman emerged, alive, at the emergency room, and sobbed. He was trying to "will" a good death much earlier than it happened. Relief finally arrived, it seems, after many near-death experiences, and a year after finishing his final book.[7]

Despite their wishes to die at home, many elders in this study found that hospitalization can change everything. As longtime geriatrician Dennis McCullough writes, "So often, the medical-care system seems to work at odds with our parents' stated wishes to die at home and avoid suffering."[8] At the time of completing this book, six study participants have passed away. Julia, Ruby, and Lore did not die in a hospital setting. Julia had a heart attack while at church. Ruby suffered from a second stroke and passed away at her family's home. And Lore died in bed at home, as she wished. The others, Christine, Olga, and Lillian were taken to a hospital for emergency health events, and for one reason or another were not able to return home.

For one thing, hospital discharge (in order to return home) requires planning. More and more hospital procedures tend to be outpatient, so once a patient's condition stabilizes, Medicare no longer covers the hospital stay. The out-of-pocket costs of extended care can bankrupt anyone. While rehabilitation is usually covered for a limited period of time, insurance provides minimal coverage for post-hospitalization in-home services. Thus, to avoid hasty decisions driven by financial concerns, elders should have home-based care plans in place, or should consult with a hospital discharge planner upon admittance to the hospital.[9] Planning ahead can make it easier to return home, where elders usually want to be.

For Lillian and Christine, there was no opportunity to return home: both passed away not long after being admitted to the hospital. Olga was in the hospital for three weeks because she did not have home-based care to return to. Ruth L.'s experience when she broke her femur highlights the importance of planning ahead. While in the hospital, her son quickly researched and chose a rehabilitation facility. Once in rehab, Ruth L. was persistent about her desire to return home, and she reports that she convinced the staff to a discharge after a traumatic month-long stay. Once at home, she struggled to care for herself in an empty home without a caregiver. Looking back, she admits they were not prepared.

Prepared or not, Alice fears that if her preferences for care are not known, well-meaning medical providers will opt for life-saving techniques, exactly what she does not want. She cites a recent *60 Minutes* episode that argued the U.S. health care system is premised on denial of death and unreasonable and expensive life extension. In 2008, Medicare paid more than fifty billion dollars to support the last two months of patients' lives in intensive care.[10] Alice prefers what is now referred to as a "slow medicine" approach in which patients can choose comfort over what they perceive as extravagant care, or a more traditional cure-based approach.[11]

Similarly, Fred has witnessed careworkers with the best of intentions force-feed a friend of his who was near death. "That man wanted to die," Fred told me. "[Force-feeding him] just wasn't right." Since advance directives may be the only way that elders can convey their wishes for end-of-life care, Alice has recently updated and filed her legal directives, and continues to make close friends aware of her preference not to be on life support.[12] She is one of less than a third of Americans who have filed advance directives. To avoid situations like the one Fred witnessed, individuals can write specific directives under the section on "feeding tubes," such as "Please do not feed me. You may place food on the table and I will choose whether I will eat or not."

In the absence of a caretaker, hospice workers can act as patient advocates and provide support and comfort for elders at the end of life. Research over the past decade shows hospice (a free service) can provide better end-of-life care than standard medical care. Instead of focusing solely on life-saving techniques, hospice workers can help elders to be at peace with their lives, and come to terms with their death. They can also enable family members and caretakers to take breaks.[13] One doctor specializing in geriatrics described hospice care this way: "Our goal is not just to change the way people die, but to change the way dying people live, and how their families experience and will remember the death."[14] Even with these advantages, only one-third of dying patients use hospice. Of the six study participants who have passed away, Ruby and Lore had hospice care.

Many barriers prevent the utilization of hospice services. A major reason is the pervasive cultural denial of death, which keeps people from accessing services in the first place. Patients or their caretakers as well as doctors need to acknowledge the dying process in order to access this service. Furthermore, in our health care system, diagnosis drives funding.[15] Medicare will not pay for hospice care until the elder has been diagnosed with a terminal condition or a doctor predicts death within six months. Given the difficulty of making these predictions and diagnoses, as well as referral delay, more than a third of patients spend less than seven days enrolled in hospice.[16] Scholars and policy institutes are now suggesting that the scope of hospice services be extended, calling for earlier referral and liberal insurance benefits to increase overall hospice use and improve end-of-life care.[17]

DEATH BECOMES THEM

When I began this research, a dear psychologist friend told me, "You're setting yourself up for a whole lot of pain and grieving." At first, all I heard in her cautionary tone was that familiar association of old age with death, and I recoiled. I responded that I was also positioning myself for a wonderful training in how to age well. In the end we were both right. As some participants in this study passed away, I began to truly understand how death shapes life and vice versa, and to empathize deeply with the participants in this study who thought about death on a regular basis. Like them, I spent more time grieving and less time on social visits. I felt as if my social network was shrinking with each "contact" I had to delete from my cell phone. I found it emotionally difficult to write and read portions of this book. At the same time, I experienced an urgency to connect with those still living, and to understand the circumstances of death for those who were gone. I devoted myself to reaching out to family members, re-reading interview transcripts, writing condolence letters, and making audio CDs for loved ones.

While grieving and reaching out, the sociologist in me couldn't help but notice how lifelike and social these deaths were. In many ways, Christine, Lore, Julia, Olga, and Lillian had death experiences that fit with their lives. They achieved a level of personal continuity in death, and this may not have been accidental.

Christine's death took place following a time of intense and gratifying connection with family and friends. In the weeks before her death, Christine had celebrated a birthday and seen her relatives from abroad (after some time). In the days before her death, Christine was not feeling well, but she invited friends over to say goodbye (including myself). She confirmed with her best friend Ileana that they would be together in death. When she was transferred to the hospital, her best friend came to hold her hand. One hour after Ileana left, Christine passed away.

Unlike Christine, Lore was always adamant about wanting to die at home. According to her granddaughter, even in death Lore got her way. Lore's granddaughter took a month off of work to ensure that her grandmother got her wish and stayed home. During Lore's final week of life, two months after her ninety-fifth birthday, she only spoke German (her native language), frustrating caretakers who could not understand her. Never a fan of religion, Lore grumbled and cleared her throat the whole time the rabbi was there. Because she was in a borrowed hospital bed, Lene was unable to get into bed with her grandmother, as she had always done. Instead, she and her sister, Lore's two nurses, friends, and neighbors spent many hours holding Lore's hand. After Lore's death, her beloved furry companion Moses curled up on Lore's empty bed, and slept.

Julia, who declined to give up her car because she valued her social life so much, had a heart attack in the pews of her church, during a service. She was surrounded by friends and loved ones. Olga was able to see her caretaking work through to the end, and her great-grandson was now being looked after by a serious girlfriend (and vice versa). While this was difficult for Olga to accept, it probably gave her good reason to let go. And I know very little about Lillian's death, except for the fact that her second husband Bernie was there with her in the hospital. That would have been what mattered most to Lillian, the lifelong romantic. Bernie passed away less than a year later.

Conclusion: New Perspectives on the Oldest Old

Mary's joint birthday party

NOBODY CAN DO IT ALONE

We learn more and more about aging everyday. As baby boomers age, a number of new books on aging attempt to offer a reality check. Two such books look to family members and classic literature to reveal stories of dementia, depression, disability, and disease. Another draws from personal experience to emphasize loss and loneliness. Yet another assumes a global perspective, forecasting increased dependency. And the last, written by a geriatric doctor, finds wisdom and vitality even in the darkest cases. All have one thing in common: they are concerned with the increasingly solitary lives of elders.[1]

This book looks to elders themselves to show the realities of aging. Their lives reflect many of these themes—from vulnerability, to dependency, to loss—while also emphasizing meaning and comfort. This book is not meant to be a romanticized view of old age, nor a portrait of heroic age-defying individuals, but rather a closer look at the ambiguities of aging by revealing elders in all their complexities, living their daily lives.[2] In many ways, this is a story about living alone and making it work. But a closer look exposes a vast web of connections, many different kinds of support, and the creative minds behind these interdependent lives. What have we learned about the oldest old? How do they maintain meaningful, connected, and comfortable lives? And how do their lives and challenges mirror our own, at any age? This section reviews the answers to these questions.

DOING IT HER WAY

If this book focused solely on "successful" or "productive aging," or the media-friendly "new old" with active and healthy lifestyles, we would miss meeting an elder like Florence, who spends much of her daily life in her recliner, relaxing her back, watching classic movies, and taking care of herself and others while in this seated position. Florence is not focused on being a productive member of society. She does not eat a particularly healthful diet, nor does she have an exercise routine. She is not in optimal health, nor does she believe that is possible at her life stage. Instead, she accepts her limitations, rests her aching body, and works toward achieving personal comfort and continuity. She takes each day as it comes. A helper comes in six days a week for a few hours. At times she is bored, lonely, and in great pain. Other times she delights in watching movies, taking phone calls from family members, and making excursions to the diner, where she is treated as a VIP. At ninety-five, Florence is just being herself. In fact, simply being herself—persistent, prudent, and responsible (and not particularly cheery)—likely contributed to her long life, according to the authors of *The Longevity Project.*[3]

In many ways, Florence is not unlike many of the oldest old aging at home. She and others in this book represent how aging is changing. First of all, Florence is a woman, like almost 70 percent of elders in her age group. Second, many of us know nonagenarians like Florence who are mostly able-bodied, relatively healthy, active decision-makers, resilient, and multifaceted. As active life span expands, they are reinventing old age. Third, many of the oldest old, like Florence, continue to value the American ideal of rugged individualism, but recognize they cannot do it alone. And fourth, while Florence will not make any headlines for her daily feats of survival, she models what it looks like to establish lifelong continuity, to create an enabling living space, to protect autonomy while also asking for help, to seek opportunities for human contact, and to prioritize comfort. These are lessons for living, at any age.

Before revisiting our thirteen lessons for living and the various local efforts to support and enable *interdependent* aging in place, I begin with six findings about the oldest old that stand in stark contrast to commonly held assumptions.

NEW PERSPECTIVES ON THE OLDEST OLD

Elders Are Agents

Far from leaving their life decisions to others, elders aged eight-five and older exert control. They are their own advocates. They network. They innovate. They grow and learn. In the context of difficulties, they try hard to lead lives of continuity and meaning. For example, Vivien, who moved to a dementia care facility, still plays piano by memory and wears colorful scarves. Joseph, now blind, does the grocery shopping by memory. Seymour communicates via e-mail. Shana weeds her garden from a standing position. And Alice feels the elevator letters with her fingers to learn what floor she is on.[4]

Elders Can Be Healthy, Able-Bodied, and Strong

Most study participants have survived major health scares, particularly in middle age. Many have chronic diseases such as diabetes and arthritis, and there is no doubt that aging weakens the body. Most individuals eighty-five and older, however, are in relatively good health. They represent important changes in aging: extended active life span and compression of morbidity. Margaret, for example, had a heart attack several years ago, but access to health care, a healthful diet, exercise, support technologies, support networks, resilience, and faith have all have contributed to her vastly improved health. At ninety-seven, she still makes her meals, reads the paper, checks in on a friend, and does her own finances.

Elders Can Be Constrained—or Enabled—By Culture

Elders, like all of us, exist in circumstances they cannot always control.[5] For example, they live in a culture that generally renders them invisible, patronizes them, or treats them as sickly or senile. [6] Sometimes, the oldest old are treated like minor celebrities, like Eddie and Alice, whose birthday parties were noted in the local paper, and Rose, who was captured beaming and clapping in a newspaper photo on the day of President Obama's inauguration. But this momentary fame does not displace ageism. Beyond age-based prejudice and discrimination, they are also constrained by structural inequalities through financial strain, sexism, racism, heterosexism, and disdain for disability. Alice worries about being able to afford the care she needs, Pauline and Juana feel vulnerable in a neighborhood transformed by racism and structural neglect, and Ruth L. feels disrespected because of her age and her ethnic background. In contrast to her late husband who embraced faith as he aged, Florence has always felt unwelcome in Judaism as a woman. Nevertheless, many have developed strategies for navigating these constraints. Alice shops on a budget and delights in using her pressure cooker to prepare hot and healthful meals, Margaret plays on beauty ideals by using cosmetics to gain respect, Ruth L. cultivates a small group of supportive medical practitioners who respect and honor her as a Holocaust survivor, and Pauline takes advantage of local services offered to arrange rides and enroll in exercise classes.

Elders Are Resilient

All elders are resilient in the context of bodily changes and age-based oppression. Oppression of all forms can translate into hardship, but it can also build resilience. Psychologists have recently begun to analyze how adversity in early life can foster adaptability in later years. Concentration camp survivors Joseph and Ruth L. are still caring for themselves at home in their nineties. Likewise, elders who grew up poor or under-educated, such as Olga and Emma, remain healthy, strong, and autonomous. They all have learned resilience. But change and adapting to it can be difficult. Ruth L. was traumatized by her stay in assisted living, for example. Others, like Diva, are so shaken by moving out of familiar spaces that confusion sets in, sometimes permanently.

Elders Are Multifaceted

Geriatric psychiatrist Gene Cohen reminds us that when it comes to aging, there is the process and the person.[7] Individuals bring life stories, personality, ingenuity, and meaning to the experience of aging; they make aging their own. One film that beautifully captures the multifaceted aspects of aging is *Strangers in Good Company*, directed by Cynthia Scott. Consider their diverse attitudes. Some make everything into something positive; others are downright cantankerous. Most, like all of us, move between these extremes. To be grumpy is one of the privileges of old age: no longer having to "perform" for anyone. Ruth L. speaks her mind, and in the process, may complain, offend, or use guilt to get what she needs. (She assumes people aren't listening, anyway.) Josie's guarded pessimism is perhaps more common. Her standard refrain, "Oh, I can't complain," hides a whole lot of hurt. She's lonely. She has aches and pains and diminished energy. She's limited in what she can do for herself and others. She's upset with her family members for never visiting. Yet, she relishes meaningful moments, like talking on the phone with friends, watching the sunrise, or participating in joking banter. There are many sides to elders' personalities and lives, and sometimes a positive attitude is less important than a sense of purpose. Josie and Ruth L. both know they have to find moments of beauty, or they end up fueling their own misery.

Elders Cannot Do It Alone

At the end of the day, social connections keep us going. Ruth L. accepted daily home health care after an injury, Ruth H. advertises for walking partners for companionship and safety, Glenn shares his home to avoid loneliness, Josie begs family members for visits, Rose moved in with her son's family, and Alice accepted her blindness and traded her condo for an apartment in assisted living. In confronting these difficulties, each learned the importance of asking for help from others to retain some control and protect their autonomy. Together their lives reveal that an aging world is an increasingly dependent world in which we all must play a part.[8]

LIFE LESSONS FOR ALL

At this moment, Ruth L. is listening to music, Bill is sharing a joke, Rose is praying, Margaret is applying lipstick, and Glenn is e-mailing his children. Simply put, they are doing what they have always done, while growing and adapting as they age. They all attend to their well-being by practicing life habits that have been meaningful and enabling. Inextricable from body, history, and social location, Pierre Bourdieu, the French social theorist, called them our habitus. Through their habitus, these elders demonstrate how behaviors that foster social connections, a balance between autonomy and dependency, care coordination, self-knowledge, creativity, and adaptability can be crucial to maintaining meaningful lives.

They remind us to:

- Identify what has consistently brought your life meaning, and continue it
- Keep growing and learning
- Design a space that works for you
- Exercise control and advocate for yourself
- Never be afraid to ask for assistance
- Embrace a routine and be open to changing it
- Belong to clubs and communities

- Contribute to a cause, a group, and/or a person's life
- Care for others
- Take time to appreciate the little things
- Use and sharpen your senses
- Make new friends
- Confront ageism
- Reach out across generations
- Accept your mortality
- Laugh and hug

Elders in this study reveal that psychosocial contexts can be just as important as functional capacity when it comes to successfully aging at home. In other words, an individual may be physically able to rise from bed, dress, and feed herself, revealing functional mastery of crucial activities of daily living, but she must have reason to do so. This is where meaning-making, relationships, and a sense of well-being become crucial.

The factors that can contribute to our well-being at age ninety can also be crucial at age nine, nineteen, or forty-nine. Most of us are engaged in creating workable living spaces, growing and learning, discovering who we are, aligning with causes, and planning for the future. We make social connections, reach out to family members, care for others, and ask for and accept assistance from these networks. Throughout our lives, we depend on others and learn to mobilize an array of resources to meet our needs, from babysitters to plumbers. We lead ageless lives, but then are forced to confront ageism when we are treated unfairly for being perceived as either too young or too old. Most of us want to retain control over the major decisions in our lives. Nearly everyone turns to family, friends, work, hobbies, and social groups in a continual quest for meaning.

In *Shock of Gray*, Ted C. Fishman reminds us that "Young people today will live in a far older world tomorrow, and it is the present that, for better or worse, will prepare them."[9] These days, we must look to our communities to experience the intergenerational connections we experienced in households over a century ago. In my classes on aging, students are matched with elder learning partners. Every semester, students discover how many similarities they share across ages and generations. This shocks them. Sadly, they have been taught that age twenty and age eighty are opposites; that the different ends of the chronological age spectrum translate into insurmountable differences. And while we know that history can shape each generation in unique ways, it is also a tragedy to overlook our human similarities. For example, both seniors in college and senior citizens are likely to be single and either embracing or preparing for new chapters of life. As we know from their comparable suicide rates, individuals in these age groups can be uniquely isolated and vulnerable. At the same time, both may have newfound time to devote to self-discovery, personal growth, creative expression, and new connections. And both may be searching for a healthy balance between autonomy and dependence in the context of family. Extended family members rarely live in close proximity, so these relationships that are forged in my classes on aging can stand in for grandchildren and grandparents.[10]

Intergenerational relationships can be most valuable when they reveal our common humanity as well as our problematic cultural valuation of young over old.[11] Students enrolled in my courses are always forced to confront ageism when they hear the inevitable ageist comments, "Why would you want to waste your time talking to an old person?" or, "Why should you care about aging?" Most of these comments come from peers, but some come from elders themselves. As we know from Alice, taking an interest in elders can be a radical act for people of any age, an acknowledgement of one's common humanity. Many elders are curious to know someone young in today's world—to compare what they have heard and experienced with the "real deal." For example, Alice says she wants to know what young people eat, what music they listen to, and what they care about. Most are pleasantly surprised to find that the young, just like the old, defy expectations and stereotypes.[12]

A NEW PARADIGM: COMFORTABLE AGING

A recent *New York Times* piece entitled "Giving Alzheimer's Patients Their Way, Even Chocolate," discusses how a dementia care facility in Arizona emphasizes therapy based on comfort.[13] Patients are allowed anything that brings them comfort, from chocolate, to perfume, to baby dolls. Caregivers, who are encouraged to scour patients' biographies and "find their strengths," offer activities related to the ones patients once enjoyed, from filling photo albums, to snapping beans, to sitting and chatting. The results of this care experiment are clear: less moody and belligerent, more active and content patients. And with less needy patients, caregivers get breaks and the facility saves money. It turns out that emphasizing comfort and continuity can be a healthy thing for all involved.[14]

The oldest old in this study prioritize aging comfortably, which directly contrasts with the popular "successful" or "productive aging" paradigms. As Margaret Cruikshank points out in *Learning to Be Old*, the latter can be simplistic and youth-focused, and misses the complex multidimensional and structural components of aging. Furthermore, in our medical world, we tend to lose sight of the social and relational aspects of health. A comfortable aging paradigm can reveal new ways of thinking about well-being and new paths for preventative health. Comfortable aging emphasizes ease and subjective health, as opposed to external signs of success and functionality.[15] Comfortable aging emphasizes learning to "be" in a culture of doing.[16] Most important, comfortable aging is universally attainable.[17] Comfortable aging has social, psychological, physiological, and policy-based dimensions unique to each elder, but there are some common threads, described below:

Comfortable Aging Requires Interdependency

Aging in place sounds like it is about autonomy. In the United States, we emphasize individualism and independence, sometimes to our own detriment.[18] In reality, aging at home works only in a social context of interdependency, or "socially inclusive independence."[19] At eighty-five, most of one's peer group is gone, and the potential for isolation, loneliness, and depression is strong. The antidote to loss is new and old connections. In fact, sociological research shows that the loss of a spouse is more likely to immediately intensify social relationships than attenuate them, and social participation rates increase a few years after the death of a spouse.[20] Social connections provide much-needed buffers and supports in the context of changing bodies, as well as personal loss and hardship. They also help us to grow. Ruth H. and Alice know this, and they swear by making new friends every year. Juana reaches out at church, Mary and Bill reach out to neighbors, and Lore dotes on her cat. Olga spent gratifying weekends with her grandson, and Pauline and Rose moved in with family. Even Ruth L., who is less social and mostly bedbound, cares for her plants as children and says telephone calls are a "lifeline," reminding her that she is still alive. And Florence, who spends most days resting her back, admits that visiting her favorite diner on Fridays is worth the physical discomfort because seeing familiar faces, experiencing human contact, and feeling respected boost her mood considerably.

Comfortable Aging Is About Accepting Bodily Changes

With time, bodies become less resilient and increasingly unreliable. This is not a disease; it is a normal process of aging.[21] Rather than deny age and health concerns, many of the oldest old accept and anticipate some loss of control. As Doris Grumbach recounts in her memoir, *Coming into the End Zone,* "We may feel eighteen years old sitting in the park, but eighty when we rise."[22] Similarly, thanatologist Edwin Shneidman admits that at ninety, he is just "wearing out like an old Oldsmobile: one of my headlamps is broken, my differential isn't differentiating, my muffler has become muffled, my distributor won't distribute—and I can't buy replacement parts at Pep Boys."[23] Stiff joints, balance issues, decreased energy, vision problems, and general weakness serve as reminders of aging that the oldest old actively negotiate. Glenn chuckles about the saliva that drips from his mouth. Shana knows that if she goes into her swimming pool, she may not have the strength to pull herself out. And Alice has come to accept that blindness in her nineties is just another stage of life and learning.

Comfortable Aging Is About Self-Acceptance

Perhaps more than any other life stage, old age can be about vulnerability, honesty, and growing into oneself. Many elders devote their time and energy to psychological growth and healing. Lore turns to art to express her painful past, Christine writes a letter to family, and Ruth H. uses memory therapy and healing rituals to confront her childhood abuse. Even accepting age can be a healthy process, as noted cultural critic Carolyn Heilbrun suggests in her memoir, *The Last Gift of Time*.[24] Heilbrun emphasizes, "Denial [of aging] is self-defeating and threatening to our integrity." Life review, in the form of reading, writing, or telling one's story, can be a way to accept or rediscover oneself. And taking time for one's self, on porches, at sewing machines, and in nature, can also contribute to comfort, continuity, and well-being.

Comfortable Aging Is about Coming to Terms with Death

Many of the oldest old have learned a Zen-like approach to death. They have watched many of their contemporaries die, and they know their own death is not far off. Philosopher Viktor Frankl has said that death gives value and meaning to life; without it, we would postpone what is most important. It follows that denying death does not allow us to truly live in the present. Those who are most comfortable with death seem to live actively in the here and now, while preparing themselves and others for death. Some, like Margaret, prepare files for their families, complete with living wills, advance directives, and favorite hymns and psalms. Glenn jokes about purchasing his own cremation for $800 twenty-five years ago. Juana tells people she is ready to be taken into the heavens when her Lord is ready. Olga gives her prized possessions away, and Josie makes plans to sell her home and enter a residential care facility. All of these can be empowering steps toward accepting the end of life. Once the dying process is acknowledged by a doctor, hospice care can enable elders to achieve some semblance of comfort in death.

Comfortable Aging Requires Structural Change

This book focuses on elders actively accomplishing and coordinating self-care. In the process, all have hit obstacles. Because countless social barriers impede elders' chances of aging comfortably, I have created my own short list of changes I would like to see in place by the time I become an elder.

My wish list includes:

- support and respect for aging in society
- public support for comprehensive health care, including preventative care, psychotherapy, in-home and community-based care, and end-of-life care
- end to over-care and over-spending in our health care system
- assistance to family members providing care
- incentives for medical students to study geriatrics
- geriatricians who oversee and prioritize their patients' comfort and care
- age-integrated, walkable neighborhoods with central gathering spaces
- expanded transportation systems with elders' needs in mind
- accessible, affordable housing, and personal and home-care services
- standardization of services across regional and state borders

Comfortable aging for all requires structural change, and change can and must begin locally. Conversations with professionals working on aging issues have left me cautiously optimistic.[25] See the "Best Practices" section in the appendix for how local, state, and federal initiatives can begin to fill in systemic gaps.

BRING BACK THE OLD NEIGHBORHOOD

Stella is slowly making her way up my downtown street, a purse in one hand, a cane in the other. I introduce myself and ask if she lives nearby. She pauses, leans on her cane, and looks me in the eye:

> I live one block over. I wanted to walk to the library today but I ended up at Dunkin Donuts instead. You know, I've been mugged three times, and hit by a car in this neighborhood. I'm in my nineties. But see, I was a nurse in World War II, and I know I have to keep going . . .

We talk for a moment, and then, as she shuffles off, she says, "It is nice to know there are still nice people out there."

Half a mile away, Juana walks proudly through her impoverished neighborhood wearing her Yankees jersey. As a single mother in a small village in Puerto Rico, Juana learned the importance of a caring community. Today, she participates in something very similar. On the streets, African American men respectfully call her "Mama." She passes the centerpiece of her support network, her bilingual Catholic church, where Juana volunteers to clean the holy linens and distribute homemade flan. Inside, the priests and deacons know and love her, and parishioners from many cultures and backgrounds hug her and treat her as their own mother. She proudly reports that she has children from all over the world.

Ninety miles away in a rural village, several households of solitary women elders build community around food, favors, and friendship. Ruth H. receives her morning call from Carol, who plans on going shopping. Ruth H. puts in her order for avocados and raves about yesterday's walk with her student friend. They both look forward to tomorrow's Fortnightly Club meeting, where two members will report about their research on immigration. Later, thirty individuals in the same rural community, including many of Ruth H.'s friends and caretakers, make the first steps in a community-wide effort to establish a local center to support aging in place. They conduct a local assessment of needs, and most agree that transportation is the biggest gap in services. Over time they hope to secure a small, centrally located space, raise money for a paid staff coordinator, and organize volunteers who can offer transportation to doctors' offices and the grocery store.

Meanwhile, a large community center in New York's capital region is hosting the twelfth annual Senior Lifetime Achievement Awards, where community members, religious leaders, and elected officials gather to honor fifty individuals over eighty-five years of age who have made a difference in education, caregiving, military service, and other forms of service. This fancy affair is the brainchild of a small group of committed elder advocates, helped by generous local benefactors. Ruth L. is there with her sons and daughter-in-law. After her short bio is read, she clings to her walker to rise and receives a standing ovation for her decades of service as a Holocaust educator. This recognition means the world to her.

That evening, on Mary and Bill's downtown block of historic row houses, a monthly supper club brings together twelve neighbors, ages three to ninety-five. Bill passes around print-outs of his favorite jokes, and we take turns reading them aloud. Meanwhile, Mary and my daughter reminisce about their joint birthday party. Last year they requested a vanilla-chocolate cake and helped each other blow out the candles and open gifts. They are already planning for the next one.

Across the country, my grandfather, who worried about a lack of purpose, seems to have embraced comfortable aging. He has started using a cane after years of claiming, "I'll use it when I really need it." He has downshifted a bit, giving into afternoon naps and new television shows, and generally accepting his lack of control when it comes to aging. In the morning he stays in bed longer, listening to music, in order to make the days feel shorter. During the day, he capitalizes on available social capital, with the help of family, friends, and even strangers. Complaints about boredom occur less often, and he says he feels healthier than ever at ninety. Perhaps most importantly Gramps has adapted by expanding his social worlds to enhance his well-being. Here are a few examples of new additions to his routine:

- On Fridays he picks up his longtime girlfriend, Linda, from the local Alzheimer's facility. They walk in the swimming pool for an hour, while listening to big band music on his transistor radio. Afterward, they go to lunch and a movie. He is caring for himself as well as Linda, and in the process, he feels as if he is contributing.
- He has befriended a waitress at one of his favorite lunch places. She brings him fresh melons from Hong Kong and generally treats him like a king. He likes the attention and returns often for lunch, to this and other establishments where he is "known."
- He joins his monthly "matinee club," which includes his daughter, son, and close friend, to see shows featuring Sinatra music or comedy. This ritual gives him something special to look forward to, a dose of humor, and a regular opportunity to connect with loved ones.
- He recently joined two friends on a road trip to Vegas, to "test" his stamina. He got to experience a new hotel and relax by the pool, and he reported that the walking did not leave him crippled. Overall, the trip was deemed a success, and he gained confidence in his abilities.
- His extended family, traveling from as far as South Africa and India, recently came together to celebrate his ninetieth birthday and review his accomplishments. He was pleasantly surprised at how much fun he had, telling stories and participating in a life review.

For Stella, Juana, Gramps, myself, and countless others, social connections generate meaning, health, and well-being. Interestingly, acquaintances and neighbors occasionally get away with being impolite and forcing sociality in a way that family members cannot. Thus, while Gramps might gruffly end a phone call with a family member, he may be more likely to shift his mood or consider a new idea in the context of an unexpected discussion with a waitress at a restaurant. Other times, family and friends do this work. With each little push and prod, individuals and communities can thrive. If everyone contributes, everyone benefits, and social networks are surprisingly easy to achieve.[26]

Participating in these communities over the past several years has enriched me and my family in countless ways. It has also revealed how important social integration can be. All of these individuals remind us how important it can be to take initiative in making connections, and, as Alice says, look elders in the eye. It doesn't take much. A phone call. A friendly wave. A greeting. A quick visit. An invitation to a community potluck. Every little attempt can mean a great deal to someone who is aging alone. In the process, it can enhance our own sense of well-being.

Before hanging up the phone, Gramps always says, "Thanks a million for the call," and he means it. But the pleasure is also mine. Those fifteen minutes once a week offer me a break from working and a reminder of the power of unconditional love. What could be better?

Postscript: On Doing Ninety (by Ann)

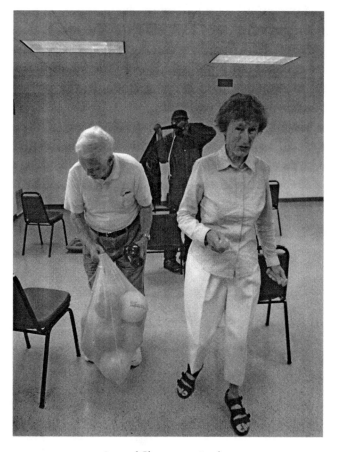

Ann and Glenn at exercise class

Dear Reader,

I remember reading an autobiography of Eva Le Gallienne, the actress. It was called "At Thirty-Three." It started with her early years. I shall do the reverse, though I'll take a little poetic license with the title.

I never expected to live this long, but I seem to be in good running condition, thanks to the six bottles of pills on my dresser and the six doctors I see: dentist, periodontist, gynecologist, dermatologist, ear doctor, and podiatrist. I go to hydroslimnastics exercises at an indoor pool twice a week, and go swimming in Lake George daily in the summer and on Memorial Day for bragging rights.

I have three sons and a daughter who take wonderful care of me: a son who calls me every evening from a suburb of Washington, DC, a son who comes to dinner two nights a week and takes me to Lake George every Sunday; a daughter who takes full charge of weekly shopping trips, keeps my wardrobe up to date, and helps me with my income taxes; and a son in Alaska who comes down every year and calls frequently to update me on the news.

Although I can no longer drive my car, I avail myself of Senior Transportation, which drives me to doctors appointments, and friends who drive me to volunteer activities, and friends who pick me up when they see me walking to the four corners. I walk about a mile a day for the fresh air and the physical exercise.

Much to my surprise I find the nineties very pleasant.

Sincerely,
Ann Donohue (age ninety-four)
January 2010

Epilogue: Updates on Study Participants

Alice, at age ninety-four and legally blind, still insists on hugs from visiting friends. She has learned to navigate public spaces, and regularly shows off her new gadgets, like her talking watch and calculator. She listens to books on tape, continues to offer a listening ear to others, and has hired an assistant to help with mail and bills. In the months ahead, with assistance from others, she plans to put her condo on the market and sell her car.

Ann fell during an unusually long walk and broke her hip. She celebrated her ninety-fifth birthday party in a rehabilitation facility, where she healed from injuries to her hip, shoulder, and heel. Still very much in control of her health, she opted against excessive testing and surgery, healed the old-fashioned way, and began a new chapter of life in a wheelchair and a care facility (in a private room that she calls her "apartment"). She still delights in her morning coffee and (seated) exercise classes. She continues to travel to her favorite local places, thanks to the used converted (wheelchair-accessible) van her family purchased. And she still does her annual Memorial Day swim (more of a quick dip now) in Lake George. She is thrilled to finally be a published author.

Bill, ninety-five, still enjoys jokes, electronic card games, and watching *M.A.S.H.* He says his neighborhood supper club keeps life interesting. Bill now literally drinks "two drops of water" or ginger ale during happy hour; he is off alcohol due to a painful stomach condition. He recently received recognition for his medic service during World War II and his community contributions as a dentist many decades after the war.

Christine was ninety-two when she died. Her memorial was attended by devoted friends and family from the United States and Ireland. To honor their agreement, her dear friend and caretaker Ileana has instructed her family to bury her next to Christine. She looks forward to when they can be together again.

Diva lives in a residence for elders with dementia. She remembers her days on campus, as a student and then as a professor, with great fondness. She is eighty-five.

Elizabeth's cleaning lady recently found her "white as a ghost" and took her to the hospital. After recovering from pneumonia, Elizabeth reports that she has a new outlook on life and has made two new friends on the hospital staff. She says she is seriously considering moving to Georgia to be near family. But, for the time being, she continues with her book groups and is learning to use a cane. She is eighty-six.

Emma, age eight-eight, had a stroke and was hospitalized in the fall of 2010. She is now back in her apartment, reading the Bible and praying. She still enjoys ordering by mail, cooking up steaks, and taking Epsom salt baths in her small apartment.

Eddie continues to play the role of informal greeter at the local gym and spends most of his days running errands for others. He is ninety-one.

Florence still enjoys her VIP lunches on Fridays and watching classic movies every day of the week from her command center, at the age of ninety-five.

Fred, age ninety-six, still lives for bocce ball and word games.

Glenn recently traveled to Norway with his daughter to visit his beloved first wife's family home and community. Although they moved out in early 2011, for five months he enjoyed two new live-in companions, a kindergarten teacher and her cat. He turned ninety-three this year.

Hy, age ninety-three, walks three miles a day and continues to facilitate a regular discussion group called "news and views" for two local community centers. He recently received a lifetime achievement award for his educational service. While still politically active, he thinks it is time to ease off and let a new generation take over. He is researching assisted living options for the future and would like to see New Zealand before he dies.

Johanna recently turned 103. She continues with her weekly Scrabble club, a highlight of her week. She recently made two seven-letter words (50 points each) in one game: "lionize" and "presume." At another game, she scored 131 points on one word by connecting triple scores. She says she is "like a child these days, more interested in games than in the work (like keeping the books)." She has increased problems with mobility, but still moves around her small home without assistance. For health reasons, she has decided against traveling to see her sister several hours away. She recently watched her grandson graduate from college online. Shortly thereafter her computer broke, and she wondered if, at her age, it was worth the investment to get a new one.

Joseph and his wife were unable to celebrate their sixty-fifth marriage anniversary after his wife, who has severe dementia, was hospitalized and subsequently moved to a nursing facility. Several months later, Joseph was able to move into the same nursing facility, honoring his promise that, after the Holocaust, they would never be separated again. He is pleasantly surprised with all of the interesting activities at the nursing facility, one that embodies Jewish values and traditions. Now that Joseph and his wife no longer need to care for one another, Joseph reports that they visit each other every day (in different wings of the nursing home) and "act like lovebirds." Joseph is ninety-two.

Josie turned 101 and soon afterwards put her house up for sale and moved to assisted living because she did not want to be alone. She put her belongings in storage so that she did not have to give them up. Several months later, she was transferred to a nursing home because of her need for regular oxygen: On her 102nd birthday, two thera-pists at the nursing home drove Josie, who is mostly blind, to a local casino to play the slot machines. Josie had the time of her life.

Juana, ninety-two years old, still cooks for her family, walks the neighborhood, writes poetry, and follows her beloved New York Yan-kees. Juana also enjoys dancing in her kitchen to Reggaeton music; her favorite song is "Gasolina."

Julia was sitting in the pews of her church, surrounded by friends, when she passed away at age ninety-five. Her sons were unable to lo-cate her homeless friend Mo.

Lillian died in the hospital with her beloved second husband Bernie by her side. She was ninety-one. Bernie passed away less than a year later.

Lore passed away two months after celebrating her ninety-fifth birth-day with family and friends. Unable to walk on her own, she sat and received guests in her self-appointed "throne." She was frustrated with her body and her memory, but still happy to have the attention. Her granddaughter and two dedicated nurses cared for Lore at home, every day until her death.

Margaret turned ninety-eight this year. She still regularly visits her friend Jackie, and Jackie continues to help Margaret monitor her health. Margaret says her recent good health report may be because she loves to eat. "If it weren't for the arthritis in the knees, I'd be in top shape," she reports. She now depends on her fancy three-wheeled honey of a walker all the time for stability. And every night before bedtime she enjoys a graham cracker with peanut butter.

Mary, who will soon turn ninety-three, has toyed with the idea of hiring a weekly housekeeper to help with vacuuming and other height- and strength-dependent tasks. Mary was recently recognized with a lifetime achievement award for her service in education. She and Bill continue to host family and attend monthly suppers with the neighbors.

Olga, age ninety-seven, continued to serve meals downstairs and hem pants for neighbors upstairs in her apartment until three weeks before her death. At that time, she was overheard saying, "I am ready to retire. I will die soon." Her daughter Carol says she finds great comfort in hearing her mother's voice while watching Olga's digital story (created collaboratively with a local university student), and has made copies for many friends and family.

Pauline went home to South Carolina, after fifty-four years in New York. She lives with her sister in a house "too big to keep up." She misses the friends who used to drop by and visit her and remains frustrated by how little she made selling her house in the city. Her arthritis makes standing for any length of time painful, but she continues to make and enjoy her sweet potato pies. She does the prep work in stages, ten minutes at a time, and then rests her back. She is eighty-five.

Rose, who turned ninety-five this year, lives in rural New York with her son and his family and reports being treated like a queen. Her son proudly reports that Rose has gained twenty-five pounds and is happy relaxing, watching wildlife out the window, and enjoying the family pets.

Ruby no longer sits on her porch watching the neighbors. After suffering a second stroke, she moved in with her daughter in a nearby town, where she had a room with a beautiful view of the woods. She was limited in her ability to move or communicate, but friends said she still smiled when she recognized them. She was cared for at home by her daughter and son-in-law and hospice nurses, and passed away at age ninety-one.

Ruth H. still lives in her large Victorian home in a small town, where community members regularly check in on her. She made five new friends this year, all local college students who are involved in the "Adopt a Grandparent" program and who take turns doing daily walks with Ruth. She still cooks for herself, takes part in the daily phone check-in, and stays in touch via email. One change: she now uses a walker to get to and from the bathroom at night. At ninety-eight, she delights in watching her two-year-old grandson develop, doing word searches (with colored pens), reading, and receiving visitors.

Ruth L., almost ninety-eight, received a lifetime service award and a standing ovation for the Holocaust education she did for decades. She still reads and cares for her plants during little spurts of energy. A loaf of fresh challah on Shabbat still brings her joy. A handful of home helpers and short hospital stays have provided some respite, as well as frustration. Ruth prefers being at home, mostly alone. She is most comfortable in her own bed with music and books nearby, and a heating pad easing her stomach pains.

Seymour, age ninety-three, focuses his energy on writing and exercise. He enjoys the warm temperatures in Florida during the winter months and believes this contributes enormously to his health. He recently participated in an exciting "90 and over" party in his large Florida apartment complex attended by three hundred nonagenarians and centenarians celebrating their unique talents, from belly dancing to speech-making. He reports that it was a "revelation" to see how many "oldsters are still fully capable of living somewhat normally."

Shana had a bumper crop of swiss chard and tomatoes this past summer, and made them available to her neighbors. For her ninety-fourth birthday, she took eighteen family members out to eat at her favorite restaurant.

Vivian, ninety-two, lives in a dementia-care unit in an assisted living center. Sometimes she ventures downstairs and surprises everyone when she plays piano pieces from memory. She still wears her scarves and jewelry and lives very much in the moment.

Best Practices in Supporting Aging in Place

This study has revealed what elders need—a mix of health care, financial support, personal services, social support network, autonomy, and respect. How can governmental, for-profit, and not-for profit entities help us to fill in the gaps and deliver the most comprehensive home-based support that those opting to age in place deserve? And how can all of us assist in supporting elders aging at home? This section reviews policy and organizational best practices models that seem to be working in New York and other states, as well as their limitations.[1]

In general, America lacks a cultural infrastructure for supporting aging. Our medically based health care structure is too narrow and insufficient to support comfortable aging and dying. In order to deliver the services that elders need, we need to expand our notion of health to include financial, personal, and social support. Many states and communities across the United States are taking a dramatic step away from institutional and even medical care and talking about a wide range of support for elders at home.[2] While programs that blur hospital and home emerge, support that goes beyond formal health care is crucial—including home care, housekeeping, meals, and transportation. In the United States, we lack these comprehensive services. Beyond this, Australian social scientist Debbie Plath recommends that, when drafting aging-in-place policies, we remind ourselves that "Independence and freedom of choice should be balanced with maximizing the social integration of older people with the goal of supported socially inclusive independence, rather than individualistic independence."[3]

U.S. NATIONAL SUPPORT PROGRAMS

President Franklin Delano Roosevelt was prescient in his approach to aging. Over seventy years ago the U.S. government, under his leadership, implemented a system that conferred earned advantages in terms of financial remittances. Today, elders could not be more appreciative of their social security checks. The oldest old have been relying on these earned benefits for decades. Most research participants say they budget for food and rent based on these monthly checks. Christine's social security checks (in combination with her savings and state and federal funding) pay for her long-term care in the Green House.

In terms of medical support, research participants are grateful for coverage through Medicare (a federally funded public health insurance that covers acute care for the disabled or those aged sixty-five and over) and Medicaid (a state and federally funded needs-based program for the poor). When it comes to Medicare, many elders proudly report discovering new perks in their health coverage as they age. For example, Alice and Margaret excitedly told me that their first walker was paid for by Medicare. Mary's preventative testing is covered by Medicare. On the other hand, they, like everyone else, identified gaps in their Medicare coverage, including support socks, eyeglasses, dental, personal care, and most types of home health care. These out-of-pocket expenses were difficult for many of the oldest old to finance. Olga talked about saving up, as she always has, for annual dental visits. Ruth L. had to visit her "leg doctor" several times to get a specific prescription for support hose for her swollen legs. Bernie told me he had to save up for an electric wheelchair for Lillian, because it wasn't covered by any health plan. Others complained about the "donut hole" in prescription benefits, translating into significant out-of-pocket costs. Because costs for home health care and long-term care are minimally covered by public insurance, most of the oldest old put off hiring a home health care aide until they are desperate. On the other hand, for those living below the poverty level, public funding through Medicaid is available. Thus, after Christine spent down her significant savings paying for long-term care in the Green House, she qualified for public funding (Medicaid) to cover her care.[4] For the three years I knew her, Christine's social security checks went toward her care, and she ended up with $25 a month in her hands, which she used to purchase cable television for her room and an occasional pair of underwear on a very rare Green House-led shopping trip.

Continuation and expansion of Social Security, Medicaid, and Medicare is crucial to making aging in place a success.[5] To some extent, this is happening with the help of federal funding due to the reauthorization of the Older Americans Act in 2006 (through 2011).[6] Expanding options for health care and psychosocial support at home can diminish structural inequities that are exacerbated in old age. Given the diversity of elder experiences, the old must be involved in developing programs to address their specific needs. I learned through following their daily experiences that despite the array of programming available, there were still major gaps in services rendered. Service providers still need to continue to consider their diverse constituencies and cater to their special needs. They need to consider elders living in impoverished areas with multiple obstacles to health and mobility. They must consider diverse women's interests and needs. And they must consider developing programming for older men, who are vastly under-represented in community programming.

Most elders participating in this study were not conducting comprehensive research on the support options in their area and mobilizing the services that fit their needs, as was Alice.[7] The lack of coordinated comprehensive services in the United States means that elders *must* coordinate their own care—which requires patiently navigating fragmented options—or go without. Nevertheless, as we know from Lesson Five ("Ask for Help"), most of the oldest old in this study utilize at least one service provider, whether it is a home care aide, a house cleaner, a meal program, or a continuing education program. Below are a few of their favorite models for à la carte (at-home) services provided by a range of for-profit, government, and nonprofit entities, followed by packaged health and personal support services for aging in place.

STATE, PRIVATE, AND NONPROFIT SUPPORT SERVICES
Health Care at Home

Many of the oldest old hire aides to care for them at home, either through an agency, or through informal networks.[8] Currently, 42 percent of long-term care is paid for by Medicaid, 20 percent by Medicare, 23 percent out-of-pocket, and 9 percent by private insurance.

Those who can afford it can pay to stay at home and can be cared for.[9] The poor increasingly use Medicaid vouchers to cover home care. On the other hand, the bias in Medicaid funding favors an institutional component, despite seniors' interest in staying at home. This bias exists because Medicaid is a medically based program, and many home and community-based programs have been viewed as less medical.[10] This social bias towards coverage of "medical needs" over and above all else is exemplified here: Medicare will pay for surgery to keep a seriously ill nonagenarian alive for a few more months, but will rarely pay for at-home care which might be able to keep her functioning and comfortable even longer.

Quite a few states are acting to expand upon the existing coverage for long-term care, to fill gaps in services.[11] And Medicare funding for community-based care has more than doubled over the last fifteen years. In 2005, spending on home and community-based care accounted for 37 percent ($35.2 billion) of total Medicaid long-term care services spending, up from 14 percent in 1991. On the other hand, despite federal assistance, many individuals who need care and who do not have long-term care insurance end up spending down their assets to pay for care at home.[12] Elders like Johanna, who never imagined she'd live into her 100s, employs daily aides and worries that she will have nothing to give her family when she dies.

Personal Support Services at Home

Because the majority of the oldest old are relatively healthy and functional, home health care may not be what they need. They can get themselves to the bathroom and bathe themselves, but they experience diminished energy, aches and pains, and general physical weakness. If they express a need for assistance, it is usually for help around the house, personal care, transportation or meals. For-profit entities, nonprofits, and municipalities try to fill in the gaps and advertise their services.

I learned about this fantastic array of services as I attended town hall meetings and conducted interviews with service providers. On the other hand, beyond talking with others or reading elder-focused newsletters, I do not know how elders living at home learn about these services. Realizing this, New York State instituted a hotline, and a local nonprofit created an excellent hourly show for public television highlighting the numerous service providers in the area. On the other hand, after watching these installments, I was amazed by the options, but also confused and frustrated. It all depended on where you lived. For example, I learned about a small nonprofit organization called Community Caregivers with a vast pool of volunteers ready to help elders in any way they needed—transportation, errands, or friendly visits. I thought of all the elders I would tell about this great organization. And then I realized that, like most organizations, their coverage area was too limited to serve the elders I knew.

For the urban and suburban participants in this study, two federal and two state-based programs stand out as models for those aging in place. A good number of participants in this research took advantage of at least one of these programs. On the other hand, they still had their downsides. Nonprofit Umbrella of the Capital District offers a home maintenance and care membership program (including carpenters, plumbers, painters, handymen, and landscaping) for elders and the disabled. Their workers are all retirees. Alice felt that more than any other service provider, Umbrella enabled her to stay at home. She paid a low annual fee for membership and then affordable hourly rates for home maintenance and a driver, who took her and her friend on picnics and shopping trips, and eventually became a close friend. One possible downside relates to liability issues; to protect themselves, their drivers can only drive elders' personal automobiles.

Medicare-funded, fitness and community-center hosted "Silver Sneaker" exercise programs, including strength-training and hydroslimnastics classes, are well received by the more active subset of the oldest old. Pauline, Glenn, and Ann appreciate these classes not only for exercise, but also for social connections. On the other hand, one needs transportation to attend these classes. In Ann's case, this means taking the bus from her apartment to a major cross street and then walking half a mile to the community center. Others, like Pauline, depend on personal rides.

The for-profit Lifeline medical alert program is popular among middle class urban elders. Many study participants living alone pay for either the necklace or wristband-based speakerphone alert program for peace of mind. The Lifeline Medical Alert website says "[the program] costs little more than a dollar a day, but the specific amount may vary slightly depending on which Lifeline program is nearest to you and which equipment and services you choose." A phone call to the center estimates a monthly bill of $28 to $38 (depending on location) with a one-time installation fee of $55. A good number of elders avoid these costs by having their own emergency call systems in place. Emma, who lives in subsidized senior housing, relies on a medical alert pull cord in her apartment in case of emergency. Ruth H., Josie, and Ruth L. all have cordless phones attached to their walkers or in purses that travel around their living spaces with them. For Ruth H., her trust in friendship networks and the independent ethic that comes with living in a remote rural location contributes to her decision to participate in a local morning call network instead of paying for a Lifeline alert system.

Finally, state and member-supported Senior Services of Albany offers an array of services to elders aging in the city, including Meals on Wheels, a grocery shopping program, a friendly home visitor program, and prearranged bus transportation to doctors' appointments. I met Diva through the grocery shopping program, and shopped for her and her husband for over a year. On the other hand, the inflexible menu associated with the hot meal program and the liability issues that constrain drivers' ability to help elders down their front stairs kept elders like Ruth L. from utilizing these services.

In rural areas, service providers are few and far between. Instead, community members work on localized levels to fill their needs. In the rural college community I studied, the residents created continuing education programs, discussion groups, and research clubs, to name a few. Ruth H., Ruby, Vivien, and others who live in the village proper are able to stay challenged and connected through these social organizations. Meanwhile, Margaret and Olga, who live at the senior apartment complex just outside the village, utilize the county-run hot food program on-site and attend their churches.

All-Inclusive Care

Three innovative New York programs are focused on protecting elder independence and providing various forms and levels of support for elders at home. Rather than expecting elders to pick and choose the services they need, these are attempts to package basic health and personal care services together. Shana, Fred, and Christine each took advantage of an all-inclusive care option.

In New York State, a program called EISEP (Expanded In-Home Services for the Elderly Program) is working to cover home-based health and personal care for all. Specifically, EISEP assists those aged sixty and older who need help with everyday activities to take care of themselves (such as dressing, bathing, personal care, shopping, and cooking), want to remain at home, and are *not* eligible for Medicaid. The program receives state and local funding, and clients pay for services on a sliding scale reflecting their income and the cost of the services they receive.[13]

Likewise, PACE (Program of All-Inclusive Care for the Elderly), which operates in many states, enables those who are in need of chronic care to stay in their community, by providing both acute and long-term care. A team of doctors, nurses, and other health professionals assess participant needs, develop care plans, and deliver all services, which are integrated into a complete health care plan. Started in 1971 for Chinatown-North Beach elders in San Francisco, this model has been adopted by an increasing number of states as a way to avoid relocating elders to nursing facilities. The comprehensive menu of services includes home help and delivered meals. This program is especially geared toward frail elders who are covered by both Medicare and Medicaid, and live in a coverage area.[14]

Designated NORCs, or Naturally Occurring Retirement Communities, attempt to pool resources for those aging in place in neighborhoods or apartment complexes. NORCs exist in twenty-six states. One such program, the Jewish Federations of North America (JFNA) Aging in Place Initiative, began in 2001. JFNA secures federal grants to improve quality of life, build community, and bring health and social services to concentrated vulnerable populations. Over half of the residents in a NORC must be aged sixty and over. In several New York State NORCs, social events are held regularly, a social worker assigned to the community assesses needs and locates assistance for residents, and potential service providers are prescreened and made available to residents at reduced costs. Shana, who shares her home-grown vegetables with neighbors, is involved in her neighborhood NORC. This involvement seems to maintain her social integration in the community as she ages.

The state and federally funded Green House program is facility-based, but is also focused on providing an alternative to traditional nursing home care. This is a care model with scientifically proven quality-of-life outcomes for meeting diverse elder needs.[15] Like PACE, this program is limited to those who qualify for skilled nursing home care. This model could serve as a guide for policy makers interested in how to support aging in place. Components of the Green House include universal design, which enables elders to utilize public (kitchen counters and drawers) and private (bathroom and bedroom) spaces, and to do this autonomously. Technologically, each elder is outfitted with an alert necklace in case they need assistance. An interdisciplinary team of health care providers, including nurses, occupational and physical therapists, and social workers, are at the elders' disposal. Cooks prepare meals to suit elders' preferences. Elders choose from and facilitate an array of activities throughout the day and night. And elders have access to laundry and barber services in their homes. There are currently fifty Green Houses in the United States. One drawback is that residents must leave their existing accommodations (and possibly their communities) to be part of this new group home. On the other hand, this was not the case for Fred and Christine, who were moved directly from a nursing home to a Green House, and their Green House community is located close to family members and friends.

Working from this short list of successful programs, a list of goods and services elders need to age in place begins to emerge. It would include, but not be limited to:

- communications technologies for emergencies and non-emergencies
- exercise opportunities
- social outlets
- culturally sensitive, nutritious hot meals
- accessible living spaces with universal design components
- safety devices such as grab bars
- prescreened health care providers, including therapists
- prescreened home care providers
- prescreened personal care providers
- laundry services
- barber services
- transportation with assistance
- mobility devices
- case workers to assess needs

- advance directive distribution
- expanded end-of-life care

Policies aimed at assisting elders as they pursue health, community, and changing forms of independence need to address the escalating costs of these services and technologies in the home. And yet, we cannot wait for policies to catch up with our changing realities. Many elders are taking it upon themselves to innovatively address their needs. We can all learn from their example, and take an active role in our own communities.

NOTES

INTRODUCTION

1. As reported in Chris Landers' article, "100: A New Centenarian Spirit," *Christian Science Monitor* (Apr. 19, 2010).
2. Bureau of the Census, "Older Americans Month: May 2009," *Facts for Features* (Mar. 3, 2009).
3. In the United States, life expectancy has increased by thirty years since 1900, when infectious disease was the leading cause of death for children. As the authors of *The Longevity Myth* point out, it is a great misconception that modern medicine has led to huge increases in longevity. Most correlate these changes with declines in infant mortality rates, as well as improvements in health care and nutrition, public infrastructure, and literacy.
4. In all of these countries, life expectancy has gone up as fertility and immigration rates decreased. Paul Taylor et al., "Growing Old in America: Expectations vs. Reality," *Pew Research Report* (June 29, 2009).
5. The oldest old are the fastest-growing age group in the world. Life expectancy at birth now exceeds eighty years in eleven countries. For census information on the oldest old in a global context, see reports such as: Kevin Kinsella and Wan He, *An Aging World: 2008*, U.S. Census Bureau, International Population Reports, P95/09-1 (Washington, DC: U.S. Government Printing Office).
6. Ibid.
7. Ibid.
8. An astounding 83 percent of baby boomers are white.
9. See Kaare Christensen et al., "Ageing Population: The Challenges Ahead," *Lancet* 374 (2010): 1196.
10. The oldest old population numbered 5.7 million in 2008, according to the U.S. Census Bureau. In 2000 this population was only 4.2 million, reflecting an increase of 1.5 million in eight years. See Julie Mayer, "Age: 2000, Census 2000 Brief," (Washington, DC: U.S. Census Bureau, 2001), and Robert Bernstein, "Census Bureau Estimates Nearly Half of Children Under Age 5 are Minorities, Estimates Find Nation's Population Growing Older, More Diverse" (Washington, DC: U.S. Census Bureau, May 14, 2009). http://www.census.gov/newsroom/releases/archives/population/cb09-75.html.
11. Federal Interagency Forum on Aging-Related Statistics, *Older Americans 2010*, (Washington, DC: US Government Printing Office, July 2010).
12. MacArthur Foundation Research Network on an Aging Society, "Facts and Fictions About an Aging America, *Contexts* 8, no. 4 (2009): 16–21.
13. Ibid.
14. MacArthur Foundation, "Facts and Fictions."

15. See, for example, medical sociologist Peter Conrad's work critiquing the medicalization of everyday life.
16. Ibid.
17. The verdict is still out on factors that contribute to longevity. One longitudinal study that traced individuals for eight decades found two traits that correlate with long life: prudence and persistence. An ethic of prudence is discussed further in Lesson 3 ("Live in Moderation"). For more on longevity research, see Howard Friedman and Leslie Martin, *The Longevity Project: Surprising Discoveries for Health and Long Life from the Landmark Eight-Decade Study* (Hudson Street Press, 2011).
18. For the purpose of this study, a "home" is both a physical place that enables self-care and autonomy as well as a state of mind centered on a sense of belonging, security, and well-being. In terms of physical spaces, I include any living environment with a hearth or a kitchen, representing the wide spectrum of elder housing options in upstate New York taken advantage of by study participants. On one end of this spectrum are houses, apartments, and condos. These living spaces require self-sufficiency and upkeep (although condo associations usually cover outdoor maintenance). On the other end of the spectrum are living environments with around-the-clock health supervision, like the Green House model. The Green House is a new alternative to the traditional nursing home, a twelve-person home with private rooms, a common-hearth area and kitchen, and care and food preparation by nursing aides. In the middle of the spectrum are apartments in HUD-subsidized senior housing complexes and in retirement communities. These age-specific complexes and communities generally offer fee-based services such as meal programs, activities, excursions, and limited transportation. The major difference between the two is cost: subsidized housing is offered on a sliding scale; retirement communities are generally more high-end. Assisted living (as opposed to independent living) apartments in a retirement community are generally the most expensive option because of on-site nursing costs.
19. Assisted living and nursing home care are different. Assisted living assumes good general health, personal autonomy, and self-sufficiency on the part of the resident. Nurses and support staff are on-site and available for general help with daily activities, but residents enjoy privacy. Nursing home residents (usually seen as patients) are believed to need twenty-four-hour nursing supervision. They have been found to require help with three or more daily tasks (e.g. walking, eating, dressing). Nursing home patients generally do not have privacy. Whether the two will merge, and elders will be able to stay in assisted living facilities and age in place in the future is unclear. Currently, based on state regulations, residents in assisted living facilities can be evicted. See Joel Sparks, "In Iowa, Moves to Regulate Facilities Spark Controversy," *National Public Radio* (2002). Continuing Care Retirement Communities (CCRC's) are on the increase nationally, but are difficult to find in New York state (thirteen total facilities). These offer on-site graduated care and housing—from independent living to nursing care. These communities can be very expensive (they charge a sizeable entrance fee and a monthly fee), but allow residents to stay and be cared for through the end of their life.
20. Federal Interagency Forum on Aging-Related Statistics, *Older Americans 2010* (Washington, DC: U.S. Government Printing Office, July 2010).
21. Even Christine and Fred who lived in Green Houses near each other had never been acquainted. Several times I attempted to introduce study participants to others, when it made sense. For example, when Mary wanted to learn more about what the Green House was like, I took her to meet Christine. Because Glenn and Ann frequented the same gym at the same time, I introduced them. And finally, since Mary and Glenn share a birthday with my daughter, they met at a joint birthday party that I hosted.

22. Many were curious to hear about other study participants and to compare their lives with others in the same age group. Each had the opportunity to choose a pseudonym for themselves, though most wanted me to use their actual names. In addition, each posed for photos wherever they were most comfortable, or opted out.

23. Federal Interagency Forum on Aging-Related Statistics, *Older Americans 2010* (Washington, DC: U.S. Government Printing Office, July 2010).

24. Calasanti (2003) defines an age relations approach as one that builds on the concept of structural ageism, exposing a system of inequality based on age that privileges the not-old at the expense of the old. Toni M. Calasanti, "Theorizing Age Relations," in *The Need for Theory: Critical Approaches to Social Gerontology*, ed. Simon Biggs, Ariela Lowenstein, and Jon Hendricks (New York: Baywood Press, 2003): 199–218. Such an approach makes explicit how ageist policies and institutional practices, as well as ageist attitudes, can be insidious, pervading everything from an individual's sense of self and others, to biomedical practices. This book not only exposes macro-level age-based stratification, but also micro-level ageism including that which may be internalized by the old themselves. I intentionally use language in this book that positions people as both agentic *and* old, to defy social stigma, to naturalize and neutralize aging, and to emphasize social stratification related to age. Language emphasizing "elderhood" comes from gerontologist Bill Thomas's (2004) influential research emphasizing three key developmental stages in life: childhood, adulthood, and elderhood. William H. Thomas, *What Are Old People For?: How Elders Will Save the World* (VanderWyck & Burnham, 2004).

25. U.S. Census Bureau, "The Older Population in the United States: 2008," Tables 2–9 (2008). http://www.census.gov/population/www/socdemo/age/older_2008.html.

26. The U.S. Census Bureau (2009) estimated that that nearly half of all children under age five are minorities. See Press Release, U.S. Census Bureau, "Census Bureau Estimates Nearly Half of Children Under Age 5 are Minorities, Estimates Find Nation's Population Growing Older, More Diverse" (May 14, 2009). http://www.census.gov/newsroom/releases/archives/population/cb09-75.html.

27. Cultural heritage is so important to this group that I was asked repeatedly about my own ethnic background, and at times, my religious background (acknowledging that the two can be intertwined). My response seemed to aid in establishing trust; one elder only agreed to speak with me because of our shared Russian Jewish heritage; another said he admired Jews and appreciated my Scandinavian roots. For more on how the Irish, Italian, and Jewish came to be perceived as white over time, see, for example, Karen Brodkin's *How Jews Became White Folks and What that Says about America* (Rutgers, 1998) and Noel Ignatiev's *How the Irish Became White* (Routledge, 1996). These authors argue that it was a mix of ethnicity and religion that fueled a sense of "otherness."

28. The question of the relationship between Jewish ethnic background and longevity in the United States is, as yet, unanswered. This may be due to the fact that census data on the oldest old does not take into account ethnic or religious backgrounds. On the other hand, studies in the UK and Canada have suggested a positive relationship. Figures compiled by the Office for National Statistics in Britain suggested that there were nearly three times as many Jewish people who are one hundred or older in the 2001 Census than there are in the general population. This may also be linked to factors such as education and resilience. For more on this, see David Graham's *Jews in Britain: A Snapshot from the 2001 Census* (2007). Similarly, in Canada, Mortimer Spiegelman published an article titled "The Longevity of Jews in Canada, 1940–1942" in the journal *Population Studies*, where he also speculated, based on life expectancy figures, and concluded: "It is, therefore, a fair assumption that the longevity and mortality characteristics of the relatively small Jewish population of Canada may be indicative of what might be found for the millions of Jews in the United States, for whom such information is not available."

29. Juana's was the only interview conducted in her native language, Spanish. The interview was translated by her daughter.
30. Eleven percent of those aged seventy-five and over are living in poverty, and older women are more likely to live in poverty than older men. See the Federal Interagency Forum on Aging-Related Statistics, *Older Americans 2010* (Washington, DC: U.S. Government Printing Office, July 2010).
31. U.S. Census Bureau *Current Population Reports, P23–209, 65+ in the United States: 2005* (Washington, DC: U.S. Government Printing Office, 2005).
32. According to the Census Bureau Population Profile 2000, the sex ratio (for every one hundred women) is fifty men. http://www.census.gov/population/pop-profile/2000/chap18.pdf. See also "Gender in the United States," adapted from U.S. Census Bureau, *Gender: 2000*, in Census 2000 Brief Series, by Denise I. Smith and Renee E. Spraggins.
33. Of the men who are not married, only one is living alone, one is living with and caring for a sister, and another is living in a group home environment.
34. Dr. David Bennett, who directs the Alzheimer's Disease Center at Rush University Medical Center in Chicago, says that most people are able to tolerate "a little bit of Alzheimers in their brains," which is compensated for by a "cognitive reserve" or extra brain capacity. On the other hand, because dementia can increase with age (and can be exacerbated by depression, loneliness, and anxiety, for example), two women in this sample developed severe dementia over the course of this three-year study, which may have been exacerbated by other changes in their lives. See Corrada et al. "Dementia Incidence Continues to Increase with Age in the Oldest Old: The 90+ Study." *Annals of Neurology* 67 no. 1 (2010): 114–121. Also see Knox, Richard, "Senior Moments, A Sign of Worse to Come?" *Morning Edition, National Public Radio* (aired Apr. 11, 2011).
35. Ibid.
36. Men in this age group are more likely than women to have a bachelor's degree or higher education. Among individuals aged eighty-five and over, 17 percent of men and 12 percent of women have achieved this level of education (Press Release, Census 2000, U.S. Census Bureau (May 20, 2003)). In this sample, eleven of the women (47 percent) and three of the men (37 percent) have a bachelor's degree or higher, and three of the women have advanced degrees.
37. More vulnerable and neglected nonagenarians living independently were difficult to locate; most are rendered further invisible in their poverty and social isolation, as discussed in Eric Klinenberg, *Heat Wave: A Social Autopsy of Disaster in Chicago.* (Chicago: Chicago University Press, 2002).
38. Daniel Morrow, (2003) "Commentary: Technology as Environmental Support for Older Adults' Daily Activities," in *Impact of Technology on Successful Aging*, eds. Neil Charness and K. Warner Schaie (New York: Springer, 2003), 290–305.
39. Marjorie H. Cantor, "Neighbors and Friends: An Overlooked Resource in the Informal Support System," *Research on Aging* 1, no. 4 (1979): 434–463.
40. For more on the "cohort effect," see G. L. Maddox, "Sociology of Later Life," *Annual Review of Sociology* 5 (1979): 113–135, and M. W. Riley, "On the Significance of Age in Sociology," *American Sociological Review* 52 no. 1 (1987): 1–14.
41. Federal Interagency Forum on Aging-Related Statistics, *Older Americans 2010* (Washington, DC: U.S. Government Printing Office, July 2010).
42. John D'Emilio and Estelle B. Freedman, *Intimate Matters: A History of Sexuality in America* (Chicago: University of Chicago Press, 1997).
43. U.S. Census 1999.
44. Melissa A. Hardy and Chardie L. Baird, "Is It All about Aging? Technology and Aging in Social Context," in *Impact of Technology on Successful Aging*, 28–42.

45. New scientific research suggests a possible link between lower caloric intake and longevity.

46. For more on social location and how it can shape a life course, see Toni M. Calasanti and Kathleen F. Slevin, *Gender, Social Inequalities, and Aging* (Walnut Creek, CA: AltaMira Press, 2001), and Toni M. Calasanti and Kathleen F. Slevin, *Age Matters: Realigning Feminist Thinking* (New York: Routledge, 2006).

47. A Pew Foundation Survey on "subjective age" in 2009 found that *the older people get, the younger they feel*—relatively speaking. Among eighteen- to twenty-nine-year-olds, about half say they feel their age, while about a quarter say they feel older than their age and another quarter say they feel younger. By contrast, among adults sixty-five and older, fully 60 percent say they feel younger than their age, compared with 32 percent who say they feel exactly their age and just 3 percent who say they feel older than their age. Among respondents ages sixty-five to seventy-four, a third say they feel ten to nineteen years younger than their age, and one in six say they feel at least twenty years younger than their actual age. Paul Taylor, et al., "Growing Old In America: Expectations vs. Realities" (Washington, DC: Pew Research Center, June 29, 2009).

48. Eric Erikson's (1950) eight psychosocial developmental stages across the life course originally extended into late adulthood (sixty-five+) with the final stage being "wisdom." Eric Erikson, *Childhood and Society* (New York: W.W. Norton, 1950). However, his wife, Joan Erikson, added a ninth stage in *The Life Cycle Completed*, describing how persons in their eighties and nineties integrate earlier stages and face the end of life. Joan M. Erikson, *The Life Cycle Completed. Extended Version with New Chapters on the Ninth Stage of Development* (New York: W.W. Norton, 1997).

49. Calasanti and Slevin call the power relations that intersect with age and other social inequalities "age relations." For more on the concept of age relations, see Calasanti and Slevin, *Gender, Social Inequalities, and Aging*, 179.

50. Ruth Reichl, the famous *New York Times* food reviewer, used disguises to stay anonymous, and her little old lady disguise was regularly met with great disrespect.

51. Robert Butler coined the word "ageism" in 1968. See Robert N. Butler, *Why Survive? Being Old in America* (Harper & Row, 1975).

52. For more on "doing gender," see Candace West and Don H. Zimmerman, "Doing Gender," *Gender and Society* 1, no. 2 (1987): 125–151. For more on "doing age" see Cheryl Laz, "Act Your Age," *Sociological Forum* 13, no. 1 (1998): 85–113.

53. For example, many women of this generation have been encouraged through adulthood to lean on others (kin, non-kin, spouses, public assistance) for emotional and financial support. This experience, which symbolizes women's limited autonomy and nonequality to men through much of the twentieth century, contributed to the feminization of poverty that women of all ages experience now. On the other hand, it may also have prepared women to better create support for themselves throughout their lives.

54. Friedman and Martin, 182.

55. Mary Pipher points out that for men, work ends, whereas women's work goes on, and this can contribute to a sense of continuity. See Mary Pipher, *Another Country: Navigating the Emotional Terrain of Our Elders* (New York: Riverhead Books, 1999): 177.

56. Betty Friedan's famous study, *The Fountain of Age* (1994), made the political personal in regards to aging, and belongs to a field of feminist work attempting to expose the intersections of ageism and sexism in semi-autobiographical books, including but not limited to Barbara Macdonald's *Look me in the Eye* (1983), Carolyn Heilbrun's *The Last Gift of Time* (1998), Gloria Steinem's *Doing Sixty and Seventy* (2006), and Lillian Rubin's *60 on Up* (2007).

57. Statistics on the oldest old are difficult to come by; many census tabulations (such as home ownership) end at age seventy-five and above, or sixty-five and up. For example, we

know that 83 percent of older Americans sixty-five and over owned their own homes in 2000, compared to 4 percent who resided in long-term care facilities. William C. Mann, "Assistive Technology," in *Impact of Technology on Successful Aging*, 177.

58. U.S. Census Bureau, "The Older Population in the United States: 2008," Table 22, Housing Tenure by Household Type and Age of Householder 55 Years and Over: 2008. http://www.census.gov/population/www/socdemo/age/older_2008.html.

59. Taylor et al., "Growing Old in America: Expectations vs. Reality," *Pew Research Report* (June 29, 2009).

60. These numbers are based on current occupancy and would be larger if they included those that have *ever* lived in nursing or assisted living facilities. According to the National Nursing Home Survey: 2004 Overview (Washington, DC: U.S. Department of Health and Human Services), of the 1.5 million total nursing home residents, 88.3 percent were sixty-five years and older, and 45.2 percent were eighty-five years and older. By 2008, the American Community Survey, published by the U.S. Census Bureau, recorded that 43 percent of nursing home patients were eighty-five+, a decrease of 2 percent. In 2008, approximately seven hundred thousand (12 percent) of the total population of Americans eighty-five and older (5.7 million) lived in a skilled nursing facility or a nursing home.

61. Two national entities have emerged to help elders to age in place by providing information and resources. NAIPC (National Aging in Place Council) is a group of professional service providers that advertise helping people to plan ahead and create local networks so seniors can take full advantage of services and aid. http://www.ageinplace.org/. The Aging in Place Initiative, a collaboration of national organization and the Metlife foundation, helps to foster sustainable communities by offering workshops, grants, and resources.

62. Home care is a $140 billion business. For an example of home-based medical care, or "telemedicine," in Denmark, see Sindya N. Bhanoo, "Denmark Leads the Way in Digital Care," *New York Times*, Jan. 11, 2010, D5. See also Laura N. Gitlin, "Commentary: Next Steps in Home Modification and Assistive Technology Research, in *Impact of Technology on Successful Aging*, 190.

63. In addition, few elders can afford another housing option, such as assisted living. Surveys conducted by AARP in 1990, 2005, and 2010 find that nine out of ten individuals over sixty-five prefer to stay in their homes for as long as possible. See AARP report, "Home and Community Preferences of the 45+ Population" (Nov. 2010). For more on elders' preferences to stay home, see, for example, Gitlin, "Commentary: Next Steps in Home Modification and Assistive Technology Research," 198.

64. Robert H. Binstock and Leighton E. Cluff, *Home Care Advances: Essential Research and Policy Issues* (New York: Springer, 2000); and Courtney Burke, "Health Care Reform: Thinking Long-Term" (Albany, NY: Nelson A. Rockefeller Institute of Government, 2009). http://www.rockinst.org/observations/burkec/2009-03-health_care_reform_thinking_long_term.aspx.

65. J. Humphreys, "Aging in Place in Upstate New York," *Upstate New York Regional Review* 2, no. 2 (2007): 1.

66. Neil Charness, "Commentary: Access, Motivation, Ability, Design and Training: Necessary Conditions for Older Adult Success with Technology," in *Impact of Technology on Successful Aging*, 15–27.

67. This innovative model of care was envisioned by a gerontologist and doctor team, Bill Thomas and Jude Rabig who spent time in nursing homes and recommended a whole new model of care centered on "elderhood." After following two nonagenarians moving into and residing in this facility (coming from the surrounding area), I chose to include them in this study to highlight that aging in place can take many forms, and that elder

control over daily lives and well-being can be prioritized in innovative care models like the Green House.

68. Emile Durkheim, *Suicide: A Study in Sociology* (1897) (The Free Press, reprint 1997).

69. Federal Interagency Forum on Aging-Related Statistics, *Older Americans 2010* (Washington, DC: U.S. Government Printing Office, July 2010).

70. In 2006, the suicide rate for young adults ages twenty to twenty-four was 12.5 per 100,000. The suicide rate increases as one ages beyond sixty-five, affecting 12.6 (per 100,000) of those sixty-five to seventy-five and 16.9 (per 100,000) of those eighty-five and older. White men over eighty-five have the greatest risk for suicide according to a 2005 report compiled by the National Center for Injury Prevention and Control (NCIPC). Divorce, widowhood, and depression are major factors in suicidality. See U.S. Department of Health and Human Services, http://mentalhealth.samhsa.gov/suicideprevention/elderly.asp, or American Association of Suicidology Fact Sheet, http://www.211bigbend.org/hotlines/suicide/SuicideandtheElderly.pdf.

71. On the quality of social ties and relationship to health, see, for example, Debra Umberson et al., "Social Relationships and Health Behavior Over the Life Course," *Annual Review of Sociology* 36 (2010): 139–157.

72. Angela M. O'Rand, "Cumulative Advantage Theory in Life course Research," in *Annual Review of Gerontology and Geriatrics*, vol. 22, eds. Stephen Crystal and Dennis Sheavol (New York: Springer, 2002), 14–20.

LESSON 1

1. See Sharon Kaufman, *The Ageless Self: Sources of Meaning in Late Life* (Madison: University of Wisconsin Press, 1994).

2. Robert C. Atchley, "A Continuity Theory of Normal Aging," *The Gerontologist* 29, no. 2 (1989): 183–190.

3. For more on a life course perspective, see Michael Shanahan and Ross McMillan, "The Life Course as a Paradigm" in *Biography and the Sociological Imagination* (New York: W.W. Norton, 2008).

4. In this case, past enjoyment of sexuality shapes one's sexuality late in life. See Victor Minichionello, David Plummer, and Anne Seal, "The Asexual Older Person: Australian Evidence," *Venereology* 9 (1996): 180–188.

5. Mark Clements, "Sex After 65," 17 *Parade Magazine* (Mar. 1996), 4–6.

6. See the Federal Interagency Forum on Aging-Related Statistics, *Older Americans 2010* (Washington, DC: U.S. Government Printing Office, July 2010).

7. Seymour's genetic disorder affected his father and brother in midlife. Thus, he and his father became deaf around the same time.

8. For more on technogenarians, Technogenarians: Studying Health and Illness Through an Aging, Science, and Technology Lens, Eds Kelly Joyce and Meika Loe, Wiley-Blackwell Monographs, 2010.

9. Kaufman, *The Ageless Self: Sources of Meaning in Late Life*, 103.

LESSON 2

1. Philips Lifeline's "aging command center" in Massachusetts averages 700,000 calls by mid-morning (out of six million members, most of whom are women whose average age is eighty-two). Philips' CEO says they are in the business of countering isolation in a world that is increasingly made up of solitary elders. Ted C. Fishman, *Shock of Gray* (New York: Scribner, 2010), 2.

2. I am borrowing the concept, "command center," from Gloria M. Gutman, "Commentary: Gerontechnology and the Home Environment," in *Impact of Technology on Successful Aging*, eds. Neil Charness and K. Warner Schaie (New York: Springer, 2003).

3. Paul B. Baltes and Margret M. Baltes, "Psychological Perspectives on Successful Aging: The Model of Selective Optimization with Compensation," in *Successful Aging: Perspectives from the Behavioral Sciences*, eds. Paul B. Baltes and Margret M. Baltes (New York: Cambridge University Press, 1990), 1–34.

4. Scholars of aging have just begun to understand how aging well goes beyond resources and activities to understand the importance of place, and how one can age in mutually compatible ways with location and environment. For more on how rural and somewhat isolated Canadian elders embrace and are shaped by what is perceived as an "unhospitable" location, see Sherry Ann Chapman, "Ageing Well: Emplaced over Time." *International Journal of Sociology and Social Policy* 29(1/2) (2009): 27–37. For more on maximizing suburban locations, see Miriam L. Knapp, "Aging in Place in Suburbia: A Qualitative Study of Older Women." PhD Dissertation, Antioch University (2009).

5. The father of the Green House movement, William Thomas, MD, calls himself an "abolitionist" who has worked hard to abolish the American system of institutional long-term care in the twenty-first century. He has written that the United States has more nursing homes than McDonald's. These systems were built en masse in the 1960s and 1970s during the rise of Medicare and Medicaid, and have become a one hundred billion dollar industry. And yet, this model of health care, to Dr. Thomas, just exacerbates "the plagues of old age"—loneliness, helplessness, and boredom. See William Thomas, *What are Old People For: How Elders Will Save the World* (Vanderwyk & Burnham, 2004).

6. Margaret proudly points out that her first walker was fully covered by Medicare, and it is a "honey of a walker."

7. Aging in place can mean "living in one's own dwelling after retirement" or "not having to move from one's present residence in order to secure necessary support services in response to changing need." See Atiya Mahmood et al., "Perceptions and Use of Gerotechnology: Implications for Aging in Place," *Journal of Housing for the Elderly* 22, no. 1 (2008): 105.

8. For resources on home modification and meaning, see Bronwyn Tanner et al. "Restoring and Sustaining Home: The Impact of Home Modifications on the Meaning of Home for Older People," *Journal of Housing for the Elderly* 22, no. 3 (2008): 195–215.

9. See Steven M. Albert, "The Dependent Elderly, Home Health Care, and Strategies of Household Adaptation," in *Aging and Everyday Life*, eds. Jaber F. Gubrium and James A. Holstein (Malden, MA: Blackwell Publications, 2000), 373–385.

10. See Eric Klinenberg *Heat Wave: A Social Autopsy of a Disaster* (Chicago: Chicago University Press, 2003).

11. See Dan Buettner, *The Blue Zones: Lessons for Living Longer from the People Who Have Lived the Longest* (National Geographic, 2009).

12. See Charles Durrett (2005). *Senior Cohousing: A Community Approach to Independent Living* (Berkeley, CA: Habitat Press, 2005).

13. See Ted Robbins, "Community Helped Change How We See Retirement," *National Public Radio* (aired Jan. 5, 2010).

14. Ibid.

15. Disability issues and aging issues are coming together now like never before. AARP recognized seniors acquired disabilities and worked with the National Association of Home Builders (NAHB) to create the certified aging in place specialist (CAPS) designation—training builders and design professionals to meet he needs of seniors through properly built and enabling environments. In an article on new elder-centered practices, Esther Greenhouse (2009) reminds us that most design standards are based on male adults within the 5th to 95th percentiles of anthropomorphic data, but these standards do not meet the needs of 90 percent of even the male population. A low

countertop can be more readily utilized by an individual in a wheelchair, an older person seated for balance, or a child. See Greenhouse's article on home modifications for aging in place in the December 2009 issue of *Capital District Quarterly*, or go to the National Association of Certified Homebuilders website to learn about the Certified Aging-in-Place Specialist (CAPS) designation program that teaches the technical, business management, and customer service skills essential to competing in the fastest growing segment of the residential remodeling industry: home modifications for the aging-in-place.

16. See Maria Luisa Gómez Jiménez and C. Theodore Koebel, "A Comparison of Spanish and American Housing Policy Frameworks Addressing Housing for the Elderly," *Journal of Housing for the Elderly* 20, no. 4 (2007): 33.

17. See Ayelet Berg-Warman et al., "The Supportive Community: A New Concept for Enhancing the Quality of Life of Elderly Living in the Community," *Journal of Aging and Social Policy* 18, no. 2 (2006): 69.

18. According to the *AARP Guide to Revitalizing Your Home: Beautiful Living for the Second Half of Life* (2010), if money is tight, elders should prioritize bathroom improvements. For the poor, these improvements are sometimes covered by Medicaid or local social service agencies. In general, things to watch out for include doors and windows that are difficult to open; poor lighting, especially in the bathroom and kitchen; tripping hazards like rugs and irregular floors; shower and tub accessibility; stair widths and heights; usable appliances and utensils; and bathroom proximity and accessibility.

LESSON 3

1. Lorraine T. Dorfman et al., "Stress and Resilience in the Oral Histories of Rural Older Women," *Journal of Women & Aging* 21, no. 4 (2009): 303–316.

2. Howard S. Friedman and Leslie R. Martin, *The Longevity Project: Surprising Discoveries for Health and Long Life from the Landmark Eight-Decade Study* (New York: Hudson Street Press, 2011).

3. See the Federal Interagency Forum on Aging-Related Statistics, *Older Americans 2010* (Washington, DC: U.S. Government Printing Office, July 2010).

4. When it comes to eating in moderation, the oldest old may be on to something. Caloric restriction (CR) movements across the country preach minimizing food intake to improve health and longevity. Scientists have shown that significant metabolic moderation and glucose handling can extend life in animal species. While endocrinologists have speculated that this trend may be associated with a narrow population of centenarians, the relationship is still unclear. Michelangela Barbieri et al., "Metabolic Journey to Healthy Longevity," *Health Research* 1, no. 71 (2009): 24–27.

5. In 1550, Italian Luigi Coronaro wrote a book that has since been translated into four languages and republished many times, *The Art of Living Long*, suggesting that living long required practicing moderation, particularly in terms of diet. More recently, international research on "blue zones" finds a link between small healthful meals and longevity. For cross-cultural research on alcohol consumption among elders, see Crystal D. Moore., et al. Drinking Among Elders: An International Perspective. Manuscript in Preparation.

6. For more on the biomedicalization of aging, see Kelly Joyce and Laura Mamo, "Graying the Cyborg," in *Age Matters*, eds. Toni Calasanti and Kevin Slevin (New York: Routledge, 2006).

7. See Center for the Evaluative Clinical Sciences, "Preference-Sensitive Care," *Dartmouth Atlas Project*, Jan. 15, 2007. http://www.dartmouthatlas.org/downloads/reports/ preference_sensitive.pdf.

8. The term, "arc of acquiescence," from Higgs and Jones, *Medical Sociology and Old Age*, might be helpful here. Or we can think of this spectrum of medical in terms of over- and under-use.

9. See Glen H. Elder, Jr., *Children of the Great Depression: Social Change in Life Experience, 25th Anniversary Edition* (Boulder, CO: Westview Press, 1999), 276.

10. Glen H. Elder Jr.'s longitudinal research following children of the Great Depression examines how life experiences relate to historical circumstances.

11. A national probability study found that individuals aged fifty-seven to eighty-five average five medications per person. For the oldest old population, this average number of medications could be even higher. Considering that older adults in the United States consume a disproportionately large and increasing share of medications, Qato et al. (2009) contend that there is a growing need to understand and account for the physiological role of medications, physical, and mental (psychological, cognitive) side effects of medications, and medication-use behavior in analyses pertinent to older adult health. See Dima M. Qato, et al., "Medication Data Collection and Coding in a Home-Based Survey of Older Adults," *Journals of Gerontology Series B: Psychological Sciences and Social Sciences* 64 (Suppl. 1) (2009): 86–93.

12. Another instance of this is in relation to disordered eating resulting in bulimia and anorexia. This restricted eating is becoming more common among the middle-aged and the old. While we hear about the health risks associated with obesity, there are also health-related reasons to avoid becoming underweight.

13. See Katherine Newman, *A Different Shade of Gray: Midlife and Beyond in the Inner City* (New York: New Press, 2006).

14. See, for example, Judith Lorber and Lisa Jean Moore, "Women Get Sicker, but Men Die Quicker: Social Epidemiology," in *Gender and the Social Construction of Illness* (Walnut Creek, CA: AltaMira Press, 2002), 13–35.

15. Authors of the Longevity Project (2011) write, "The longest living are not necessarily risk averse but they tend to be sensible in evaluating how far to push the envelope" (16).

LESSON 4

1. See David J. Ekerdt, "The Busy Ethic: Moral Continuity Between Work and Retirement," *The Gerontologist* 26, no. 3 (1986): 239–244.

2. See Margaret Cruikshank, "Prescribed Busyness and its Antidotes," in *Learning to be Old: Gender, Culture, and Aging* (Rowman and Littlefield, 2002), 163–178.

3. See Amanda Clarke and Lorna Warren, "Hopes, Fears and Expectations About the Future: What Do Older People's Stories Tell Us About Active Ageing?," *Ageing and Society* 27, no. 4 (2007): 465–488.

4. This quote is actually from *Gone with the Wind*.

5. See, for example, the now-famous "nun study." Robert S. Wilson et al., "Participation in Cognitively Stimulating Activities and Risk of Incident Alzheimer Disease," *JAMA* 287, no. 6 (2002): 742–748.

6. See Julia Twigg, *Bathing: the Body and Community Care* (New York: Routledge, 2000); and "Carework as a Form of Bodywork," *Ageing and Society* 20, no. 4 (2000): 389.

7. Laura Hurd Clarke and Melanie Griffin, "Visible and Invisible Ageing: Beauty Work as a Response to Ageism," *Ageing and Society* 28 (2008): 653–674.

8. See Laura Hurd Clarke and Andrea Bundon, "From 'The Thing to Do' to 'Defying the Ravages of Age': Older Women Reflect on the Use of Lipstick," *Journal of Women and Aging* 21, no. 3 (2009): 198–212.

9. See Frida Kerner Furman, Facing the Mirror (New York: Routledge, 1997), and Martha B. Holstein, "On Being an Aging Woman," in *Age Matters: Realigning Feminist Thinking*, eds. Toni M. Calasanti and Kathleen F. Slevin (New York: Routledge, 2006), 313–334.

10. See Julia Twigg, "Carework as a Form of Bodywork," *Ageing and Society* 20, no. 4 (2000): 389.

11. As throughout life, these body projects can be classed, reflecting the availability of time and resources, as well as ethnic and cultural pressures.

12. Baker and Gringart (2009) show that while old women tend to focus on appearance, old men focus on bodily functionality. See "Body Image and Self-Esteem in Older Adulthood," *Aging and Society* 29 (2009): 977–995.

13. Toni M. Calasanti and Kathleen F. Slevin, *Gender, Social Inequalities, and Aging* (Walnut Creek, CA: AltaMira Press, 2001).

14. See Gene Cohen, "Research on Creativity and Aging: The Positive Impact of the Arts on Health and Illness," *Generations* 30, no. 1 (2006): 7–15.

15. As a professional ceramicist and ceramics teacher in New York City, Lore's ceramic work was shown publicly decades ago.

16. Paula J. Gardner and Jennifer M. Poole, "One Story at a Time: Narrative Therapy, Older Adults, and Addictions," *Journal of Applied Gerontology* 28, no. 5 (2009): 600–620.

17. Marc E. Agronin, *How We Age: A Doctor's Journey into the Heart of Growing Old* (Philadelphia: DeCapo Press, 2011).

18. See National Council on Aging, "Myths and Realities of Aging in America" (2000).

19. In a 2010 a study published in *Proceedings of the National Academy of Sciences*, authors Stone and others found that from age fifty, individuals get happier as they age. In this study eighty-five-year-olds were generally more satisfied with themselves than they had been at age eighteen. A Gallup survey (2010) corroborated these findings.

20. See Mihaly Csikszentmihalyi, *Beyond Boredom and Anxiety: Experiencing Flow in Work and Play* (San Francisco: Jossey-Bass, 1975).

21. See Jonathan Haidt, *The Happiness Hypothesis: Finding Modern Truth in Ancient Wisdom* (New York: Basic Books 2006), 7.

22. Gene Cohen, "Research on Creativity and Aging: The Positive Impact of the Arts on Health and Illness," *Generations* 30, no. 1 (2006): 7–15.

23. Hundreds of social science studies have revealed the importance of social capital (networks) across the life course, using empirical evidence to show how mortality risk (a mix of psychological health, physiological health, and health behaviors) can be reduced with advantageous social ties. At the same time, it is important to remember that damaging social ties can undermine health.

24. Carolyn Heilbrun (1997), noted author and critic, writes about the gifts of time, or the unexpected pleasures she encounters in her sixties, including discoveries associated with place, time, family, fashion, mortality, and living in the moment. She writes, "The greatest oddity about one's sixties is that if one dances for joy, one always supposes it is for the last time. Yet this supposition provides the rarest and most exquisite flavor for one's later years." She ended her life at age seventy-seven (in 2003) to achieve closure on a life well lived.

25. Gloria Steinem, *Doing Sixty and Seventy* (San Francisco, CA: Elders Academy Press, 2006), 5.

26. Gene Cohen has proposed looking at aging as a series of overlapping phases, each rich with its own possibilities. Cohen's phases include the following:

Liberation (fifties to seventies), in which individuals take advantage of increased freedom from personal responsibilities, such as parenting, to explore new avenues.
Summing-up (sixties to nineties), in which individuals engage with the larger meaning of life and often search for ways to make a contribution.
Encore (seventies to nineties), in which individuals reflect, reaffirm, and celebrate.

27. For more on nonagenarians using everyday technologies, see Meika Loe, "Doing it My Way: Old Women, Technology, and Wellbeing, *Sociology of Health and Illness* 32, no. 2 (2010): 319–334.

LESSON 5

1. One exception is work by Duner and Nordstrom (2005) that reveals elders sixty-five and over managing and coping in active, adaptive and passive ways. See "Intentions and

Strategies Among Elderly People: Coping in Everyday Life," *Journal of Aging Studies* 19 (2005): 437–451.

2. One interview-based study found that for women, asking for help was perceived as a loss of independence and an invasion of privacy. Concerns about nudity were also mentioned. For men, assistance was viewed more pragmatically. After receiving formal or informal help, elders lost independence but exerted autonomy in terms of choice, payment, and decision-making. See B. Roe et al., "Elders' Perceptions of Formal and Informal Care: Aspects of Getting and Receiving Help for Their Activities of Daily Living,"*Journal of Clinical Nursing* 10, no. 3 (2001): 398–416.

3. In other areas, Meals on Wheels does offer vegetarian meals.

4. Jonathan Haidt, *The Happiness Hypothesis: Finding Modern Truth in Ancient Wisdom* (New York: Basic Books, 2006), 93.

5. For cross-cultural research on alcohol consumption among elders, see Crystal D. Moore, et al. Drinking Among Elders: An International Perspective. Manuscript in Preparation.

6. Ten percent of elderly people experience some form of identity theft. A New York study found that elders who were financially exploited were, on average, in their late seventies and tended to be cognitively impaired. Approximately 60 percent of the perpetrators were relatives, mostly their adult children. See, for example, Namkee G. Choi et al., "Financial Exploitation of Elders," *Journal of Elder Abuse and Neglect* 10, no. 3/4 (1999): 39–62.

7. See Maryanne Sacco-Petersen et al., "Struggles for Autonomy in Self-Care: The Impact of the Physical and Socio-Cultural Environment in a Long-Term Care Setting," *Scandinavian Journal of Caring Sciences* 18, no. 4 (2004): 376–386.

8. As of 2005, Oregon, New York, and California (in that order) had the highest spending on home- and community-based services, according to Jeffrey A. Burr et al., "State Commitment to Home and Community-Based Services" *Journal of Aging and Social Policy* 17, no. 1 (2005): 9.

9. Andrew E. Reed, et al., "Older Adults Prefer Less Choice than Young Adults," *Psychology and Aging* 23, no. 3 (2008): 671–675.

10. A study of Korean-American elders found that they were more likely to prefer formal care if Medicaid covered this care. In terms of a health event, most chose informal or mixed care in the case of a hip fracture, and formal care in a stroke situation. See Jong Won Min, "Preference for Long-Term Care Arrangement and its Correlates for Older Korean Americans," *Journal of Aging and Health* 17, no. 3 (2005): 363–395.

11. Paul Taylor et al., "Growing Old in America: Expectations vs. Reality," *Pew Research Report* (Washington, DC: Pew Research Center, June 29, 2009).

12. Ruth H.'s friends found her a somewhat local nursing student who is willing to work a night shift at a moment's notice. Ruth H. keeps her name and number handy. Thus far, Ruth H. has used her once, more for peace of mind than anything.

LESSON 6

1. This body of literature begins with Durkheim's (1897) work on the symbolic meaning of social ties and health habits. More recently, sociologist Debra Umberson has made a career out of research linking social ties to health, and is one of the few to use a life course perspective to explore how health behaviors and social connections shift and intertwine across the life course. Umberson et al. (2010) make this argument in "Social Relationships and Health Behavior Across the Life Course," *Annual Review of Sociology* 36 (2010): 139–157. For a classic scientific study that makes the link between health and social ties, see James S. House, Kark R. Landis, and Debra Umberson, "Social Relationships and Health," in *Science* 241, no. 4865 (1988): 540–545. And for more recent work on social ties, health, and the life course, see Steven Haas, "Trajectories of Functional Health: The

'Long Arm' of Childhood Health and Socioeconomic Factors," *Social Science and Medicine* 66, no. 4 (2008): 849–861.

2. Gene Cohen conducted a 2006 study inviting elders to take part in a year of community-based cultural programs and then asking participants about health and well-being. Compared to the control group, those who participated in the programming reported a higher overall rating of physical health, fewer doctor visits, less medication use, fewer instances of falls, less loneliness, and fewer other health problems than the comparison group. See Gene Cohen et al., "The Impact of Professionally Conducted Cultural Programs on the Physical Health, Mental Health, and Social Functioning of Older Adults," *Gerontologist* 46, no. 6 (2006): 726–734.

3. Some elders are true "independents" who, for a variety of reasons, do not form close friendships. See Sarah Matthews' work on three types of friends—independents, acquisitive, and discerning, in *Friendships through the Life Course: Oral Biographies in Old Age* (Newbury Park, CA: Sage, 1986).

4. See, for example, Rosemary Blieszner, "'She'll Be on My Heart': Intimacy among Friends," *Generations* 25, no. 2 (2001): 48–54.

5. Laurel L. Carstensen, Selectivity Theory: Social Activity in Life-Span Context, in *Annual Review of Gerontology and Geriatrics*, vol. 11, ed. K. Warner Schaie (New York: Springer, 1991), 195–217.

6. Mark S. Granovetter, "The Strength of Weak Ties" *American Journal of Sociology* 78, No. 6 (1973): 1360–1380.

7. Holstein (2006) and Furman (2007) both argue that these mostly women-focused microworlds can be communities of resistance against ageism. Also see Susan L. Hutchinson et al., "Beyond Fun and Friendship: The Red Hat Society as a Coping Resource for Older Women," *Aging and Society* 28, no. 7 (2008): 979–999.

8. For more on the Fortnightly Club and others like it, see my article "What a Colgate Professor Learned from the Women's Academy Down the Hill…" The Colgate Scene, May 2007. Also listen to Margot Adler's "Women's Clubs Evolve for New Generation," NPR Weekend Edition (April 13, 2008) http://www.npr.org/templates/story/story.php?storyId=89598533.

9. See Krishnavelli Nadasen (2008), "'Life Without Line Dancing and the Other Activities Would be Too Dreadful to Imagine': An Increase in Social Activity for Older Women." *Journal of Women and Aging* 20, no. 3/4 (2008): 329–342, and Denise A. Copelton, "Output that Counts: Pedometers, Sociability and the Contested Terrain of Older Adult Fitness Walking," *Sociology of Health and Illness* 32, no. 2 (2009): 304–318.

10. Patricia Leigh Brown, "Invisible Immigrants, Old and Left with 'Nobody to Talk To,'" *New York Times*, Aug. 31, 2009.

LESSON 7

1. For more on the physiological and psychosocial effects of humor, see David Guttmann, *Finding Meaning in Life, at Midlife and Beyond: Wisdom and Spirit From Logotherapy* (New York: Praeger Publishers, 2008).

2. For more on the physiological aspects of humor, see William F. Fry, "Humor, Physiology, and the Aging Process," In *Humor and Aging*, eds. Lucille Nahemow, Kathleen McCluskey-Fawcett, and Paul McGhee (Orlando, FL: Academic Press, 1986), 81–98.

3. See Carol D. Ryff, "In the Eye of the Beholder: Views of Psychological Well-Being among Middle-Aged and Older Adults." *Psychology and Aging* 4, no. 2 (1989): 195–210.

4. A 2010 psychological study measured age-related changes in humor and found an increase in humor after age fifty, a trend that is statistically significant in men. Ruch et al., "Humor As a Character Strength among the Elderly: Theoretical Considerations," *Zeitschrift Für Gerontologie Und Geriatrie* 43, no. 1 (2010): 8–12.

5. For more on this, see Helga Kotthoff, "Gender and Humor: The State of the Art," *Journal of Pragmatics* 38, no. 1 (2006): 4–25.

6. Palmore found that jokes about old women do tend to be more negative than jokes about old men, and joke content is generally related to longevity, physical and mental abilities, appearance, sexual ability and interest, and age concealment. See Erdman Palmore, "Attitudes Toward Aging Shown by Humor: A Review," in *Humor and Aging,* eds. Lucille Nahemow, Kathleen McCluskey-Fawcett, and Paul McGhee (Orlando, FL: Academic Press, 1986).

7. Kothoff, "Gender and Humor."

8. See Mary Crawford, "Gender and Humor in Social Context," *Journal of Pragmatics* 35 (2003): 1413–1430.

9. For more on how Japanese and Swedish women elders use humor, see Yoshiko Matsumoto, "Dealing with Life Changes: Humour in Painful Self-Disclosures by Elderly Japanese Women," *Ageing and Society* 29, no. 6 (2009): 929–952, and Annika Foressen, "Humour, Beauty, and Culture as Personal Health Resources: Experiences of Elderly Swedish Women" *Scandinavian Journal of Public Health* 35 (2007): 228–234.

10. Ibid.

11. Lore is usually asked by her granddaughter to be on "good behavior" with me when I visit (although she has been nothing but respectful since I met her at her art opening).

12. In contrast, Ruth H. says she has been known to utter offensive things without thinking. She explains, "I have to go and apologize and explain that my brain inhibitor [frontal cortex] is shrinking with age."

13. In any marginalized group, humor can give voice to the "underdog." Nancy Datan, "The Last Minority: Humor, Old Age, and Marginal Identity" in *Humor and Aging,* eds. Lucille Nahemow, Kathleen McCluskey-Fawcett, and Paul McGhee (Orlando, FL: Academic Press, 1986).

14. Elsa Marziali et al., "The Role of Coping Humor in the Physical and Mental Health of Older Adults," *Aging and Mental Health* 12, no. 6 (2008): 713–718.

15. See Margaret Hellie Huyck, and James Duchon, "Over the Miles: Coping, Communicating, and Commiserating through Age-Theme Greeting Cards," in *Humor and Aging,* eds. Lucille Nahemow, Kathleen McCluskey-Fawcett, and Paul McGhee (Orlando, FL: Academic Press, 1986).

LESSON 8

1. See Carol D. Ryff, "In the Eye of the Beholder: Views of Psychological Well-Being Among Middle-Aged and Older Adults," *Psychology and Aging* 4, no. 2 (1989): 195–210.

2. See Stephanie L. Brown, Randolph M. Nesse, Amiram D. Vinokur, and Dylan M. Smith, "Providing Support may be More Beneficial than Receiving It: Results from a Prospective Study of Mortality," *Psychological Science* 14 (2003): 320–327, and Jonathan Haidt, *The Happiness Hypothesis: Finding Modern Truth in Ancient Wisdom* (New York: Basic Books, 1996), 133.

3. Judith C. Barker, "Neighbors, Friends, and Other Nonkin Caregivers of Community-Living Dependent Elders," *Journal of Gerontology Psychology and Social Sciences* 57(B), no. 3 (2002): 158–167.

4. One day Joseph told me that he wanted to "make another a test." He followed with, "I want to know if I remember Ruth L.'s ex-husband's first name. Was it Donald?" He explains that he and Ruth L., both Holocaust survivors, were neighbors at one time. When I tell him he is right about the name, he beams with pride.

5. When Ruth L. does venture out and finds an individual who defies her expectations, she is thrilled.

6. A few social gerontologists have explored how engaging with living things like plants and animals can help one to celebrate life and living in old age. As a practicing medical doctor

working in a nursing home, Bill Thomas, who later founded the Green House concept, advocated for elders to engage with multiple forms of life in care facilities.

7. Herd and Harrington Meyer (2002) call for a fuller slate of social policies that will both redistribute the burden of care work and reinvigorate civic engagement. See "Care Work: Invisible Civic Engagement," *Gender & Society* 16, no. 5 (2002): 665–688.

8. Marc E. Agronin, *How We Age: A Doctor's Journey into the Heart of Growing Old* (Philadelphia: DeCapo Press, 2011), 255.

9. Deferred giving may be the strongest evidence of elders as caretakers, and yet it is rarely acknowledged in the scholarship on aging or carework. Desire for financial privacy, mixed with avoidance of death, have likely led to silences on this topic. I heard the oldest old talk about this mostly in passing—when Olga says she has put aside envelopes with money for family members, or when Glenn says that life will go on after his death, and his family will be fine.

10. See Toni Calasanti, "Gender and Old Age: Lessons From Spousal Carework," in *Age Matters: Realigning Feminist Thinking*, eds. Toni M. Calasanti and Kathleen F. Slevin (New York: Routledge, 2006), 269–294.

LESSON 9

1. One important exception to this is for the children of most Holocaust survivors. Joseph's daughter told me she never had grandparents or old people in her life, so she especially appreciates seeing her father as an old man.

2. Paul Taylor et al., "Growing Old in America: Expectations vs. Reality," *Pew Research Center* (June 29, 2009).

3. "In a striking illustration of the impact of changes in longevity for connections across generations, Uhlenberg (1996) found that a child born in 2000 will be more likely to have a grandmother alive by the time he or she reaches 20 years old (91% chance) than was a child in 1900 to have his or her mother still living at the same age (83%). Co-survivorship of generations may have important implications for multigenerational families and the potential role of grandparents (Bengtson 1996, 2001)." Teresa Toguchi Swartz, "Intergenerational Family Relations in Adulthood: Patterns, Variations, and Implications in the Contemporary United States," *Annual Review of Sociology* 35, no. 1 (2009): 191–212.

4. Paul Taylor et al., "The Return of the Multi-Generational Household," *Social and Demographic Trends* (Pew Research Center, Mar. 18, 2010). http://pewsocialtrends.org/pubs/752/the-return-of-the-multi-generational-family-household.

5. Teresa Toguchi Swartz (2009) argues that some college-aged children depend on their families for longer periods of time, and they receive social and financial resources (in the form of invisible advantages) from parents that can extend into adulthood. In contrast, children with more challenged socioeconomic backgrounds may not be able to depend on similar forms of family capital. I argue here that in similar ways, children can be enabling to parents in terms of passing on social resources. See Teresa Toguchi Swartz, "Intergenerational Family Relations in Adulthood," *Annual Review of Sociology* 35 (2009): 191–212.

6. For more on family capital in the context of parenting children and young adults, see Annette Lareau, *Unequal Childhoods* (Berkeley, CA: University of California Press, 2003), and Toguchi Swartz, "Family Capital and the Invisible Transfer of Privilege: Intergenerational Support and Social Class in Early Adulthood," *New Directions for Child and Adolescent Development* 119 (2008):11–24.

7. See Sharon Hays, *Flat Broke with Children: Women in the Age of Welfare Reform* (New York: Oxford University Press, 2003) and Lareau, *Unequal Childhoods*, on intensive parenting and concerted cultivation.

8. Ted C. Fishman, *Shock of Gray* (New York: Scribner, 2010), 269.

9. Fishman, *Shock of Gray*, 8.

10. Toguchi Swartz, "Intergenerational Family Relations in Adulthood."

11. For more on support networks among childless elders, see Zheng Wu and Randy Hart, "The Mental Health of the Childless Elderly," *Sociological Inquiry* 72, no. 1 (2002): 21–42.

12. Steve McDonald and Christine A. Mair, "Social Capital Across the Life Course," *Sociological Forum* 25, no. 2 (2010): 335–359.

13. Taylor et al. "Growing Old in America: Expectations vs. Reality."

14. John Wallis Rowe and Robert L. Kahn, *Successful Aging: The MacArthur Foundation Study* (New York: Dell Publishing, 1998).

15. Exceptions include birthday parties and chance meetings at a hospital, care facility, or a home. For example, I met a goddaughter of Alice's when I helped her to move out of her condo. I also spoke with a few family members by phone. For example, I brainstormed over the phone with Diva's family about her care options.

16. Robert H. Binstock and Leighton E. Cluff, *Home Care Advances: Essential Research and Policy Issues* (New York: Springer, 2000), and Courtney Burke, *Health Care Reform: Thinking Long-Term* (Albany, NY: Nelson A. Rockefeller Institute of Government, 2009). http://www.rockinst.org/observations/burkec/2009-03-health_care_reform_thinking_long_term.aspx.

17. See Marjorie L. DeVault, *Feeding the Family: The Social Organization of Caring as Gendered Work* (Chicago: University of Chicago Press, 1991).

18. Fishman, *Shock of Gray*, 171–172.

19. Those who had only sons preferred to hire caretakers over asking daughters-in-law for assistance. Those who hadn't married, had married more than two times, or had married for only a short time depended the least on family members for care.

20. In her 1997 account of the unexpected pleasures of living into her seventies, Carolyn Heilbrun, distinguished author and critic, recounts: "The most potent reward of parenthood I have known has been delight in my fully grown progeny. They are friends with an extra dimension of affection."

21. For more on this, see Meika Loe, "Doing it My Way: Aging, Technology and Wellbeing," *Technogenarians: Studying Health and Illness Through an Aging, Science, and Technology Lens*, Special Issue of *Sociology of Health and Illness*, eds. Kelly Joyce and Meika Loe (Wiley-Blackwell Publishers, 2010). Also see William C. Mann, "Assistive Technology," in *Impact of Technology on Successful Aging*, eds. Neil Charness and K. Warner Schaie (New York: Springer, 2003), 177–187.

22. Martha Holstein, "On Being an Aging Woman," in *Age Matters: Realigning Feminist Thinking*, eds. Toni M. Calasanti and Kathleen F. Slevin (New York: Routledge, 2006), 313–334.

23. See Peter Townsend, *The Family Life of Old People: An Inquiry in East London* (London: Routledge & Kegan Paul, 1957).

24. Taylor et al., "Growing Old in America: Expectations vs. Reality."

25. For more on India and changing ideas about aging and familial duty, see Lawrence Cohen's *No Aging In India: Alzheimer's, the Bad Family, and other Modern Things* (1998) and Sarah Lamb's *White Saris and Sweet Mangoes: Aging, Gender and Body in North India* (2000). See Kristin Schultz Lee, "Gender, Care Work, and the Complexity of Family Membership in Japan," *Gender and Society* 24, no. 5 (2010): 647–671.

26. Ibid.

LESSON 10

1. See Carol Stack's original work, *All Our Kin* (1974), on the family-like relationships that were created and maintained in a working-class black community near Chicago.

2. On the degree of social integration in America, see Benjamin Cornwell, Edward O. Laumann and L. Philip Schumm, "The Social Connectedness of Older Adults: A National Profile," *American Sociological Review* 73, no. 2 (2008): 185–203.

3. In the Internet age, we see the potential strengths of weak ties in relation to new dimensions of social networking. Mark S. Granovetter, "The Strength of Weak Ties," *American Journal of Sociology* 78, no. 6 (May 1973): 1360–1380.

4. Miller McPherson et al., "Social Isolation in America: Changes in Core Discussion Networks over Two Decades," *American Sociological Review* 71, no. 3 (2006): 353–375.

5. For more on the Canadian social capital study, see Hazel Mac Rae, "Fictive Kin as a Component of the Social Networks of Older People," *Research on Aging* 14, no. 2 (1992): 226–247.

6. National Academy on an Aging Society, "Caregiving: Helping the Elderly with Activity Limitations," *Challenges for the Twenty-First Century: Chronic and Disabling Conditions* 7 (2000): 1–6.

7. For more on the differences in embrace of extended kin by blacks and whites, see work by Johnson and Barer including: "Families and Networks Among Older Inner City Blacks," *Gerontologist* 30 (1990): 726–733, and "Childlessness and Kinship Organization: Comparisons of Very Old Whites and Blacks," *Cross-Cultural Gerontology* 10, no. 4 (1995).

8. See Hazel Mac Rae, "Fictive Kin."

9. See Rachelle A. Dorfman et al., "Old, Sad and Alone: The Myth of the Aging Homo-sexual," *Journal of Geronotological Social Work* 24, no. 1/2 (1995): 29–44.

10. Excerpted from Colleen Ryan's article, "Social Networks Build Stronger Neighborhoods," in *Albany Center Square Newsletter*, Spring 2010.

11. Ann Cronin and Andrew King, "Care for Gay Elders," Carework Panel, International Sociological Association, Gothenberg, Sweden (2010).

12. See Carole Haber and Brian Gratton, *Old Age and the Search for Security* (Bloomington, IN: Indiana University Press, 1994).

13. See Paul Taylor et al., "The Return of the Multi-Generational Household," *Social and Demographic Trends* (Pew Research Center, Mar. 18, 2010). http://pewsocialtrends.org/pubs/752/the-return-of-the-multi-generational-family-household.

14. One possible explanation for the recent trend reversal is an increase in what demographers refer to as "kin availability." The outsized baby boom generation offers its elderly parents about 50 percent more grown children with whom they can share a household if and when their life circumstances (such as widowhood, declining health, or poverty) take them in that direction. Another possible explanation is that cuts to Medicare enacted in 1997 have increased the financial incentives for those who are elderly and infirm to move in with a grown child who is able to take on the role of informal caregiver. (Pew Research Center).

15. According to Pew Research Center (2010), 6 percent of Americans live in a "skipped" generation household made up of a grandparent and grandchild (like Lore and her granddaughter) but no parent. See Pew Research Center, "The Return of the Multi-Generational Household."

16. When I shared with elders that one of the chapters in the book would be about intergen-erational lives, many told me of the joys they receive from their family members, particularly grandchildren, and even great-grandchildren. This is discussed specifically by Joseph, Olga, and Johanna in Lessons 8, 9, and 11. The literature on grandparenting is growing; and Olga's story, as a weekend caretaker of her grandson, fits with national trends. On the other hand, what may not be addressed in the literature is the role that is evident in the story of Lore, who lives with her granddaughter, and Johanna, who sees her granddaughter as the family member who cares for her the most.

17. For more on gated communities and taxation, see Andrew Blechman, *Leisureville: Adventures in America's Retirement Utopias* (Atlantic Monthly Press, 2008).

18. Alice's insistence on being seen as a human being has been repeated by several generations of feminist scholars confronting ageism, from Barbara MacDonald's watershed essay "Look Me in the Eye" (1984), to Martha Holstein's (2006) essay, "On Being an Aging Woman." Holstein insists that she is still objectified in old age, but "now not in terms of sexual desirability but rather as one without importance sexual or otherwise." (p. 327).

LESSON 11

1. The case histories of feral children like Victor, popularly referred to as "The Wild Boy of Aveyron," who was raised among animals in the wild in France at the end of the eighteenth century, are often used to show how human traits are learned.
2. Bodywork is carework that physically relates to touching the body; it can be "medical, therapeutic, pleasurable, aesthetic, erotic, hygienic, and symbolic." See Julia Twigg, "Carework as a Form of Bodywork," *Ageing and Society* 20, no. 4 (2000): 389.
3. Ted C. Fishman, *Shock of Gray* (New York: Scribner, 2010), 171.
4. Jaylie I. L. Beckenhauer and Joyce Armstrong, "Exploring Relationships Between Normative Aging, Technology, and Communication," *Marriage and Family Review* 45, no. 6–8 (2009): 825–844.
5. See Laura Hurd Clarke, "Remarriage in Later Life: Older Women's Negotiation of Power, Resources and Domestic Labor," *Journal of Women and Aging* 17, no. 4 (2005): 21–41.
6. See William Thomas, *In the Arms of Elders: A Parable of Wise Leadership and Community Building* (VanderWyk and Burnham, 2006).

LESSON 12

1. See Sharon R. Williams et al., "Measures of Chronic Conditions and Diseases Associated with Aging in the National Social Life, Health, and Aging Project," *Journal of Gerontology: Psychological Sciences and Social Sciences* 64B (2009): 67–75.
2. NSHAP developed a test for physical mobility called the "get-up-and-go test." For this test, respondents are asked to, from a seated position, get up from a chair, walk three meters (premeasured) at a normal pace, turn around, walk back three meters toward the chair, and sit down again.
3. Ben Schott (2009) sums up recent National Social Life Health and Aging Project (NSLHAP) key findings in his op-chart, "When I'm 57–85" published in the *New York Times*, Dec. 14, 2009. http://www.nytimes.com/interactive/2009/12/14/opinion/20091214_opart.html?em.
4. One of the most common effects of losing a loved one was that the bereaved had a great appreciation of and tolerance for the other people in his or her own life. Jonathan Haidt, *The Happiness Hypothesis: Finding Modern Truth in Ancient Wisdom* (New York: Basic Books, 2006), 138–139.
5. See Haidt, *The Happiness Hypothesis*, 151. Also, in a recent study, authors found that eighty-five-year-olds were generally happier than they had been at age eighteen. See Arthur Stone et al., "A Snapshot of the Age Distribution of Psychological Well-Being in the United States," *Proceedings of the National Academy of Sciences* (May 17, 2010).
6. Approximately one in ten thousand women over sixty-five experience hip fractures annually in the United States. Fracture rates for men are lower. Hip along with femur fracture are common after falls, particularly in the frail old or those with osteoporosis. Mortality rates following fractures have declined, but comorbidity rates are high. In a study of nonagenarians who had experienced a hip fracture, 54 percent were independent before the hip fracture occurred, and only 16 percent three months later. Only 12 percent of patients who survived were unable to return to their preadmission dwelling. See Carmen A. Brauer, "Incidence and Mortality of Hip Fractures in the United States," *JAMA: Journal of the American Medical Association* 302, no. 14 (2009): 1573–1579, and

F. Formiga et al., "Mortality and Morbidity in Nonagenarian Patients following Hip Fracture Surgery," *Gerontology* 49, no. 1 (2003): 41–45.

7. See David A. Karp, "A Decade of Reminders: Changing Age Consciousness between Fifty and Sixty Years Old," *Gerontologist* 28, no. 6 (1988): 727–738.

8. In a study of elders with multiple morbidities, many indicated that they simply no longer pursued certain activities because of limitations imposed by their chronic conditions. See Nancy E. Schoenberg et al., "'It's a Toss Up between My Hearing, My Heart, and My Hip': Prioritizing and Accommodating Multiple Morbidities by Vulnerable Older Adults," *Journal of Health Care for the Poor and Underserved* 20, no. 1 (2009): 134–151.

LESSON 13

1. Add cite: Susan Jacoby makes this argument in *Never Say Die* (2011).

2. See Barbara Myerhoff, *Number Our Days: A Triumph of Continuity and Culture Among Jewish Old People in an Urban Ghetto* (Austin, TX: Touchstone, 1980) and the 1976 documentary feature by the same name.

3. See Amanda Clarke and Lorna Warren, "Hopes, Fears and Expectations about the Future: What Do Older People's Stories Tell Us about Active Ageing?" *Ageing and Society* 27, no. 4 (2007): 465–488.

4. For a nice collection of essays on death and choice, see Final Acts: Death, Dying, and the Choices We Make (2010), edited by Nan Bauer-Maglin and Donna Perry, Rutgers University Press.

5. See Edwin Shneidman, *A Commonsense Book of Death: Reflections at Ninety of a Lifelong Thanatologist* (Lanham, MD: Rowman & Littlefield, 2008), 101.

6. See Edwin Shneidman, "Criteria for a Good Death," *Suicide and Life-Threatening Behavior* 37, no. 3 (June 2007): 245–247.

7. Dr. Shneidman's powerful slideshow is *Waiting for the End, Alone and Unafraid*, http://www.latimes.com/news/local/ed_shneidmanff_ss,0,3414993.htmlstory.

8. See Dennis McCullough, *My Mother, Your Mother: Embracing "Slow Medicine," the Compassionate Approach to Caring for Your Aging Loved Ones* (New York: Harper Collins, 2008).

8. Hospital discharge planners are usually social workers whose job is to assist individuals in preparing the patient for the next step. Getting to know your discharge planner from the day you or a loved one is admitted to the hospital can be crucial to knowing and understanding your options.

10. "The Cost of Dying," *60 Minutes*, CBS News, Nov. 20, 2009.

11. McCullough, *My Mother, Your Mother*.

12. Advance directives are legal documents that allow you to convey your decisions about end-of-life care ahead of time. They provide a way for you to communicate your wishes to family, friends, and health care professionals, and to avoid confusion later on. The living will sets forth how you feel about care intended to sustain life. You can accept or refuse medical care related to assisted breathing, tube feeding, and resuscitation, and you can also accept or refuse organ or tissue donation. The health care proxy or durable power of attorney names your proxy, or the person you trust to make health decisions if you are unable to do so.

13. Bruce Jennings et al., *Access to Hospice Care: Expanding Boundaries, Overcoming Barriers,* a special supplement to the *Hastings Center Report* (Mar.–Apr. 2003).

14. According to a report in the *New York Times*, when Dr. Domer and his staff first visited patients on a Navaho reservation, none had signed advance directives for health care, and the subject of death was avoided out of cultural sensitivity. With the help of a cultural translator, Dr. Domer began to approach the topic using a Navaho poem: "When that time comes, when my last breath leaves me, I choose to die in peace to meet Shi' dy' in"—the creator. Now, almost 90 percent of the patients in the program have signed the poem and other standard directives.

15. Much like countless Americans, Marie, my husband's grandmother, came up against many barriers to hospice care in her final year of life. Her doctor and daughters believed very strongly that she was dying, and requested hospice care several times. On the other hand, because Medicare will only pay for hospice care with a terminal diagnosis, this put Marie's caretakers in a bind. All involved believed that putting her through a health assessment process (in this case, a biopsy) in order to receive a diagnosis while living in a state of severe dementia and a "failure to thrive" mode was medically unethical. Thus, Marie was rejected for hospice care twice, and only qualified in her last two weeks of life. In the interim, contrary to her wishes, Marie's life was needlessly extended because her well-meaning caretakers in her assisted living facility continued to feed her. Only with hospice care was she able to have around-the-clock advocates who followed her final wishes to help her to comfortably embrace death.

16. The difficulty of predicting death to within six months was cited by 37 percent of doctors as the foremost barrier to hospice referral. See Leslea Brickner, Kate Scannell, Stephanie Marquet, and Lynn Ackerson, "Barriers to Hospice Care and Referral," *Journal of Palliative Medicine* 7, no. 3 (June 2004): 411–418.

17. See study by Claire M. Spettell et al. in *Journal of Palliative Medicine* (2009), and Jennings et al., *Access to Hospice Care: Expanding Boundaries, Overcoming Barriers,* a special supplement to the *Hastings Center Report* (Mar.–Apr. 2003).

CONCLUSION

1. *Never Say Die: The Myth and Marketing of the New Old Age* (New York: Pantheon, 2011), by cultural critic Susan Jacoby, argues that "real" old age (in comparison to media messaging) is not pleasant and carefree. Professor of comparative literature Arnold Weinstein, in *Morning, Noon, and Night: Growing Up and Growing Old with Literature* (New York: Random House, 2011), suggests that like Shakespeare's King Lear, we must come to terms with vulnerability and death. Fiction writer Joyce Carol Oates, in *A Widow's Story: A Memoir* (New York: Ecco, 2011), emphasizes small treasures in the context of great loss and loneliness. Journalist Ted Fishman's *Shock of Gray: The Aging of the World's Population and How It Pits Young Against Old, Child Against Parent, Worker Against Boss, Company Against Rival, and Nation Against Nation* (New York: Scribner, 2010), emphasizes aging, stratification, and globalization. And geriatric psychiatrist Marc Agronin, in *How We Age: A Doctor's Journey into the Heart of Growing Old* (Philadelphia: DeCapo Press, 2011), finds wisdom even in the context of dementia and dying.

2. I am borrowing the term "ambiguities of aging" from Martha Holstein, "On Being an Aging Woman," in *Age Matters*, eds. Toni Calasanti and Kevin Slevin (New York: Routledge, 2006), 313–331.

3. Howard S. Friedman and Leslie R. Martin, *The Longevity Project: Surprising Discoveries for Health and Long Life from the Landmark Eight-Decade Study* (New York: Hudson Street Press, 2011).

4. Geriatrician Marc Agronin reminds us that even in the most severe cases of disability, sparks of humanity persist. Even without mental rationality, there is perception, emotion, and imagination; without mobility, there is still movement and sensation. Thus, seeing elders as victims denies their agency.

5. Experiences of aging are circumscribed by physical health, personal resources, historical events, and cultural norms often outside of our control.

6. The ways in which culture shapes the aging process is the focus of a vital interdisciplinary sub-field within gerontology. One scholar in this field, Margaret Morganroth Gullette (2011), calls on her readers to become ageist-conscious to counter ubiquitous decline narratives in marketing, politics, and the larger culture. (See *Agewise: Fighting the New*

Ageism in America, University of Chicago Press, 14.) For more on cultural aging, see works by Stephen Katz (2005), and Toni Calasanti and Kathleen Slevin (2006).

7. Gene Cohen is quoted in a conversation with Marc Agronin in *How We Age*, 31.
8. Fishman, *Shock of Gray*.
9. Fishman, *Shock of Gray*, 17.
10. As a testament to this social need, the Adopt-a-Grandparent program thrives on countless college campuses.
11. In the process of sharing their life stories and opening up their lives to students, elders may be able to guide young adults to know themselves, slow down, live in the moment and in moderation, deepen sensory perception, and be more in control of their lives. In other words, elders can model balanced lives, something that many college students need to learn. They can educate young adults about their own experiences with social entitlement programs, advance directives, and housing options. They can also offer a sense of history, honest feedback, and a perspective separate from peer or family influence. Students also have much to offer in the form of interest, respect, a listening ear, and even advocacy. I'll never forget when one student told me that she opened up more to her elder than anyone on campus, because she longed for an outside perspective on her life. Others reported instrumental benefits through exchanging books and travel stories, or collecting relationship or career advice from their elders. And some students, after collecting life histories, were taking new interest in historical events, the surrounding college community, and their own grandparents. Most important, after being matched with elders, students have newly complicated perspectives on aging, and their fear of aging is diminished.
12. Students studying aging can engage elders in discussions about the lessons they are receiving in the classroom and in textbooks. And finally, when students openly receive an elder's life story, this receiving is one of the best gifts they can give another human being. The ability to aid in a process of life review can be crucial for a sense of continuity and closure, particularly for the very old. See Barbara Haight, "Sharing Life Stories: Acts of Intimacy," *Generations* 25, no. 2 (2001): 90–95.
13. See Pam Belluck's *New York Times* article dated Dec. 31, 2010.
14. For research on staff satisfaction in a care facility, see Meika Loe and Crystal Dea Moore (March 18, 2011), "From Nursing Home to Green House: Changing Contexts and Outcomes of Elder Care in the U.S." *Journal of Applied Gerontology*.
15. See Margaret Cruikshank, *Learning to Be Old: Gender, Culture, and Aging* (Lanham, MD: Roman & Littlefield, 2003), 3.
16. Robert Butler, Pulitzer prize-winning author and psychiatrist of aging who helped to create the field of geriatrics, believed that "aging successfully" required realism and the ability to accept mortality. In his last interview before his death in July 2010, he stated, "I think we ought to have a realistic portrait of all different periods of life and not try to romanticize old age as the most wonderful, all these great old wise people. I think that goes too far." Kate Zernicke's July 10, 2010, *New York Times* piece entitled "Turn 70. Act Your Grandchild's Age," memorializes Butler and reflects on the "successful aging" movement in the United States, which has imposed expectations on elders that may not be universally attainable.
17. While we can fail at being "successful" or "productive," personal comfort is subjectively defined and attainable.
18. In *Another Country: Navigating the Emotional Terrain of Our Elders* (New York: Berkeley Publishing, 1999), Mary Pipher writes "At some point getting old is like the game of falling back and trusting others will catch you. That game goes better when the person falling is relaxed and the person doing the catching is strong and loving."
19. Debbie Plath, "International Policy Perspectives on Independence in Old Age," *Journal of Aging and Social Policy* 21, no. 2 (2009): 209–223.

20. See Kenneth Ferraro, "Widowhood and Social Participation in Later Life," *Research on Aging* 6, no. 4 (1984): 451–468.
21. Barbara Hillyer, "The Embodiment of Old Women: Silences," *Frontiers: a Journal of Women's Studies* 19, no. 1 (1998): 48–60.
22. Doris Grumbach, *Coming into the End Zone: A Memoir* (New York: W.W. Norton, 1991).
23. Edwin Shneidman, *A Commonsense Book of Death: Reflections at Ninety of a Lifelong Thanatologist.* (Lanham, MD: Rowman & Littlefield, 2009), xv.
24. Heilbrun is adamant about accepting chronological age as a fact of life, cautioning that we ought not impersonate youth. See Carolyn G. Heilbrun, *The Last Gift of Time: Life Beyond Sixty* (New York: Ballantine Books, 1997).
25. I convened a group of professionals who work on aging issues in policy, social work, and social services to brainstorm about social change and identify gaps in the system. The majority of these professionals were women under age forty. Even in their short careers, all were frustrated by the social barriers they saw impeding elders' chances of aging comfortably. They too agreed that structural changes were necessary to enable comfortable aging.
26. In *Aging in America: The Years Ahead* (2003), photo essayist Ed Kashi says we are unprepared for our aging population and envisions a "rehumanization of America" and the genesis of a Care Corps (perhaps patterned after Americorps), with minimally trained workers who are maximally inspired to do local intergenerational community-building and outreach. *Aging in America: The Years Ahead* (powerHouse Books, 2003), 248–249.

APPENDIX

1. As of 2005, Oregon, New York, and California (in that order) had the highest spending on home and community-based services, according to Jeff Burr et al., "State Commitment to Home and Community-Based Services," *Journal of Aging and Social Policy* 17, no. 1 (2005): 9.
2. In Albany, New York, the issue of whether to close or rebuild the county nursing home is contentious, and this debate is playing out in numerous communities around the nation. County Executive Michael Breslin wants to take those funds and support community-based aging at home, which is much more cost-effective. He adds that the 1999 *Olmstead* Supreme Court decision makes it a violation of civil rights to institutionalize a disabled individual when that person could be treated in the community. Olmstead v. L.C., 527 U.S. 581 (1999). On the other hand, Mr. Breslin believes that communities will need nursing homes in fifteen years when our aged population expands considerably. See interview in *Metroland*, January 28–February 3, 2010.
3. Debbie Plath, "International Policy Perspectives on Independence in Old Age," *Journal of Aging and Social Policy.* 21, no. 2 (2009): 209–223.
4. This is an ongoing policy dilemma. Since Medicaid pays for most long-term care, but qualification is income-based, to get the services you need, you need to impoverish yourself. A nice discussion of this is included in Timothy Diamond, *Making Gray Gold: Narratives of Nursing Home Care* (Chicago: University of Chicago Press, 1995).
5. Contrary to what we might expect, Medicaid pays 42 percent of long-term care costs, while Medicaid pays only 20 percent. Medicare does not cover long-term skilled nursing care, and covers home care in very limited circumstances.
6. The Older Americans Act of 1965 was the first federal-level initiative aimed at providing comprehensive services for older adults. The network provides funding—based primarily on the percentage of an area's population aged sixty and older—for nutrition and supportive home and community-based services, disease prevention/health promotion services, elder rights programs, the National Family Caregiver Support Program, and the

Native American Caregiver Support Program. In 2006, Congress reauthorized the Act in its entirety, effective through 2011. Congress is currently considering reinstating OAA in 2012.

7. Barriers to service participation were fivefold. First, many experienced feeling overwhelmed and confused by the array of options. Psychological research suggests that elders (as opposed to young adults) want fewer choices; too many options can be a burden. Conversely, some elders may not have been aware of services, particularly if they were homebound or lacking in networks. Second, like most of us, elders act out of acute need. If they need a plumber, they call one. On the other hand, signing up for a home maintenance membership program like Umbrella requires long-term planning. Third, as we know from sociological research, most turn to informal sources of assistance (family, friends, neighbors) before turning to formal service providers. And finally, without a personal reference, elders may be cautious about providers, fearing exploitation.

8. According to the Bureau of Labor Statistics Occupational Handbook (2010–2011), *home health aides* typically are directly supervised by a medical professional and work for certified home health or hospice agencies that receive government funding. They provide basic health-related services and can assist with medication administration. In contrast, *personal and home care aides*—also called homemakers, caregivers, companions, and personal attendants—work for various public and private agencies that provide home care services. Some personal and home care aides are hired, supervised, and assigned tasks directly by the patient or the patient's family. U.S. Department of Labor, Bureau of Labor Statistics, *Occupational Outlook Handbook, 2010–11 Edition*. http://www.bls.gov/oco/ocos326.htm (last modified Dec. 17, 2009).

9. Burr et al., in "State Commitment to Home and Community-Based Services," refer to this phenomenon as purchasing independence. The average (mean) hourly wage for nursing aides nationwide in 2009 was $10.39. Many home health care organizations require three-hour shifts at minimum. Bureau of Labor Statistics (2009). http://www.bls.gov/oes/current/oes311011.htm.

10. Burr et al. "State Commitment to Home and Community-Based Services."

11. According to The Kaiser Commission on Medicaid and the Uninsured, thirty-three states allow the "medically needy"—those with high medical bills—to spend down to a state-set eligibility standard. In addition, because few people can afford the high cost of long-term care, thirty-eight states allow individuals needing nursing home care to qualify under the "300 percent rule." Under this option, individuals with income up to 300 percent of SSI ($1,806 per month in 2006) can qualify for Medicaid assistance with institutional care. See Kaiser Commission on Medicaid and the Uninsured, "Medicaid and Long-Term Care Facts" (July 2006). http://www.kff.org/medicaid/upload/Medicaid-and-Long-Term-Care-Services-PDF.pdf.

12. Currently, most available long-term care (LTC) policies require that an individual have at least two limitations out of six common ADLs or be cognitively impaired in order to qualify for benefits. For more on LTC insurance, see Marc A. Cohen et al., "Patterns of Informal and Formal Caregiving Among Elders With Private Long-Term Care Insurance," Gerontologist 41, no. 2 (2001): 180–187.

13. This information was accessed from the EISEP website (2010), New York State, Department of Health. http://www.health.state.ny.us/health_care/medicaid/program/longterm/expand.htm.

14. Read about PACE and other all-inclusive care providers in Miriam K. Aronson and Marcella Bakur Wiener, *Aging Parents, Aging Children: How to Stay Sane and Survive* (Lanham, MD: Roman & Littlefield, 2007).

15. Rosalie A. Kane et al., "Resident Outcomes in Small-House Nursing Homes: A Longitudinal Evaluation of the Initial Green House Program," *Journal of the American Geriatrics Society* 55, no. 6 (2007): 832–839.

INDEX

quality of life and, 223
computers, 44, 96, 106, 125, 236
conflict, humor and, 147
connection, 26, 133
  humor and, 149–50
  intergenerational, 208–12, 261–62
  maintaining, 135
  social, 107, 142, 260, 268
  solitude and, 105
Conrad, Peter, 288n15
conscientious living, 6
context, humor and, 149
continuing care retirement community
  (CCRC), 125
continuity, xi, 174
  across lives, 44–46
  theory, 33
contributing, 46, 161
  to a cause, 162, 170–171
  to others' lives, 25, 38, 148, 174,
    268
  strategies for, 162
control, xi, 104, 111, 123
  asking for help and, 113–14
  of daily life, 15
  decreased, 238
cooking, 71, 100–101, 117
co-residence, intergenerational, 181
Coronaro, Luigi, 295n5
correspondence, 165
County Office for Aging, 38, 118
CR. *See* caloric restriction
creativity, 98–101
  of daily practices, 28
  expression of, 55, 104
  of kitchen rituals, 120
  strategies, 29
"Criteria for a Good Death"
  (Schneidman), 249
Cruikshank, Margaret, 263
Csikszentmihalyi, Mihaly, 104
culture
  age and, 18
  ageism and, 19
  elders and, 258
  heritage of, 11, 289n27
  youth-obsessed, 10
cumulative advantage 21, 293n71
curiosity, 100
cutting ties, 249
cycle of birth/death, xii

daily routines, 46
dance, 275
Dartmouth Atlas Medical Research, 73
dating, 24, 32, 101
deafness, 220, 293n7
death and dying, 254
  active, 246–48
  circumstances of, 247
  coming to terms with, 265
  cycle of, xii
  denial of, 252
  diagnosis of, 252–53
  good, 248–50
  in hospital, 247–49, 250–53
  leading causes of, 14
  predicting, 306n15
  preparation for, 247–48
  prolonged, 248–49
  ritual meaning 247
  social construction of, 248
death dips, 247
decline, 5
deferred giving, 301n9
dementia, 13, 262, 290n34. *Also see*
  Alzheimer's
demographics, 195
  change of, 4
denial
  of aging, 265
  of death, 252
dentistry 56, 75, 271, 279
dependency, 118, 236, 249
depression, 26, 107
  suicidality and, 293n69
designers, of homes, 63–67
desperation, 184
development, 18
diabetes, 14, 258
diagnosis, of death, 252–53
diet, 7, 70–72, 295n4
A Different Shade of Gray (Newman),
  21, 82
dignity, 15, 111
disability, 229, 294n15, 306n4. *See also*
  blindness; deafness
  ability and, 243–44
  avoiding, 5
  isolation and, 143
  rates, 5
  resource mobilization and, 128
  of women, 20

spending time with, 181, 183–85
women's roles in, 176, 182
Family Medical Leave Act (FMLA), 192
fear, 64, 296n3
  bad news, 63
  dependency, 192
  exploitation, 207
  falling, 45, 63
  loss, 122
  violence, 58, 64
federal programs, 282
feminism, and aging, 291n56
feral children, 304n1
fertility, high rates of, 17
finances, 70, 76–77, 125
  contributing to, 171
  help with, 187
  support and, 186, 285
Fishman, Ted C., 180, 216, 261
Florence, 47, 53, 256–57, 273
  affection/pleasure of, 218–19
  comfortable aging of, 257
  command center of, 47–48
  media consumption and, 90–94
flow, 104, 180
FMLA. See Family Medical Leave Act
food, 75–76. See also cooking
  preparation of, 100–101, 116, 120
formal service providers, 128
Fortnightly Club, 136, 267
The Foundation of Age (Friedan), 291n56
fourth age, 246–47
France, 4
Frankl, Viktor, 265
Fred, xii, 9, 14, 50, 60–62, 273
  family and, 186–87
  friendships of, 137–38
Freud, Sigmund, 147, 156
Friedan, Betty, 291n56
Friedman, Howard, 6
friendships, 135–37, 195, 197, 264
  accidental, 134
  cultivating, 165
  intergenerational, 196
  new, 198–99
  types of, 299n3
friendship families, 196
frugality, 16–17, 77
functional capacity, 228, 261
functional health, 227
Furman, Frida Kerner, 135, 216

gambling, 275
games, 94–95, 137–38
gardening, 85, 104
gay elders, 196, 207, 303n11
gay grandchildren, 185
gender. See also men; women
  age and, 19–20
  caregiving and, 176
  carework and, 182
  doing, 148, 153, 291n52
  family capital and, 181
  humor and, 148, 154
  mortality/morbidity and, 83
  peer networks and, 143
  scholars of, 148
  socialization, 19, 33, 130
generations, 4, 80
  differences of, 16
  membership of, 15
genetics, longevity and, 69
geography
  location, 130
  of vulnerability, 64
Germany, 4
get-up-and-go test, 304n2
GI Bill, 16
GI Generation, 15
"Giving Alzheimer's Patients Their Way,
  Even Chocolate," 262
Glenn, 20, 145, 205–7, 270, 273
  caregiving by, 163–66
  family and, 186–87
  humor of, 145–46
  risk avoidance by, 79–80
global contexts of aging, 4, 66, 149, 191,
  216, 287n5. See also specific countries
good death, 248–50
Gramps (author's grandfather), 23–25,
  268–69
grandchildren, 179, 184
  closeness to, 164, 222, 303n16
  as strangers, 222
  caring for, 177, 187
grandparents, 179, 180, 187
gratification, sensory, 217
gratitude, 103
Great Depression, 15, 24, 33, 70
Greatest Generation, 15–16, 67, 75, 186
great-grandparenting, 168–69
Great Recession, 179
Greenhouse, Esther, 294n15

Pauline, 11, 27, 58–59
    family of, 190–91
    home of, 49
    neighborhood of, 51, 64–65
    pleasures of, 276
peer networks, 142–43
perceived age, 18
Perlman, Itzhak, 98
persistence, 70, 288n17
personal agency, 33
personal care providers, 285, 309n8. *Also
    see care*
personal fulfillment, 84
personal histories, 9, 101, 135. *Also
    see* interviews
personalized care systems, 127–30
personal shoppers, 188
personal support services, 281–82
personality theory, 33
pets 214–15, 217–8, 223
Pew Research Report, 11, 12t, 181, 186,
    189, 291n47
phone calls, 186
    network of, 119
physical activity, regular, 43
physical affection, 214–16
physical appearance, 19, 97, 297n12
physical decline. *See* decline
physical functioning, 230
physical health, 13, 59
physical location, 21. *Also see* rural
    location
physical strength. *See* strength-training
physicians. *See* doctors
Pipher, Mary, 291n54
place, 48–51, 61, 130
plagues of old age, 104
planning ahead, 251
plants, 173, 300n6
Plath, Debbie, 278
pleasure, 215, 217–23, 302n21
    bodily obstacles to, 107
    experience of, 33
    Lillian and, 30–32
    sensory, 104
    solitary, 28, 85
poetry, 161–2
population
    Jewish, 13
    of oldest old, 287n10
    sex ratio of, 290n32

Posada, Jorge, 34–35
poverty, 64, 290n30
practicality, 81
pranks, 148
prejudice, 210
prescription medication, 32, 74
"Presto Presto, Do Your Very Best-O"
    (song), 37
pride, 154, 173, 185, 242
privacy, 176
productive aging, 88, 256
Program of All-Inclusive Care for the
    Elderly (PACE), 284
prostate, enlarged, 14
Protestants, 26
proximity, 16, 143
prudence, 70, 288n17
psychiatry, geriatric, 175, 259, 266
psychosocial aspects, 23
psychosocial challenges, 228
psychosocial development stages,
    291n48
public insurance, 279
Puerto Ricans, 16, 34
purpose, 46
Putnam, Robert, 142

qualitative research, 9
quality of life, 32
    affection and, 223
    care and
    companionship and, 223
    exercise and, 43
    location and, 51
    social contexts of, 5
    social networks and, 86
"Que Sera Sera" (song), 37

Rabig, Jude, 292n66
race, 11, 89, 194. *See also specific races*
    baby boomers and, 287n8
racism, 89, 156, 207, 214, 258
reaching out, 223
reading, 93–4, 226
recipes, 117
reciprocity, 168, 196
    carework and, 162, 174
    familial, 179, 191
    social bonds and, 174
Red Leather Diary (Koppel), 106
reflection, 101–3

CPSIA information can be obtained at www.ICGtesting.com
Printed in the USA
BVOW01s1150160114

341980BV00004B/45/P